JEFFERSON ABROAD

JEFFERSON

ABROAD

Edited by

DOUGLAS L. WILSON

and

LUCIA STANTON

THE MODERN LIBRARY

NEW YORK

1999 Modern Library Edition

Copyright © 1999 by Random House, Inc.

Grateful acknowledgment is made to Princeton University Press for permission to
include excerpts from *The Papers of Thomas Jefferson, Volumes 7–16*. Copyright ©
1953–1961 by Princeton University Press. Reprinted by permission of Princeton
University Press.

LIBRARY OF CONGRESS CATALOGING-IN-PUBLICATION DATA
Jefferson, Thomas, 1743–1826.
Jefferson abroad/edited by Douglas L. Wilson and Lucia
Stanton.—Modern Library ed.
p.   cm.
Includes index.
ISBN 0-679-60319-0
1. Jefferson, Thomas, 1743–1826—Correspondence.   2. Presidents—
United States—Correspondence.   3. Diplomats—France—Paris—
Correspondence.   4. Jefferson, Thomas, 1743–1826—Homes and haunts—
France—Paris.   5. Jefferson, Thomas, 1743–1826—Journeys—Europe.
6. Paris (France)—Intellectual life—18th century.   7. Europe—
Description and travel.   I. Wilson, Douglas L.   II. Stanton, Lucia C.
III.   Title.
E332.45.J44   1999
973.4'6'092—dc21
[b]   98-31431

Modern Library website address: www.modernlibrary.com

Printed in the United States of America on acid-free paper

2   4   6   8   9   7   5   3   1

PREFACE

This collection of selected writings focuses attention on what were arguably the most memorable five years of Thomas Jefferson's life. By the time he returned to America in 1789, Paris—with its music, its architecture, its savants and salons, its learning and enlightenment, not to mention its elegant social life and distinctive sexual mores—had worked its enchantments on this rigidly self-controlled Virginia gentleman, and had stimulated him to say and do and write remarkable things.

"Behold me at length on the vaunted scene of Europe!"[1] Jefferson's famous remark to his friend Charles Bellini gives voice to an American's awareness of having finally arrived to see for himself how the "vaunted" civilization of Europe measured up to his own expectations and to its supposed superiority to everything American. His findings, which punctuate and flavor his correspondence, were decidedly mixed. He loved the French people but deplored their government. He admired the friendliness and courtesy that characterized social relations among the French but was aghast at their sexual morality. "Conjugal love having no existence among them, domestic happiness, of which that is the basis, is utterly unknown." He also deplored the rigidity of French society, which lacked the kinds of options and social mobility afforded in America. "The truth of Voltaire's observation offers itself perpetually," he wrote, "that every man here must be either the hammer or the anvil."

Jefferson's European experience provided a new stage for his lifelong role as a defender of the reputation of his homeland—its climate and natural phenomena as well as its government and people. Whether combating the aspersions of the British press or the "degrading" degeneracy theories of French naturalists, he missed no opportunity to display everything American in the best possible light. In his country's interest Jefferson also made himself the center of a busy import-export network for both ideas and more tangible objects. He distributed his own Virginia statute for religious freedom and presented the Comte de Buffon with the skeleton of an American moose (to prove that it towered over the European reindeer), while shipping home books to inform the constitutional thought of James Madison and olive trees and rice to benefit the economy of South Carolina. He gratified French gardeners with seeds of novel southern trees and sought to establish "colonies" of desirable European animals on the American continent. "What a bird the nightingale would be in the climates of America!" he exclaimed, after listening to its song in the South of France. Quick as he was to dispute the Old World's claims of ascendancy over the New, he was eager to apprise his countrymen of the best that Europe had to offer.

———

Thomas Jefferson was born in 1743 and raised in the sparsely populated piedmont of Virginia, which was then almost the frontier. His education, the finest available in colonial Virginia, prompted a keen interest in the cosmopolitan attractions of Europe, and taking the Grand Tour was one of his earliest aspirations. The successive demands of his studies, his profession as a lawyer, his obligations as a husband and father, and finally the conditions of revolutionary warfare all combined to foil his hopes for European travel, but an unexpected combination of circumstances eventually cleared the way. His wife of ten years, to whom he was deeply devoted, died in 1782, and his friends sought to ease the effects of bereavement by reengaging Jefferson in political affairs. He resisted until the enticement took the form of a diplomatic appointment to France, which held out the prospect of joining a much-needed change of scene to the opportunity to see Europe and, at the same time, serve his country. Before he could sail, his post was rendered unnecessary by the signing of the Treaty of Paris in 1783, but the following year he was again appointed to represent the American Congress in France.

Leaving his two younger daughters in the care of their maternal aunt, Jefferson sailed for France from Boston in July 1784 with his daughter Martha, who was then almost twelve. Once in Paris, they found themselves in brilliant company—the remarkable Adams family and the great Benjamin Franklin. But they had practical problems to contend with. The first was the French language. While Jefferson could read and write French fluently, he at first had great difficulty conversing in it. For Martha, who was called Patsy, the problem was solved by placing her in a convent school, where she quickly gained facility with the language. And then there was the problem of where to live. Though he eventually ended up in splendid quarters in a handsome residence called the Hôtel de Langeac, finding a suitable place took Jefferson over a year. Perhaps most trying of all was the adjustment to the new climate that kept this irrepressibly active man virtually out of commission for six months. "A seasoning as they call it is the lot of most strangers," Jefferson wrote to a friend, "and none I beleive have experienced a more severe one than myself. The air is extremely damp, and the waters very unwholesome."[2] In typical fashion, he devised his own scheme for reestablishing his health—walking four or five miles a day in the Bois de Boulogne and exposing himself to the sun, which he described as "my almighty physician."

At his elegant new house on the Champs-Elysées, which had been designed by Jean F. T. Chalgrin, Jefferson offered a hospitable welcome to Europeans and Americans alike. The rooms of the Hôtel de Langeac were filled with furniture in the neoclassical style, bought from the most fashionable *marchand-merciers*. Fine silk damask curtains adorned the windows and bed alcoves, and copies of the European masters, found at auctions of indebted estates, covered the walls. The household staff numbered seven or eight, including a coachman and footman, a valet, and the indispensable *frotteur*, or floor-polisher. At its head was the *maître-d'hôtel,* Adrien Petit, who later served in the same position in Philadelphia, when Jefferson was secretary of state. Jefferson's chef from 1787 on was his own slave, James Hemings, brought from Monticello to learn the art of French cookery. Jefferson's younger daughter Mary (also called Polly or Maria) arrived from Virginia that year, accompanied by James Hemings's fourteen-year-old sister, Sally. Patsy and Polly lived in the convent school and visited their father once or twice a week.

Jefferson's private secretary, William Short, lived with Jefferson when he was not in Saint-Germain-en-Laye learning the French language. Young Americans abroad wrote of going to the Hôtel de Langeac for chess games or discussions of literature with their nation's minister. French scientists, *littérateurs,* and politicians dined at Jefferson's table or walked in his garden. And every July Fourth Americans in Paris, and honorary Americans like the Marquis de Lafayette, came to the Hôtel de Langeac to celebrate.

———

Although Jefferson's efforts as a diplomat were constantly frustrated and mostly unavailing, he enjoyed conspicuous recognition in the most cultivated society in Europe as a man of ability and accomplishments. In truth, the man who disingenuously described himself as "a savage of the mountains of America" could hardly disguise his relish for the excitement and amenities of urban life. Never having lived in a city for an extended period, and a vocal champion of the superiority of country life, Jefferson nonetheless took full advantage of the special attractions of Parisian life. He had been cultivating all his life a taste for things that flourish mainly in cities, particularly the fine arts, and he found them in abundance in Paris. "Were I to proceed to tell you how much I enjoy their architecture, sculpture, painting, music," he wrote a friend, "I should want words. It is in these arts they shine. The last of them particularly is an enjoiment, the deprivation of which with us cannot be calculated. I am almost ready to say it is the only thing which from my heart I envy them, and which in spight of all the authority of the decalogue I do covet."[3]

It was not only the arts that beguiled him. The bookshops of Paris were treasure troves for a man who later said he couldn't live without books. "While residing in Paris," he later recalled, "I devoted every afternoon I was disengaged, for a summer or two, in examining all the principal bookstores, turning over every book with my own hand, and putting by everything which related to America, and indeed whatever was rare and valuable in every science."[4] Great feats of engineering were a special fascination for him. He marveled at the hydraulic pumping system that provided the water for the royal gardens and called attention to the quiet magnificence of Parisian bridges. His fellow American Gouverneur Morris noted in his diary: "Visit Mr. Jefferson and ride with him in the Bois de Boulogne and then at his Request visit the Bridge of Neuilly, which I had crossed four Times without remarking it and which he says is the handsomest in the World."[5]

Nor was Jefferson immune to the allurements of the social realm. When he was introduced to the beautiful artist Maria Cosway, his infatuation was apparently immediate and all-consuming. In spite of his avowed disapproval of such behavior, he found himself engaged in the common French practice of coveting another man's wife. In fact, he yielded to his milieu in much the same manner that plants and animals, as he believed, responded to their environment. "A poet," he wrote, "is as much the creature of climate as an orange or palm tree."

On his tours, especially in the wine country and the South of France in 1787, his pen was kept busy recording his rapid-fire observations—on soil, on crops and livestock, on roads and canals, and on local customs. When he was out in the countryside and away from the vexations of office, his mood became, by turns, animated and serene. His idea of leisure was the opposite of idleness. He luxuriated in the freedom to indulge his inclinations, and these, characteristically, were mostly dictated by a ceaseless and insatiable curiosity. In praising Jefferson during these years, his friend John Adams wrote, "I only fear that his unquenchable thirst for knowledge may injure his health."[6]

———

Jefferson's writings during the Paris years were voluminous. Facility with the written word was something that Jefferson had assiduously cultivated as a student, and it was a principal reason he had distinguished himself with his contemporaries. Writing appears to have been for Jefferson more than a talent and an interest, but almost a necessary activity. In providing a constant source of novelty and stimulation, his European experiences served to accentuate this trait. He wrote down not only what was happening on the public stage but what was new in science, in technology, and in virtually all the fields of learning. He wrote about the people and personalities he encountered, but also the buildings and machines. Wherever he went, he investigated his new surroundings with a sharply observant eye, and what he observed he diligently set down in notes, letters, and journals.

One of the reasons that Jefferson's surviving works bulk so large is that he took care to retain copies of everything he wrote. Together with his incoming correspondence (which he also carefully preserved), the writings of the Paris years fill more than eight large volumes of the Princeton edition of Jefferson's *Papers*, and this does not include the sizeable book he offered the public in 1787, *Notes on the State of Virginia*. Not surprisingly, a very substantial portion of Jefferson's writing in this period relates to his work as a diplomat. The reader of the Princeton edition will find its pages replete with diplomatic correspondence and other writings deriving from his official duties: drafts of treaties, reports on the tobacco trade and whale oil imports, discussions of Dutch loans and Barbary pirates and the perfidy of the British. Important as these historical documents are to scholars, few appear in the present collection, for the editors have chosen to minimize this category of official writing in favor of material that is more personal and more personally revealing. In addition to some of the most famous of his Paris writings, the editors have opted for selections that reflect Jefferson's broad array of interests and that bring out telling aspects of his character and personality.

His letters to women are a case in point. Abraham Lincoln once wrote to a female well-wisher: "The truth is I have never corresponded much with ladies; and hence I postpone writing letters to them, as a business which I do not understand."[7] By contrast, in his years in Paris Jefferson kept up an avid correspondence with a great many women, leaving no doubt that it was a business that he not only understood but delighted in. His early letters to Maria Cosway are very close to courtship, but those to a number of other women friends—Angelica Church, Madame de Corny, Madame de Tott—are also written in something akin to the language of love, the witty and flirtatious style of an admiring gallant. Even his letters to older women, such as Abigail Adams and Madame de Tessé, are often cast in the conventions of the courtly tradition.

One of the pleasures of history is that it legitimizes our reading of other people's private letters. However, a few caveats are in order. The first is that personal letters, being addressed to a particular person, have a specific context, and the reader should be on guard against inferring that a view expressed in any given letter is a definitive expression of the writer's thinking on the subject. In Jefferson's case, the opposite is probably a safer assumption: that to a different correspondent he would probably have put the matter differently. Whether this be diplomacy or duplicity is a question each reader must decide. A related caveat is that Jefferson frequently expressed himself in broad and even sweeping language. His power as a writer in part depended on this trait, but readers will be led astray if they do not take into account what his biographer Merrill D. Peterson has observed, that Jefferson's was a temperament that "did not often bother to qualify felicitous generalizations."[8]

Because he was the author of the Declaration of Independence and became president of the United States, Thomas Jefferson is universally identified with politics. But as these writings make clear, politics was far from his only concern. His interests were exceptionally diverse, and his years in Paris brought out aspects of his character and personality that were either absent or less evident before and afterward. These five years abroad provided him with an extraordinary opportunity not just to pursue his interests and ideas but to commit them to writing. It was an opportunity he did not miss.

LUCIA STANTON
DOUGLAS L. WILSON
Charlottesville, Va.

ACKNOWLEDGMENTS

The editors are grateful to their colleagues at the Thomas Jefferson Memorial Foundation for faithful assistance and support; to Jenny Shaw Clay and the classics department at the University of Virginia, Olivier Zunz, and Gabriele Rausse for help with translations; and to Susan DiSesa and Ian Jackman for their patience. The editors are particularly grateful to Princeton University Press for permission to reprint these selections.

CONTENTS

A NOTE ON THE TEXT

The texts of all selections in this book are taken from *The Papers of Thomas Jefferson*, edited by Julian P. Boyd et al., Princeton University Press, 1950–. Scrupulously edited and the most authoritative of all editions of Jefferson's writings, the *Papers* gives both sides of Jefferson's voluminous correspondence, personal and diplomatic, and prints in chronological order all of his known letters and incidental writings. The footnotes given here have been supplied by the editors of the present work; readers seeking further information on these and other documents from Jefferson's Paris years may consult the headnotes and annotation in Volumes 7 through 15 of the *Papers*.

PRINCIPAL CORRESPONDENTS

ABIGAIL (1744–1818) and JOHN ADAMS (1735–1826). John Adams, Jefferson's fellow commissioner for negotiating commercial treaties, his wife, and their children, Abigail and John Quincy, lived in Auteuil, on the outskirts of Paris. Their home was a haven to Jefferson until their departure in May 1785 for London, where Adams took up his post as American minister to Great Britain. The Adamses hosted Jefferson's visit to England in 1786 and looked after his daughter Mary on her arrival from Virginia in the summer of 1787.

ABIGAIL ADAMS, daughter of Abigail and John Adams. *See* Abigail Adams Smith.

ANNE WILLING BINGHAM (1764–1801). Anne Bingham and her husband, wealthy banker William Bingham, resided in Paris and other European capitals from 1783 to 1786, when they returned to the United States to become leaders of Philadelphia society.

PETER CARR (1770–1815). After the death in 1773 of Jefferson's brother-in-law Dabney Carr, "the dearest friend I possessed on earth," Jefferson became a second father to Carr's six children. Even from a distance in Paris, he superintended the education of his nephew Peter Carr, who became an attorney and Virginia legislator. Carr settled near Monticello, where he was an intimate in Jefferson's family.

FRANÇOIS JEAN DE BEAUVOIR, MARQUIS DE CHASTELLUX (1734–1788). In Paris, Jefferson and Chastellux resumed a friendship begun in 1782, when the Frenchman passed through Virginia on a tour of the new United States after serving in the American Revolution. His account of Monticello and its owner appeared in his *Travels in North America*, published in Paris in 1786.

ANGELICA SCHUYLER CHURCH (1756–1815). Daughter of General Philip Schuyler and sister-in-law of Alexander Hamilton, Mrs. Church was an intimate friend of Maria Cosway. Her daughter Kitty was a schoolmate of Jefferson's daughters at the Abbaye Royale de Panthemont.

MARIA COSWAY (1760–1838). Born to English parents who had settled in Italy, Maria Hadfield married prominent English miniaturist Richard Cosway in 1781. A talented artist and musician, Mrs. Cosway established with her husband one of the most fashionable *salons* in London. They visited Paris in the late summer of 1786 and Mrs. Cosway returned alone for several months in 1787. She spent most of the last part of her life in Italy, where she founded a convent school for girls in Lodi. She and Jefferson continued to correspond intermittently until his death.

ELIZABETH WAYLES EPPES (1752–1810) and FRANCIS EPPES (1747–1808). On his departure for France in 1784, Jefferson had left his daughters Mary and Lucy in the care of his sister- and brother-in-law at Eppington in Chesterfield County, Virginia. Eppes, with Jefferson, was an executor of John Wayles's encumbered estate. The Eppeses' son John Wayles Eppes (1773–1823) married Jefferson's younger daughter in 1797.

DAVID HUMPHREYS (1752–1818). Former aide-de-camp to George Washington, Connecticut-born Humphreys served as secretary to the commissioners for negotiating commercial treaties and lived in Jefferson's Paris household from 1784 to 1786.

MARTHA JEFFERSON (1772–1836). Patsy, as she was usually called, was Jefferson's oldest child; she and her sister Mary were his only children who lived to adulthood. In 1784 she accompanied her father to Paris, where she was a boarding student at a fashionable convent school, the Abbaye Royale de Panthemont. A few months after their return to Virginia in 1789, she married her third cousin Thomas Mann Randolph. The Randolphs had eleven children and lived with Jefferson at Monticello during his retirement years, from 1809 to 1826.

MARY JEFFERSON (1778–1804). Jefferson's younger daughter Polly, as she was usually called, arrived in Paris in the summer of 1787 from Virginia, where she had been living with her Eppes relations. She joined her sister at the Abbaye Royale de Panthemont. Known as Maria after her return to Virginia in 1789, she married her cousin John Wayles Eppes in 1797.

MARIE JOSEPH PAUL YVES ROCH GILBERT DU MOTIER, MARQUIS DE LAFAYETTE (1757–1834). Well known to each other since the last years of the American Revolution, Jefferson and the Marquis were most closely associated in Paris. Lafayette's Paris residence was like a second home to Jefferson, who later called Lafayette his "most powerful auxiliary" in forwarding the interests of the United States at this time. In 1789, during the opening acts of the French Revolution, Jefferson collaborated with Lafayette in drafting the document that became the Declaration of the Rights of Man. Lafayette made two memorable visits to Monticello during his triumphal tour of the United States in 1824–1825.

NICHOLAS LEWIS (1734–1808). A close friend and neighbor, Lewis superintended Jefferson's Albemarle County affairs during his absence in France. He was married to Mary Walker, daughter of Dr. Thomas Walker, an executor of Peter Jefferson's estate.

JAMES MADISON (1751–1836). Jefferson's lifelong friend and political associate, Madison served in the Virginia assembly from 1784 to 1786, working for the enactment of the laws (including the statute for religious freedom) drafted by Jefferson in the Revisal of 1777–1779. Jefferson's extensive Parisian book purchases contributed to Madison's developing views on an American constitution, which culminated in his celebrated essays in *The Federalist* in 1788. Madison was secretary of state in both of Jefferson's presidential administrations and succeeded him as president.

REVEREND JAMES MADISON (1749–1812). A professor at the College of William and Mary, and then its president, Madison became the first Episcopal bishop of Virginia in 1790. He and Jefferson shared an interest in science, and Madison's map of Virginia, published in 1807, was the standard for many years.

PATSY. *See* Martha Jefferson.

POLLY. *See* Mary Jefferson.

THOMAS MANN RANDOLPH, JR. (1768–1828). Oldest son of Jefferson's cousin Thomas Mann Randolph, Sr., Randolph studied at the University of Edinburgh from 1784 to 1788. He married Jefferson's daughter Martha in March 1790 and, except for brief service in Congress and as governor of Virginia, lived mainly at Edgehill, adjoining Monticello, and at Monticello after Jefferson's 1809 retirement.

WILLIAM SHORT (1759–1849). This Virginian, Jefferson recalled, "put himself under my guidance at 19. or 20. years of age. He is to me therefore as an adoptive son." Short came to France at Jefferson's invitation to act as his private secretary and lived in Jefferson's Paris household. On Jefferson's departure in 1789, Short became American chargé d'affaires. He served in various diplomatic capacities in Europe and finally returned to live in Philadelphia.

ABIGAIL ADAMS SMITH (1765–1813) and WILLIAM STEPHENS SMITH (1755–1816). John and Abigail Adams's daughter and Adams's secretary of legation were married in London in the summer of 1786. They returned to the United States in 1788, settling in New York City.

ADRIENNE CATHERINE DE NOAILLES, COMTESSE DE TESSÉ (1741–1814). Madame de Tessé, introduced to Jefferson by her niece Madame de Lafayette, became one of his closest friends in Paris. He frequented the brilliant *salons* at her *hôtel* in the Faubourg

Saint-Germain and at Chaville, her country estate on the road to Versailles, and participated in her horticultural interests.

SOPHIE ERNESTINE DE TOTT (c. 1759–c. 1840). Daughter of the Baron de Tott, Sophie de Tott was a protégée of Madame de Tessé and resident in her household. Described by Jefferson as "a native Greek," she shared his interest in art and literature.

ELIZABETH HOUSE TRIST (c. 1754–1828). The widowed Mrs. Trist, whom Jefferson had first met in 1782 at her mother's Philadelphia boardinghouse, spent much of her later life in Virginia, often staying for long periods at Monticello. Her grandson Nicholas P. Trist married Jefferson's granddaughter Virginia J. Randolph in 1824.

JOHN TRUMBULL (1756–1843). This American painter lived in London in the 1780s, pursuing his career and making several visits to Paris. He stayed with Jefferson at the Hôtel de Langeac and worked on his canvases depicting the American Revolution. Jefferson considered him second only to Jacques Louis David as a historical painter.

GEORGE WASHINGTON (1732–1799). After resigning as commander in chief of the Continental Army in 1783, Washington returned to Mount Vernon, but was drawn from retirement to participate in the constitutional convention in 1787. He was inaugurated president of the United States on April 30, 1789. While in Paris, Jefferson commissioned the French sculptor Jean Antoine Houdon to make for the Virginia capitol a statue of the man he later called "our first and greatest revolutionary character." Washington offered Jefferson the post of the nation's first secretary of state in 1789.

JEFFERSON ABROAD

1. REASONS IN SUPPORT OF THE NEW PROPOSED ARTICLES IN THE TREATIES OF COMMERCE . . .[1]

[Nov. 10, 1784]

By the original Law of Nations war and extirpation was the punishment of injury. Humanizing by degrees, it admitted slavery instead of death. A farther step was the exchange of prisoners instead of slavery. Another, to respect more the property of private persons under conquest, and be content with acquired dominion. Why should not this Law of Nations go on improving? Ages have intervened between its several steps; but as knowledge of late encreases rapidly, why should not those steps be quickened? Why should it not be agreed to as the future law of Nations that in any war hereafter the following discriptions of men should be undisturbed, have the protection of both sides, and be permitted to follow their employments in surety, viz.

1. Cultivators of the earth, because they labour for the subsistance of mankind.
2. Fishermen, for the same reason.
3. Merchants and Traders in unarmed ships; who accomodate different Nations by communicating and exchanging the necessaries and conveniencies of life.
4. Artists and Mechanics inhabiting and working in open towns.

It is hardly necessary to add that the Hospitals of Enemies should be unmolested, they ought to be assisted.

It is for the interest of humanity in general, that the occasions of war, and the inducements to it should be diminished.

If rapine is abolished, one of the encouragements to war is taken away, and peace therefore more likely to continue and be lasting.

The practice of robbing merchants on the high seas, a remnant of the antient piracy, tho' it may be accidentally beneficial to particular persons, is far from being profitable to all engaged in it or to the nation that authorizes it. In the beginning of a war some rich ships, not upon their guard, are surprized and taken. This encourages the first adventurers to fit out more armed vessels, and many others to do the same, but the Enemy at the same time, become more careful, arm their merchant ships better and render them not so easy to be taken; they go also more under the protection of convoys. Thus while the privateers to take them are multiplied, the vessels subject to be taken and the chances of profit are diminished, so that many cruises are made wherein the expences overgo the gains; as it is the case in other lotteries, tho' particulars have got prizes the mass of Adventurers are losers, the whole expence of fitting out all the privateers during a war, being much greater than the whole amount of goods taken. Then there is the national loss of all the labour of so many men during the time they have been employed in robbing; who besides spend what they get in riot, drunkenness, and debauchery, lose their habits of industry, are rarely fit for any sober business after a peace, and serve only to encrease the number of Highwaymen and House-breakers. Even the Undertakers who have been fortunate, are by sudden wealth led into expensive living, the habit of which continues, when the means of supporting it cease, and finally ruins them. A just punishment for their having wantonly and unfeelingly ruined many honest innocent Traders and their families, whose substance was employed in serving the common interests of Mankind.

2. TO JAMES MADISON

Dear Sir   *Paris Nov. 11. 1784.*

Your letters of Aug. 20. Sep. 7. and 15. I received by the last packet. That by Mr. Short is not yet arrived. His delay is unaccountable. I was pleased to find by the public papers (for as yet I have no other information of it) that the assembly had restrained their foreign trade to four places. I should have been more pleased had it been to one. However I trust that York and Hobbs' hole will do so little that Norfolk and Alexandria will get possession of the whole. Your letter first informs me of the exception in favor of citizens, an exception which by the contrivance of merchants will I fear undo the whole. The popular objection which you mention that the articles passing thro' so many hands must come at a higher price to the consumer, is much like the one which might be made to a pin passing thro' the hands of so many workmen. Each being confined to a single operation will do it better and on better terms. This act of our assembly has been announced in all the gazettes of Europe with the highest commendations.—I am obliged to you for your information as to the prospects of the present year in our farms. It is a great satisfaction to know it, and yet it is a circumstance which few correspondents think worthy of mention. I am also much indebted for your very full observations on the navigation of the Missisipi. I had thought on the subject, and sketched the anatomy of a memorial on it, which will be much aided by your communications.—You mention that my name is used by some speculators in Western land jobbing, as if they were acting for me as well as themselves. About the year 1776 or 1777 I consented to join Mr. Harvey and some others in an application for lands there: which scheme however I beleive he dropped in the threshold, for I never after heard one syllable on the subject. In 1782. I joined some gentlemen in a project to obtain some lands in the Western parts of North Carolina. But in the winter of 1782. 1783. while I was in expectation of going to Europe and that the title to Western lands might possibly come under the discussion of the ministers, I withdrew myself from this company. I am further assured that the members never prosecuted their views. These were the only occasions in which I ever took a single step for the acquisition of Western lands, and in these I retracted at the threshold. I can with truth therefore declare to you, and wish you to repeat it on every proper occasion, that no person on earth is authorized to place my name in any adventure for lands on the Western waters, that I am not engaged in any one speculation for that purpose at present, and never was engaged in any, but the two before mentioned. I am one of eight children to whom my father left his share in the loyal company; whose interests however I never espoused, and they have long since received their quietus. Excepting these, I never was nor am now interested in one foot of land on earth, off of the waters of James river.

I shall subjoin the few books I have ventured to buy for you. I have been induced to do it by the combined circumstances of their utility and cheapness. I wish I had a catalogue of the books you would be willing to buy, because they are often to be met with on stalls very cheap, and I would get them as occasions should arise. The subscription for the Encyclopedie is still open.[1] Whenever an opportunity offers of sending you what is published of that work (37 vols) I shall subscribe for you and send it with the other books purchased for you. Probably no opportunity will occur till the spring when I expect the packets will be removed from L'Orient to Havre. The communication between this place and l'Orient is as difficult as it is easy with Havre. From N. York packages will be readily sent to Richmond by the care of Mr. Neill Jamieson, a very honest refugee now living at New York but who certainly ought to be permitted to return to Norfolk. Whatever money I may lay out for you here in books, or in any thing else which you may desire, may be replaced, crown for crown (without bewildering ourselves in the Exchange) in Virginia, by making paiments for the instruction or boarding of my nephews, and I wish you to be assured that this will be as perfectly convenient to me as the replacing the money here, that you may with freedom order any thing from hence of which you have occasion. If the bearer Colo. Le Maire can take charge of a pamphlet on Animal magnetism, another giving an account of Robert's last voiage thro' the air,[2] and of some Phosphoretic matches, I will send them to you. These matches consist of a small wax taper, one end of which has been dipped in Phosphorus, and the whole is inclosed in a glass tube hermetically sealed. There is a little ring on the tube to shew where it is to be broken. First warm the phosphorized end (which is the furthest one from the ring) by holding it two or three seconds in your mouth, then snap it at or near the ring and draw the phosphorized end out of the tube. It blazes in the instant of it's extraction. It will be well always to decline the tube at an angle of about 45°. (the phosphorized end lowest) in order that it may kindle thoroughly. Otherwise though it blazes in the first instant it is apt to go out if held erect. These cost about 30 sous the dozen. By having them at your bedside with a candle, the latter may be lighted at any moment of the night without getting out of bed. By keeping them on your writing table, you may seal three or four letters with one of them, or light a candle if you want to seal more which in the summer is convenient. In the woods they supply the want of steel, flint and punk. Great care must be taken in extracting the taper that none of the phosphorus drops on your hand, because it is inextinguishable and will therefore burn to the bone if there be matter enough. It is said that urine will extinguish it. There is a new lamp[3] invented here lately which with a very small consumption of oil (of olives) is thought to give a light equal to six or eight candles. The wick is hollow in the middle in the form of a hollow cylinder, and permits the air to pass up thro' it. It requires no snuffing. They make shade candlesticks of them at two guineas price, which are excellent for reading and are much used by studious men.—Colo. Le Maire, whom you know, is the bearer of this. He comes to Virginia to obtain the 2000 acres of land given him for his services in procuring us arms, and what else he may be entitled to as having been an officer in our service. Above all things he wishes to obtain the Cincinnatus eagle, because it will procure him here the order of St. Louis, and of course a pension for life of 1000 livres. He is so extremely poor that another friend and myself furnish him money for his whole expences from here to Virginia. There I am in hopes the hospitality of the country will be a resource for him till he can convert a part of his lands advantageously into money. But as he will want some small matter of money, if it should be convenient for you to furnish him with as much as ten guineas from time to time on my account I will invest that sum in books or any thing else you may want here by way of paiment. He is honest and grateful, and you may be assured that no aid which you can give him in the forwarding his claims will be misplaced.

The lamp of war is kindled here, not to be extinguished but by torrents of blood. The firing of the Dutch on an Imperial vessel going down the Scheld, has been followed by the departure of the Imperial minister from the Hague without taking leave. Troops are in motion on both sides towards the Scheld, but probably nothing will be attempted till the spring. This court has been very silent as to the part they will act. Yet their late treaty with Holland, as well as a certainty that Holland would not have proceeded so far without an assurance of aid furnish sufficient ground to conclude they will side actively with the republic. The king of Prussia it is beleived will do the same. He has patched up his little disputes with Holland and Dantzic. The prospect is that Holland, France, Prussia and the Porte will be engaged against the two Imperial courts. England I think will remain neuter. Their hostility towards us has attained an incredible height. Notwithstanding the daily proofs of this, they expect to keep our trade and cabotage[4] to themselves by the virtue of their proclamation. They have no idea that we can so far act in concert as to establish retaliating measures. Their Irish affairs will puzzle them extremely. We expect every moment to hear whether their Congress took place on the 25th Ult. Perhaps before I seal my letter I may be enabled to inform you. Should things get into confusion there, perhaps they will be more disposed to wish a friendly connection with us.

There is a dictionary of law, natural, civil and political in 13. vols. 4to. published here. It is well executed, by Felice, Jaurat, De la lande and others. It supplies the diplomatic dictionary of which you saw some volumes in Philadelphia and which degenerated into a trifling thing. This work costs half a guinea a volume. If you want De Thou, I can buy it on the stalls in perfect condition, 11. vols. 4to. in French @ 6. livres a vol. Moreri is to be bought cheap on the stalls.

The inclosed papers being put into my hands by Mr. Grand I cannot do better than to forward them to you and ask your attention to the case should the party present himself to you. I am with great sincerity Your affectionate friend & servt.,

Th: Jefferson

3. TO JAMES CURRIE[1]

[Jan. 14, 1785]

Various conversations with Mr. Short on the situation of things in Richmd. seem to render it very evident that the improvement of ground in that place is of certain and great profit. I have been induced to reflect on the subject as it furnishes a resource for subsistence independent of the usual one which spreads our couch with thorns. A particular building[2] lately erected here which has greatly enriched the owner of the ground, has added one of the principal ornaments to the city and increased the convenience of it's inhabitants [and] has suggested to us that a whole square in Richmd. improved on some such plan, but accommodated to the circumstances of the place, would be very highly advantageous to the proprietors, convenient to the town and ornamental. A detail of this is beyond the limits of a letter. The principal circumstances in it are the giving to all the tenants of the building a common in the whole ground of the square uncovered, the establishing in and about that such improvements as will make it the resort of everyone for either business or pleasure, thus rendering it the best stand for persons of every object and of course entitling it to the highest rents. Our plan would be of 8. or 10 years' execution, completing certain parts annually so that the rents of the parts completed might after 2. or 3. years relieve us from the subsequent expense of the work. For the 1st. 2. or 3. year the annual expense would be of about 800£ to be furnished in money labor or necessaries. The 1st. object is to procure a complete square level, and well situated. We have cast our eyes on one of Mr. Ross's, on the N. side of the main street on Sh[ockoe] hill where that street terminates on the brow of the hill. We have concluded to ask your intervention in this business and should be glad to have yourself or Mr. R. or both associated in the business, each holding an undivided 3d. or 4th. and indivisible also as to the common grounds. Should you be willing to join us in this, make the purchase of him on such terms as you think reasonable. Should you not chuse to join us, we must then give you the trouble of explaining the matter to Mr. R. and of knowing from him the lowest sum he will take in ready money for the square giving us time to send our definitive answer which may be from 6. to 10. weeks from the time we receive a notification of his terms. He will at the same time be so good as to say who he chuses to be concerned for a 3d. or 4th. part. Should the purchase be made I propose to bring proper master workmen when I return from Eur. to Amer. These need not exceed 4. in number and every other person employed may be of the common slaves of the country to be furnished by the partners. I have directed 500£ of mine in the treasury to be left for this purpose and in case of your making the purchase Mr. E[ppes]. (on sight of this letter) will be so good as to give an order for my part of the money. Mr. S.'s money is in the hands of Mr. Han. and he writes you on the subject. Should you be unable to purchase Mr. R.'s square we are willing you should proceed as to a square of Turpin's as we have desired in the case of Mr. R.'s, only that we should confine the partnership to you and ourselves or to ourselves alone if you decline it. The square of T.'s we have in view is on the same side of the same street with Mr. R.'s, but higher up the town by 2. or 3. squares. We wish this matter to be committed to no person whose agency is not necessary to fulfill it, and to hear from you as soon as possible on the subject.

4. TO JAMES MONROE[1]

Dear Sir   *Paris Mar. 18. 1785.*
... I have had a very bad winter, having been confined the greatest part of it. A seasoning as they call it is the lot of most strangers: and none I beleive have experienced a more severe one than myself. The air is extremely damp, and the waters very unwholesome. We have had for three weeks past a warm visit from the sun (my almighty physician) and I find myself almost reestablished. I begin now to be able to walk 4. or 5. miles a day, and find myself much the better for it. If the state of our business will permit I wish much to take a tour through the South of France for three or four weeks. The climate and exercise would, I think, restore my health....

Your's affectionately,

Th: Jefferson

5. TO ABIGAIL ADAMS

Dear Madam   *Paris June 21. 1785*
I have received duly the honor of your letter, and am now to return
you thanks for your condescension in having taken the first step for
settling a correspondence which I so much desired; for I now consider
it as *settled* and proceed accordingly. I have always found it best to remove obstacles first. I will do so therefore in the present case by telling
you that I consider your boasts of the splendour of your city and of it's
superb hackney coaches as a flout, and declaring that I would not give
the polite, self-denying, feeling, hospitable, goodhumoured people of
this country and their amability in every point of view, (tho' it must be
confessed our streets are somewhat dirty, and our fiacres rather indifferent) for ten such races of rich, proud, hectoring, swearing, squib-
bing, carnivorous animals as those among whom you are; and that I do
love this *people* with all my heart, and think that with a better religion
and a better form of government and their present governors their
condition and country would be most enviable. I pray you to observe
that I have used the term *people* and that this is a noun of the masculine
as well as feminine gender. I must add too that we are about reforming
our fiacres, and that I expect soon an Ordonance that all their drivers
shall wear breeches unless any difficulty should arise whether this is a
subject for the police or for the general legislation of the country, to
take care of. We have lately had an incident of some consequence, as
it shews a spirit of treason, and audaciousness which was hardly
thought to exist in this country. Some eight or ten years ago a Chevalier —— was sent on a message of state to the princess of —— of
—— of (before I proceed an inch further I must confess my profound
stupidity; for tho' I have heard this story told fifty times in all it's
circumstances, I declare I am unable to recollect the name of the ambassador, the name of the princess, and the nation he was sent to; I
must therefore proceed to tell you the naked story, shorn of all those
precious circumstances) some chevalier or other was sent on some
business or other to some princess or other. Not succeeding in his negociation, he wrote on his return the following song.

Ennivré du brillant poste
Que j'occupe récemment,
Dans une chaise de poste
Je me campe fierement:
Et je vais en ambassade
Au nom de mon souverain
Dire que je suis malade,
Et que lui se porte bien.

Avec une joue enflée
Je debarque tout honteux:
La princesse boursoufflée,
Au lieu d'une, en avoit deux;
Et son altesse sauvage
Sans doute a trouvé mauvais
Que j'eusse sur mon visage
La moitié de ses attraits.

Princesse, le roi mon maitre
M'a pris pour Ambassadeur;
Je viens vous faire connoitre
Quelle est pour vous son ardeur.
Quand vous seriez sous le chaume,
Il donneroit, m'a-t-il dit,
La moitié de son royaume
Pour celle de votre lit.

La princesse à son pupitre
Compose un remerciment:
Elle me donne une epitre
Que j'emporte lestement,
Et je m'en vais dans la rue
Fort satisfait d'ajouter
A l'honneur de l'avoir vue
Le plaisir de la quitter.[1]

This song run through all companies and was known to every body. A book was afterwards printed, with a regular license, called 'Les quatres saisons litteraires' which being a collection of little things, contained this also, and all the world bought it or might buy it if they would, the government taking no notice of it. It being the office of the Journal de Paris to give an account and criticism of new publications, this book came in turn to be criticised by the redacteur, and he happened to select and print in his journal this song as a specimen of what the collection contained. He was seised in his bed that night and has been never since heard of. Our excellent journal de Paris then is suppressed and this bold traitor has been in jail now three weeks, and for ought any body knows will end his days there. Thus you see, madam, the value of energy in government; our feeble republic would in such a case have probably been wrapt in the flames of war and desolation for want of a power lodged in a single hand to punish summarily those who write songs. The fate of poor Pilatre de Rosiere[2] will have reached you before this does, and with more certainty than we yet know it. This will damp for a while the ardor of the Phaetons of our race who are endeavoring to learn us the way to heaven on wings of our own. I took a trip yesterday to Sannois and commenced an acquaintance with the old Countess d'Hocquetout.[3] I received much pleasure from it and hope it has opened a door of admission for me to the circle of literati with which she is environed. I heard there the Nightingale in all it's perfection: and I do not hesitate to pronounce that in America it would be deemed a bird of the third rank only, our mockingbird, and fox-coloured thrush being unquestionably superior to it. The squibs against Mr. Adams are such as I expected from the polished, mild tempered, truth speaking people he is sent to. It would be ill policy to attempt to answer or refute them. But counter-squibs I think would be good policy. Be pleased to tell him that as I had before ordered his Madeira and Frontignac to be forwarded, and had asked his orders to Mr. Garvey as to the residue, which I doubt not he has given, I was afraid to send another order about the Bourdeaux lest it should produce confusion. In stating my accounts with the United states, I am at a loss whether to charge house rent or not. It has always been allowed to Dr. Franklin. Does Mr. Adams mean to charge this for Auteuil and London? Because if he does, I certainly will, being convinced by experience that my expences here will otherwise exceed my allowance. I ask this information of you, Madam, because I think you know better than Mr. Adams what may be necessary and right for him to do in occasions of this class. I will beg the favor of you to present my respects to Miss Adams. I have no secrets to communicate to her in cypher at this moment, what I write to Mr. Adams being mere commonplace stuff, not meriting a communication to the Secretary. I have the honour to be with the most perfect esteem Dr. Madam Your most obedient & most humble servt.

Th: Jefferson

6. TO ELIZABETH HOUSE TRIST

Dear Madam   *Paris Aug. 18. 1785.*
Your favor of Dec. 25. came to hand on the 22d. of July, and on the next day I had the pleasure of receiving that of May. 4. I was happy to find that you had taken the first step for a return to your own country, tho' I was sensible many difficult ones still remained. I hope however these are surmounted, and that this letter will find you in the bosom of your friends. Your last letter is an evidence of the excellence of your own dispositions which can be so much excited by so small a circumstance as the one noticed in it. Tho' I esteem you too much to wish you may ever need services from me or any other person, yet I wish you to be assured that in such an event no one would be more disposed to render them, nor more desirous of receiving such a proof of your good opinion as would be your applying for them. By this time I hope your mind has felt the good effects of time and occupation.[1] They are slow physicians indeed, but they are the only ones. Their opiate influence lessens our sensibility tho their power does not extend to dry up the sources of sorrow. I thought there was a prospect the last winter of my taking a trip to England. Tho' I did not know who and where were Browse's relations in that country, yet I knew he had some so nearly connected as to claim their attention. I should have endeavored to have seen them, and disposed them to feel an interest both in you and him. Tho' the probability of my going there is very much lessened, yet it is not among impossible events. Will you be

so good as to let me know what relations he has there and where they live, and if I should at any time go there I will certainly see them. Patsy is well, and is happily situated in the Convent of Panthemont the institutions of which leave me nothing to wish on that head. It is attended by the best masters. The most disagreeable circumstance is that I have too little of her company. I am endeavoring by some arrangements to alter this. My present anxiety is to get my other daughter over to me; for tho' my return is placed at a period not very distant, yet I cannot determine to leave her so long without me. But indeed the circumstances of such a passage, to such an infant, under any other care than that of a parent, are very distressing. My wishes are fixed, but my resolution is wavering.

I am much pleased with the people of this country. The roughnesses of the human mind are so thoroughly rubbed off with them that it seems as if one might glide thro' a whole life among them without a justle. Perhaps too their manners may be the best calculated for happiness to a people in their situation. But I am convinced they fall far short of effecting a happiness so temperate, so uniform and so lasting as is generally enjoyed with us. The domestic bonds here are absolutely done away. And where can their compensation be found? Perhaps they may catch some moments of transport above the level of the ordinary tranquil joy we experience, but they are separated by long intervals during which all the passions are at sea without rudder or compass. Yet fallacious as these pursuits of happiness are, they seem on the whole to furnish the most effectual abstraction from a contemplation of the hardness of their government. Indeed it is difficult to conceive how so good a people, with so good a king, so well disposed rulers in general, so genial a climate, so fertile a soil, should be rendered so ineffectual for producing human happiness by one single curse, that of a bad form of government. But it is a fact. In spite of the mildness of their governors the people are ground to powder by the vices of the form of government. Of twenty millions of people supposed to be in France I am of opinion there are nineteen millions more wretched, more accursed in every circumstance of human existence, than the most conspicuously wretched individual of the whole United states.—I beg your pardon for getting into politics. I will add only one sentiment more of that character. That is, nourish peace with their persons, but war against their manners. Every step we take towards the adoption of their manners is a step towards perfect misery.—I pray you to write to me often. Do not you turn politician too; but write me all the small news; the news about persons and not about states. Tell me who die, that I may meet these disagreeable events in detail, and not all at once when I return: who marry, who hang themselves because they cannot marry &c. &c. Present me in the most friendly terms to Mrs. House, and Browse, and be assured of the sincerity with which I am Dear Madam your affectionate friend & servant,

Th: Jefferson

7. TO PETER CARR

Dear Peter   *Paris Aug. 19. 1785.*
I received by Mr. Mazzei your letter of April 20. I am much mortified to hear that you have lost so much time, and that when you arrived in Williamsburgh you were not at all advanced from what you were when you left Monticello. Time now begins to be precious to you. Every day you lose, will retard a day your entrance on that public stage whereon you may begin to be useful to yourself. However the way to repair the loss is to improve the future time. I trust that with your dispositions even the acquisition of science is a pleasing employment. I can assure you that the possession of it is what (next to an honest heart) will above all things render you dear to your friends, and give you fame and promotion in your own country. When your mind shall be well improved with science, nothing will be necessary to place you in the highest points of view but to pursue the interests of your country, the interests of your friends, and your own interests also with the purest integrity, the most chaste honour. The defect of these virtues can never be made up by all the other acquirements of body and mind. Make these then your first object. Give up money, give up fame, give up science, give the earth itself and all it contains rather than do an immoral act. And never suppose that in any possible situa-

tion or under any circumstances that it is best for you to do a dishonourable thing however slightly so it may appear to you. Whenever you are to do a thing tho' it can never be known but to yourself, ask yourself how you would act were all the world looking at you, and act accordingly. Encourage all your virtuous dispositions, and exercise them whenever an opportunity arises, being assured that they will gain strength by exercise as a limb of the body does, and that exercise will make them habitual. From the practice of the purest virtue you may be assured you will derive the most sublime comforts in every moment of life and in the moment of death. If ever you find yourself environed with difficulties and perplexing circumstances, out of which you are at a loss how to extricate yourself, do what is right, and be assured that that will extricate you the best out of the worst situations. Tho' you cannot see when you fetch one step, what will be the next, yet follow truth, justice, and plain-dealing, and never fear their leading you out of the labyrinth in the easiest manner possible. The knot which you thought a Gordian one will untie itself before you. Nothing is so mistaken as the supposition that a person is to extricate himself from a difficulty, by intrigue, by chicanery, by dissimulation, by trimming, by an untruth, by an injustice. This increases the difficulties tenfold, and those who pursue these methods, get themselves so involved at length that they can turn no way but their infamy becomes more exposed. It is of great importance to set a resolution, not to be shaken, never to tell an untruth. There is no vice so mean, so pitiful, so contemptible and he who permits himself to tell a lie once, finds it much easier to do it a second and third time, till at length it becomes habitual, he tells lies without attending to it, and truths without the world's beleiving him. This falshood of the tongue leads to that of the heart, and in time depraves all it's good dispositions.

An honest heart being the first blessing, a knowing head is the second. It is time for you now to begin to be choice in your reading, to begin to pursue a regular course in it and not to suffer yourself to be turned to the right or left by reading any thing out of that course. I have long ago digested a plan for you, suited to the circumstances in which you will be placed. This I will detail to you from time to time as you advance. For the present I advise you to begin a course of antient history, reading every thing in the original and not in translations. First read Goldsmith's history of Greece. This will give you a digested view of that feild. Then take up antient history in the detail, reading the following books in the following order. Herodotus. Thucydides. Xenophontis hellenica. Xenophontis Anabasis. Quintus Curtius. Justin. This shall form the first stage of your historical reading, and is all I need mention to you now. The next will be of Roman history. From that we will come down to Modern history. In Greek and Latin poetry, you have read or will read at school Virgil, Terence, Horace, Anacreon, Theocritus, Homer. Read also Milton's paradise lost, Ossian, Pope's works, Swift's works in order to form your style in your own language. In morality read Epictetus, Xenophontis memorabilia, Plato's Socratic dialogues, Cicero's philosophies. In order to assure a certain progress in this reading, consider what hours you have free from the school and the exercises of the school. Give about two of them every day to exercise; for health must not be sacrificed to learning. A strong body makes the mind strong. As to the species of exercise, I advise the gun. While this gives a moderate exercise to the body, it gives boldness, enterprize, and independance to the mind. Games played with the ball and others of that nature, are too violent for the body and stamp no character on the mind. Let your gun therefore be the constant companion of your walks. Never think of taking a book with you. The object of walking is to relax the mind. You should therefore not permit yourself even to think while you walk. But divert your attention by the objects surrounding you. Walking is the best possible exercise. Habituate yourself to walk very far. The Europeans value themselves on having subdued the horse to the uses of man. But I doubt whether we have not lost more than we have gained by the use of this animal. No one has occasioned so much the degeneracy of the human body. An Indian goes on foot nearly as far in a day, for a long journey, as an enfeebled white does on his horse, and he will tire the best horses. There is no habit you will value so much as that of walking far without fatigue. I would advise you to take your exercise in the afternoon. Not because it is the best time for exercise for certainly it is not: but because it is the best time to spare from your studies; and habit will soon reconcile it to health, and render it nearly as useful as if you gave to that the more precious hours of the day. A little walk of half an hour in the morning when you first rise is adviseable also. It shakes off sleep, and produces other good effects in the animal œconomy. Rise at a fixed and an early hour, and go to bed at a fixed and early hour also. Sitting up late at night is injurious to the health, and not useful to the mind.—Having ascribed proper hours to exercise, divide what remain (I mean of your vacant hours) into three portions. Give the principal to history, the other two, which should be shorter, to Philosophy and Poetry. Write me once every month or two and let me know the progress you make. Tell me in what manner you employ every hour in the day. The plan I have proposed for you is adapted to your present situation only. When that is changed, I shall propose a corresponding change of plan. I have ordered the following books to be sent to you from London to the care of Mr. Madison. Herodotus. Thucydides. Xenophon's Hellenics, Anabasis, and Memorabilia. Cicero's works. Baretti's Spanish and English dictionary. Martin's philosophical grammar and Martin's philosophia Britannica. I will send you the following from hence. Bezout's mathematics. De la Lande's astronomy. Muschenbroek's physics. Quintus Curtius. Justin, a Spanish grammar, and some Spanish books. You will observe that Martin, Bezout, De la Lande and Muschenbroek are not in the preceding plan. They are not to be opened till you go to the University. You are now I expect learning French. You must push this: because the books which will be put into your hands when you advance into Mathematics, Natural philosophy, Natural history, &c. will be mostly French, these sciences being better treated by the French than the English writers. Our future connection with Spain renders that the most necessary of the modern languages, after the French. When you become a public man you may have occasion for it, and the circumstance of your possessing that language may give you a preference over other candidates. I have nothing further to add for the present, than to husband well your time, cherish your instructors, strive to make every body your friend, & be assured that nothing will be so pleasing, as your success, to Dear Peter yours affectionately,

Th: Jefferson

8. TO JOHN JAY[1]

Dear Sir   *Paris Aug. 23, 1785.*
I shall sometimes ask your permission to write you letters, not official but private. The present is of this kind, and is occasioned by the question proposed in yours of June 14 'Whether it would be useful to us to carry all our own productions, or none?' Were we perfectly free to decide this question, I should reason as follows. We have now lands enough to employ an infinite number of people in their cultivation. Cultivators of the earth are the most valuable citizens. They are the most vigorous, the most independant, the most virtuous, and they are tied to their country and wedded to it's liberty and interests by the most lasting bands. As long therefore as they can find emploiment in this line, I would not convert them into mariners, artisans, or any thing else. But our citizens will find emploiment in this line till their numbers, and of course their productions, become too great for the demand both internal and foreign. This is not the case as yet, and probably will not be for a considerable time. As soon as it is, the surplus of hands must be turned to something else. I should then perhaps wish to turn them to the sea in preference to manufactures, because comparing the characters of the two classes I find the former the most valuable citizens. I consider the class of artificers as the panders of vice and the instruments by which the liberties of a country are generally overturned. However we are not free to decide this question on principles of theory only. Our people are decided in the opinion that it is necessary for us to take a share in the occupation of the ocean, and their established habits induce them to require that the sea be kept open to them, and that that line of policy be pursued which will render the use of that element as great as possible to them. I think it a duty in those entrusted with the administration of their affairs to conform themselves to the decided choice of their constituents: and that therefore we should in every instance preserve an equality of right to them in the transportation of commodities, in the right of fishing, and in the other uses of the sea. But what will be the consequence? Frequent wars without a doubt. Their property will be violated on the

sea, and in foreign ports, their persons will be insulted, emprisoned &c. for pretended debts, contracts, crimes, contraband &c. &c. These insults must be resented, even if we had no feelings, yet to prevent their eternal repetition. Or in other words, our commerce on the ocean and in other countries must be paid for by frequent war. The justest dispositions possible in ourselves will not secure us against it. It would be necessary that all other nations were just also. Justice indeed on our part will save us from those wars which would have been produced by a contrary disposition. But how to prevent those produced by the wrongs of other nations? By putting ourselves in a condition to punish them. Weakness provokes insult and injury, while a condition to punish it often prevents it. This reasoning leads to the necessity of some naval force, that being the only weapo[n] with which we can reach an enemy. I think it to our interest to punis[h] the first insult: because an insult unpunished is the parent of many oth[ers]. We are not at this moment in a condition to do it, but we should put ourselv[es] into it as soon as possible. If a war with England should take place it see[ms] to me that the first thing necessary would be a resolution to abandon the carrying trade because we cannot protect it. Foreign nations must in that case be invited to bring us what we want and to take our productions in their own bottoms. This alone could prevent the loss of those productions to us and the acquisition of them to our enemy. Our seamen might be emploied in depredations on their trade. But how dreadfully we shall suffer on our coasts, if we have no force on the water, former experience has taught us. Indeed I look forward with horror to the very possible case of war with an European power, and think there is no protection against them but from the possession of some force on the sea. Our vicinity to their West India possessions and to the fisheries is a bridle which a small naval force on our part would hold in the mouths of the most powerful of these countries. I hope our land office will rid us of our debts, and that our first attention then will be to the beginning a naval force of some sort. This alone can countenance our people as carriers on the water, and I suppose them to be determined to continue such.

I wrote you two public letters on the 14th. inst. since which I have received yours of July 13. I shall always be pleased to receive from you in a private way such communications as you might not chuse to put into a public letter. I have the honor to be with very sincere esteem Dr. Sir your most obedient humble servt.,

Th: Jefferson

9. TO FRANCIS EPPES

Dear Sir   *Paris Aug. 30. 1785.*
I have received no letter from you of later date than Oct. 14. 1784. Since that date I have written to you Nov. 11. Jan. 13. Feb. 5. and May 11. and to Mrs. Eppes Nov. 11. and Feb. 5. The letters of November were carried by Colo. Lemaire. He has been so kind as to write to me from Richmond Apr. 30. and to inform me of Polly's welfare and that of your family at that date. He also said in his letter that you would be glad of some seeds both for the kitchen and flower garden. The Mr. Fitzhughs being to go from here to Virginia I shall endeavor to get them to take a small packet of seeds for you, which I am obliged to make very small to enable them to take it at all. Not knowing the French names, which distinguish the best species of every kind of plant, I could only desire a good seedsman to pack up a few of what are deemed the best kinds in this country: there is only enough of each to begin a stock with. You will soon see whether any of them are preferable to what you already have. I must observe only that the Peach Apricot is one of the most valuable fruits in this country and very lately known. It is therefore worth your utmost care. I will state a list of the seeds at the end of this letter. I must now remind you that I expect from you the seeds I desired in my letter of July 1. 1784. to wit, Cypress, cedar, magnolia and myrtle, and in great quantities each. I mentioned then the method of sending them. I take the liberty of inviting the elder Mr. Fitzhugh, who we understand is elected for his county, to pay his respects to Mrs. Eppes and yourself some Saturday afternoon from Richmond. I must now repeat my wish to have Polly sent to me next summer. This however must depend on the circum-

stance of a good vessel sailing from Virginia in the months of April, May, June, or July. I would not have her set out sooner or later on account of the equinoxes. The vessel should have performed one voiage at least, but not be more than four or five years old. We do not attend to this circumstance till we have been to sea, but there the consequence of it is felt. I think it would be found that all the vessels which are lost are either in their first voiage, or after they are five years old. At least there are few exceptions to this. With respect to the person to whose care she should be trusted, I must leave it to yourself and Mrs. Eppes altogether. Some good lady passing from America to France, or even England would be most eligible. But a careful gentleman who would be so kind as to superintend her would do. In this case some woman who has had the small pox must attend her. A careful negro woman, as Isabel for instance if she has had the small pox, would suffice under the patronage of a gentleman. The woman need not come further than Havre, l'Orient, Nantes or whatever other port she should land at, because I would go there for the child myself, and the person could return to Virginia directly. My anxieties on this subject would induce me to endless details. But your discretion and that of Mrs. Eppes saves me the necessity. I will only add that I would rather live a year longer without her than have her trusted to any but a good ship and a summer passage. Patsy is well. She speaks French as easily as English, whilst Humphries, Short and myself are scarcely better at it than when we landed. She writes to Mrs. Eppes.

Europe is likely to enjoy quiet. The affair between the Emperor and Dutch is settled, tho the treaty is not yet published, and there is no other storm hovering over us as yet. Perhaps one may be brewing between him and the Turks: but not for this year.

Besides anxieties on the more important branches of my affairs I feel others also for the preservation of my improvements at home. I have no doubt but proper charges are given on this subject. It would be grievous to me to have to begin them anew. I look with impatience to the moment when I may rejoin you. There is nothing to tempt me to stay here. Present me with the most cordial affection to Mrs. Eppes, the children, and the family at Hors dumonde.[1] I commit to Mrs.

Eppes my kisses for dear Poll who hangs on my mind night and day. Adieu my dear Sir and be assured of the affection with which I am Your sincere friend & servt.

Th: Jefferson

James is well and salutes all his friends.[2]

10. TO JAMES MADISON, WITH A LIST OF BOOKS

Dear Sir   *Paris Sep. 1. 1785.*
My last to you was dated May 11. by Monsr. de Doradour. Since that I have received yours of Jan. 22. with 6. copies of the revisal, and that of Apr. 27. by Mr. Mazzei.

All is quiet here. The Emperor and Dutch are certainly agreed tho' they have not published their agreement. Most of his schemes in Germany must be postponed, if they are not prevented, by the confederacy of many of the Germanic body at the head of which is the K. of Prussia, and to which the Elector of Hanover is supposed to have acceded. The object of the league is to preserve the members of the empire in their present state. I doubt whether the jealousy entertained of this prince, and which is so fully evidenced by this league, may not defeat the election of his nephew to be king of the Romans, and thus produce an instance of breaking the lineal succession. Nothing is as yet done between him and the Turks. If any thing is produced in that quarter it will not be for this year. The court of Madrid has obtained the delivery of the crew of the brig Betsy taken by the Emperor of Marocco. The Emperor had treated them kindly, new-cloathed them, and delivered them to the Spanish minister who sent them to Cadiz. This is the only American vessel ever taken by the Barbary states. The Emperor continues to give proofs of his desire to be in friendship with us, or in other words, of receiving us into the number of his tributaries. Nothing further need be feared from him. I wish the Algerines may be as easily dealt with. I fancy the peace expected between them and Spain is not likely to take place. I am well informed that the late proceedings in America have produced a wonderful sensation in England in our favour. I mean the disposition which seems to be becoming general to invest Congress with the regulation of our commerce, and in the mean time the measures taken to defeat the avidity of the British government, grasping at our carrying business. I can add with truth that it was not till these symptoms appeared in America that I have been able to discover the smallest token of respect towards the United states in any part of Europe. There was an enthusiasm towards us all over Europe at the moment of the peace. The torrent of lies published unremittingly in every day's London paper first made an impression and produced a coolness. The republication of these lies in most of the papers of Europe (done probably by authority of the governments to discourage emigrations) carried them home to the belief of every mind. They supposed every thing in America was anarchy, tumult, and civil war. The reception of the M. Fayette gave a check to these ideas. The late proceedings seem to be producing a decisive vibration in our favour. I think it possible that England may ply before them. It is a nation which nothing but views of interest can govern. If it produces us good there, it will here also. The defeat of the Irish propositions is also in our favor.

I have at length made up the purchase of books for you, as far as it can be done for the present. The objects which I have not yet been able to get, I shall continue to seek for. Those purchased, are packed this morning in two trunks, and you have the catalogue and prices herein inclosed. The future charges of transportation shall be carried into the next bill. The amount of the present is 1154 livres 13 sous which reckoning the French crown of 6. livres at 6/8 Virginia money is £64-3. which sum you will be so good as to keep in your hands to be used occasionally in the education of my nephews when the regular resources disappoint you. To the same use I would pray you to apply twenty five guineas which I have lent the two Mr. Fitzhughs of Marmion, and which I have desired them to repay into your hands. You will of course deduct the price of the revisals and any other articles you may have been so kind as to pay for me. Greek and Roman authors are dearer here than I believe any where in the world. No body here reads them, wherefore they are not reprinted. Don Ulloa in the original not to be found. The collection of tracts on the œconomics of different nations we cannot find; nor Amelot's travels into

China. I shall send these two trunks of books to Havre there to wait a conveiance to America; for as to the fixing the packets there it is as incertain as ever. The other articles you mention shall be procured as far as they can be. Knowing that some of them would be better got in London, I commissioned Mr. Short, who was going there, to get them. He is not yet returned. They will be of such a nature as that I can get some gentleman who may be going to America to take them in his portmanteau. Le Maire being now able to stand on his own legs there will be no necessity for your advancing him the money I desired if it is not already done. I am anxious to hear from you on the subject of my Notes on Virginia.[1] I have been obliged to give so many of them here that I fear their getting published. I have received an application from the Directors of the public buildings to procure them a plan for their Capitol. I shall send them one taken from the best morsel of antient architecture[2] now remaining. It has obtained the approbation of fifteen or sixteen centuries, and is therefore preferable to any design which might be newly contrived. It will give more room, be more convenient and cost less than the plan they sent me. Pray encourage them to wait for it, and to execute it. It will be superior in beauty to any thing in America, and not inferior to any thing in the world. It is very simple. Have you a copying press?[3] If you have not, you should get one. Mine (exclusive of paper which costs a guinea a ream) has cost me about 14. guineas. I would give ten times that sum that I had had it from the date of the stamp act. I hope you will be so good as to continue your communications both of the great and small kind which are equally useful to me. Be assured of the sincerity with which I am Dr. Sir Your friend & servt.,

Th: Jefferson

ENCLOSURE

	livres	sous	den
Dictionnaire de Trevoux. 5. vol. fol. @ 5f12	28–	0–	0
La Conquista di Mexico. De Solis. fol. 7f10.			
relieure 7f	14–	10	

	livres	sous	den
Traité de morale et de bonheur. 12mo. 2. v. in 1	2–	8	
Wicquefort de l'Ambassadeur. 2. v. 4to	7–	4	
Burlamaqui. Principes du droit Politique 4to. 3f12 relieure 2f5	5–	17	
Conquista de la China por el Tartaro por Palafox. 12mo.	3		
Code de l'humanité de Felice. 13. v. 4to	104–	0	
13. first livraisons of the Encyclopedie 47. vols. 4to. (being 48f less than subscription)	348–	0	
14th. livraison of do. 4. v. 4to	24–	0	
Peyssonel	2–	0	
Bibliotheque physico-œconomique. 4. v. 12mo. 10f4. rel. 3f	13–	4	
Cultivateur Americain. 2. v. 8vo. 7f17. rel. 2f10	10–	7	
Mirabeau sur l'ordre des Cincinnati. 10f10. rel. 1f5 (prohibited)	11–	15	
Coutumes Anglo-Normands de Houard. 4. v. 4to. 40f rel. 10f	50–	0	
Memoires sur l'Amerique 4. v. 4to	24–	0	
Tott sur les Turcs. 4. v. in 2. 8vo. 10f. rel. 2f10	12–	10	
Neckar sur l'Administration des Finances de France. 3. v. 12mo. 7f10 rel. 2f5	9–	15	
le bon-sens. 12mo. 6f rel. 15s (prohibited)	6–	15	

Mably. Principes de morale.

1. v. 12mo.	3^{lt} 12^4		
etude de l'histoire 1	2 10		
maniere d'ecrire l'histoire 1	2 8		
constitution d'Amerique 1	1 16	relieure	
sur l'histoire de France. 2. v.	6	de 11	
droit de l'Europe 3. v.	7 10	vols. @	
ordres des societies	2	15 s. 8f5	41– 1
principes des negotiations	2 10		
entretiens de Phocion	2		
des Romains	2 10		
	32 16		

	livres	sous	den
Wanting to complete Mably's works which I have not been able to procure			
les principes de legislation			
sur les Grecs			
sur la Pologne.			
Chronologie des empires anciennes de la Combe. 1. v. 8vo.	5–	0–	0
de l'histoire universelle de Hornot 1. v. 8vo. 4f	4–	0–	0
de l'histoire universelle de Berlié 1. v. 8vo. 2f10 rel. 1f5	3–	15	
des empereurs Romains par Richer 2. v. 8vo. 8f rel. 2f10	10–	10	
des Juifs 1. v. 8vo. 3f10. rel. 1f5	4–	15	
de l'histoire universelle par Du Fresnoy 2. v. 8vo. 13f rel. 2f10	15–	10	
de l'histoire du Nord par La Combe 2. v. 8vo. 10f. rel. 2f10	12–	10	
de France. par Henault. 3. v. 8vo. 12f rel. 3f15	15–	15	
Memoires de Voltaire. 2. v. in 1. 2f10 rel. 15s	3–	5–	0
Linnaei Philosophia Botanica. 1. v. 8vo. 7f rel. 1f5	8–	5	
Genera plantarum 1. v. 8vo. 8f rel. 1f5	9–	5	
Species plantarum. 4. v. 8vo. 32f rel. 5f	37–	0	
Systema naturae 4. v. 8vo. 26f rel. 5f	31–	0	
Clayton. Flora Virginica. 4to. 12f. rel. 2f10	14–	10	
D'Albon sur l'interet de plusieurs nations. 4. v. 12mo. 12f. rel. 3f	15–	0	
Systeme de la nature de Diderot. 3. v. 8vo. 21f (prohibited)	21–	0	
Coussin [*sic*] histoire Romaine. 2. v. in 1. 12mo. / de Constantinople 8. v. in 10. } 16. vols. 12mo. / de l'empire de l'Occident 2. v. / de l'eglise. 5. v. in 3.	36–	0–	0
Droit de la Nature. por Wolff. 6. v. 12mo. 15f rel. 4f10	19–	10	

	livres	sous	den
Voyage de Pagét 8vo. 3. v. in 1	9		
Mirabeau. Ami des hommes 5. v. 12mo.	12		
Theorie de l'impot 2. v. in 1. 12mo.			
Buffon. Supplement 11. 12. Oiseaux 17. 18.			
Mineraux 1. 2. 3. 4.	24.		
Lettres de Pascal. 12mo. 2f. rel. 15s.	2–	15	
Le sage à la cour et le roi voiageur (prohibited)	10–	15	
Principes de legislation universelle 2. v. 8vo.	12–	0	
Ordonnances de la Marine par Valin. 2. v. 4to.	22		

Diderot sur les sourds and muets 12mo.
          3f12. sur les   4. v. 12mo.   13–   7
aveugles 3f. sur la nature 3f. sur la
                morale 3f15

	livres	sous	den
Mariana's history of Spain 11. v. 12mo.	21		
2 trunks & packing paper	43–	0	
	1154–	13	

11. TO CHASTELLUX, WITH ENCLOSURE

Dear Sir   *Paris Sep. 2. 1785.*
You were so kind as to allow me a fortnight to read your journey through Virginia.[1] But you should have thought of this indulgence while you were writing it, and have rendered it less interesting if you meant that your readers should have been longer engaged with it. In fact I devoured it at a single meal, and a second reading scarce allowed me sang froid enough to mark a few errors in the names of persons and places which I note on a paper herein inclosed, with an inconsiderable error or two in facts which I have also noted because I supposed you wished to state them correctly. From this general approbation however you must allow me to except about a dozen pages in the earlier part of the book which I read with a continued blush from beginning to end, as it presented me a lively picture of what I wish to be, but am not. No, my dear Sir, the thousand millionth part of what you there say, is more than I deserve. It might perhaps have passed in Europe at the time you

wrote it, and the exaggeration might not have been detected. But consider that the animal is now brought there, and that every one will take his dimensions for himself. The friendly complexion of your mind has betrayed you into a partiality of which the European spectator will be divested. Respect to yourself therefore will require indispensably that you expunge the whole of those pages except your own judicious observations interspersed among them on Animal and physical subjects. With respect to my countrymen[2] there is surely nothing which can render them uneasy, in the observations made on them. They know that they are not perfect, and will be sensible that you have viewed them with a philanthropic eye. You say much good of them, and less ill than they are conscious may be said with truth. I have studied their character with attention. I have thought them, as you found them, aristocratical, pompous, clannish, indolent, hospitable, and I should have added, disinterested, but you say attached to their interest. This is the only trait in their character wherein our observations differ. I have always thought them so careless of their interests, so thoughtless in their expences and in all their transactions of business that I had placed it among the vices of their character, as indeed most virtues when carried beyond certain bounds degenerate into vices. I had even ascribed this to it's cause, to that warmth of their climate which unnerves and unmans both body and mind. While on this subject I will give you my idea of the characters of the several states.

In the North they are	*In the South they are*
cool	fiery
sober	Voluptuary
laborious	indolent
persevering	unsteady
independant	independant
jealous of their own liberties, and just to those of others	zealous for their own liberties, but trampling on those of others
interested	generous
chicaning	candid
superstitious and hypocritical in their religion	without attachment or pretentions to any religion but that of the heart.

These characteristics grow weaker and weaker by gradation from North to South and South to North, insomuch that an observing traveller, without the aid of the quadrant may always know his latitude by the character of the people among whom he finds himself. It is in Pennsylvania that the two characters seem to meet and blend and to form a people free from the extremes both of vice and virtue. Peculiar circumstances have given to New York the character which climate would have given had she been placed on the South instead of the North side of Pennsylvania. Perhaps too other circumstances may have occasioned in Virginia a transplantation of a particular vice foreign to it's climate. You could judge of this with more impartiality than I could, and the probability is that your estimate of them is the most just. I think it for their good that the vices of their character should be pointed out to them that they may amend them; for a malady of either body or mind once known is half cured.

I wish you would add to this peice your letter to Mr. Madison on the expediency of introducing the arts into America. I found in that a great deal of matter, very many observations, which would be useful to the legislators of America, and to the general mass of citizens. I read it with great pleasure and analysed it's contents that I might fix them in my own mind. I have the honor to be with very sincere esteem Dear Sir Your most obedient & most humble servt.,

Th: Jefferson

ENCLOSURE

1.2.3. *Kent* should be Newkent.
   4. Button's bridge should be Bottom's bridge.
5.6. Bothwell   should be Boswell.
   7. montagnes de l'Ouest, should be South-west mountains. They are so called from their direction which is from North-East to South-west. All our mountains run in the same course, but these being the first discovered appropriated the name to themselves.
   8. The expression 'il avoit conquis tout le pais entre l'Appamatoc et le bay de Chesapeak,' gives an idea of Powhatan, perhaps not exactly true, and certainly defective. He was the head of all the tribes of Indians below the falls of the rivers from Susquehanna to the mid-

lands of James and Roanoke rivers. What was the nature of his power over them, is not known; probably it was like that of the chiefs among the modern tribes of Indians, which we now know to consist in persuasion and respectability of personal character. It would be more accurate also to say that 'Powhatan county takes it's name from the river on which it lies, now called James river, but formerly Powhatan from a tribe and chief of that name famous in the history of Virginia.' The truth is that the county of Powhatan was not occupied by the Powhatans, but was the chief habitation of the Monacans, the rivals and perpetual enemies of the Powhatans.

9. The town of Pocahuntas does not send delegates to the assembly. The county, in which it is, sends delegates as all the other counties do.

10. Ross should be Rolfe.

11. Carter should be Cary.

12. Mr. Beverley Randolph, should be Mr. Randolph.

13. Colchester, should be, Manchester.

14. The first Congress was at Philadelphia and not New York.

15. *du Congrés* should be *du Conseil du roi.* He was a tory.

16. Maryland was never purchased by the crown. It was always a proprietary government.

17. The government is divided into three departments, legislative, executive and judiciary. No person can hold an office in any two of them. Consequently all the members in any one department are excluded from both the other. Hence the judges and Attorney general cannot be of the legislature.

The clergy are excluded, because, if admitted into the legislature at all, the probability is that they would form it's majority. For they are dispersed through every county in the state, they have influence with the people, and great opportunities of persuading them to elect them into the legislature. This body, tho shattered, is still formidable, still forms a *corps,* and is still actuated by the *esprit de corps.* The nature of that spirit has been severely felt by mankind, and has filled the history of ten or twelve centuries with too many atrocities not to merit a proscription from meddling with government. Lawyers, holding no public office, may act in any of the departments. They accordingly constitute the ablest part both of the legislative and executive bodies.

12. TO ABIGAIL ADAMS

Dear Madam   *Paris Sep. 4. 1785.*
... We have little new and interesting here. The Queen has determined to wear none but French gauzes hereafter. How many English looms will this put down? You will have seen the affair of the Cardinal de Rohan so well detailed in the Leyden gazette that I need add nothing on that head. The Cardinal is still in the Bastille. It is certain that the Queen has been compromitted without the smallest authority from her: and the probability is that the Cardinal has been duped into it by his mistress Madme. de la Motte. There results from this two consequences not to his honour, that he is a debauchee, and a booby. The Abbés are well.[1] They have been kept in town this summer by the affairs of the Abbé Mably. I have at length procured a house in a situation much more pleasing to me than my present.[2] It is at the grille des champs Elysees, but within the city. It suits me in every circumstance but the price, being dearer than the one I am now in. It has a clever garden to it. I will pray you to present my best respects to Miss Adams and to be assured of the respect & esteem with which I have the honour to be Dear Madam Your most obedient & most humble servt.,

Th: Jefferson

13. TO JAMES MADISON

Dear Sir   *Paris Sep. 20. 1785.*
By Mr. Fitzhugh you will receive my letter of the 1'st inst. He is still here, and gives me an opportunity of again addressing you much sooner than I should have done but for the discovery of a great peice of inattention. In that letter I send you a detail of the cost of your books, and desire you to keep the amount in your hands, as if I had forgot that a part of it was in fact your own, as being a balance of what I had remained in your debt. I really did not attend to it in the moment of writing, and when it occurred to me, I revised my memorandum book from the time of our being in Philadelphia together, and stated our account from the beginning lest I should forget or mistake any

part of it: I inclose you this state. You will always be so good as to let me know from time to time your advances for me. Correct with freedom all my proceedings for you, as in what I do I have no other desire than that of doing exactly what will be most pleasing to you.

I received this summer a letter from Messrs. Buchanan and Hay as directors of the public buildings desiring I would have drawn for them plans of sundry buildings, and in the first place of a Capitol. They fixed for their receiving this plan a day which was within one month of that on which their letter came to my hand. I engaged an Architect of capital abilities in this business.[1] Much time was requisite, after the external form was agreed on, to make the internal distribution convenient for the three branches of government. This time was much lengthened by my avocations to other objects which I had no right to neglect. The plan however was settled. The gentlemen had sent me one which they had thought of. The one agreed on here is more convenient, more beautiful, gives more room and will not cost more than two thirds of what that would. We took for our model what is called the Maisonquarrèe of Nismes, one of the most beautiful, if not the most beautiful and precious morsel of architecture left us by antiquity. It was built by Caius and Lucius Caesar and repaired by Louis XIV. and has the suffrage of all the judges of architecture who have seen it, as yeilding to no one of the beautiful monuments of Greece, Rome, Palmyra and Balbec which late travellers have communicated to us. It is very simple, but it is noble beyond expression, and would have done honour to our country as presenting to travellers a morsel of taste in our infancy promising much for our maturer age. I have been much mortified with information which I received two days ago from Virginia that the first brick of the Capitol would be laid within a few days. But surely the delay of this peice of a summer would have been repaid by the savings in the plan preparing here, were we to value it's other superiorities as nothing. But how is a taste in this beautiful art to be formed in our countrymen, unless we avail ourselves of every occasion when public buildings are to be erected, of presenting to them models for their study and imitation? Pray try if you can effect the stopping of this work. I have written also to E. R. on the subject.[2] The loss will be only of the laying the bricks already laid, or a part of them. The bricks themselves will do again for the interior walls, and one side wall and one end wall may remain as they will answer equally well for our plan. This loss is not to be weighed against the saving of money which will arise, against the comfort of laying out the public money for something honourable, the satisfaction of seeing an object and proof of national good taste, and the regret and mortification of erecting a monument of our barbarism which will be loaded with execrations as long as it shall endure. The plans are in good forwardness and I hope will be ready within three or four weeks. They could not be stopped now but on paying their whole price which will be considerable. If the Undertakers are afraid to undo what they have done, encourage them to it by a recommendation from the assembly. You see I am an enthusiast on the subject of the arts. But it is an enthusiasm of which I am not ashamed, as it's object is to improve the taste of my countrymen, to increase their reputation, to reconcile to them the respect of the world and procure them it's praise.

I shall send off your books, in two trunks, to Havre within two or three days to the care of Mr. Limozin, American agent there. I will advise you as soon as I know by what vessel he forwards them. Adieu. Your's affectionately,

Th: Jefferson

14. TO ABIGAIL ADAMS

Dear Madam   *Paris Sep. 25. 1785.*
Mr. Short's return the night before last availed me of your favour of Aug. 12. I immediately ordered the shoes you desired which will be ready tomorrow. I am not certain whether this will be in time for the departure of Mr. Barclay or of Colo. Franks, for it is not yet decided which of them goes to London. I have also procured for you three plateaux de dessert with a silvered ballustrade round them, and four figures of Biscuit. The former cost 192^{tt}, the latter 12^{tt} each, making together 240 livres or 10. Louis. The merchant undertakes to send them by the way of Rouen through the hands of Mr. Garvey and to have them delivered in London. There will be some additional ex-

pences of packing, transportation and duties here. Those in England I imagine you can save. When I know the amount I will inform you of it, but there will be no occasion to remit it here. With respect to the figures I could only find three of those you named, matched in size. These were Minerva, Diana, and Apollo. I was obliged to add a fourth, unguided by your choice. They offered me a fine Venus; but I thought it out of taste to have two at table at the same time. Paris and Helen were presented. I conceived it would be cruel to remove them from their peculiar shrine. When they shall pass the Atlantic, it will be to sing a requiem over our freedom and happiness. At length a fine Mars was offered, calm, bold, his faulchion not drawn, but ready to be drawn. This will do, thinks I, for the table of the American Minister in London, where those whom it may concern may look and learn that though Wisdom is our guide, and the Song and Chase our supreme delight, yet we offer adoration to that tutelar god also who rocked the cradle of our birth, who has accepted our infant offerings, and has shewn himself the patron of our rights and avenger of our wrongs. The groupe then was closed, and your party formed. Envy and malice will never be quiet. I hear it already whispered to you that in admitting Minerva to your table I have departed from the principle which made me reject Venus: in plain English that I have paid a just respect to the daughter but failed to the mother. No Madam, my respect to both is sincere. Wisdom, I know, is social. She seeks her fellows. But Beauty is jealous, and illy bears the presence of a rival—but, Allons, let us turn over another leaf, and begin the next chapter. I receive by Mr. Short a budget of London papers. They teem with every horror of which human nature is capable. Assassinations, suicides, thefts, robberies, and, what is worse than assassination, theft, suicide or robbery, the blackest slanders! Indeed the man must be of rock, who can stand all this; to Mr. Adams it will be but one victory the more. It would have illy suited me. I do not love difficulties. I am fond of quiet, willing to do my duty, but irritable by slander and apt to be forced by it to abandon my post. These are weaknesses from which reason and your counsels will preserve Mr. Adams. I fancy it must be the quantity of animal food eaten by the English which renders their character insusceptible of civilisation. I suspect it is in their kitchens and not in their churches that their reformation must be worked, and that Missionaries of that description from hence would avail more than those who should endeavor to tame them by precepts of religion or philosophy. But what do the foolish printers of America mean by retailing all this stuff in our papers? As if it was not enough to be slandered by one's enemies without circulating the slanders among his friends also.

To shew you how willingly I shall ever receive and execute your commissions, I venture to impose one on you. From what I recollect of the diaper and damask we used to import from England I think they were better and cheaper than here. You are well acquainted with those of both countries. If you are of the same opinion I would trouble you to send me two sets of table cloths and napkins for 20 covers each, by Colo. Franks or Mr. Barclay who will bring them to me. But if you think they can be better got here I would rather avoid the trouble this commission will give. I inclose you a specimen of what is offered me at 100. livres for the table cloth and 12 napkins. I suppose that, of the same quality, a table cloth 2. aunes wide and 4. aunes long, and 20 napkins of 1. aune each, would cost 7. guineas.—I shall certainly charge the publick my house rent and court taxes. I shall do more. I shall charge my outfit.[1] Without this I can never get out of debt. I think it will be allowed. Congress is too reasonable to expect, where no imprudent expences are incurred, none but those which are required by a decent respect to the mantle with which they cover the public servants, that such expences should be left as a burthen on our private fortunes. But when writing to you, I fancy myself at Auteuil, and chatter on till the last page of my paper awakes me from my reverie, and tells me it is time to assure you of the sincere respect and esteem with which I have the honour to be Dear Madam your most obedient & most humble servt.,

Th: Jefferson

P.S. The cask of wine at Auteuil, I take chearfully. I suppose the seller will apply to me for the price. Otherwise, as I do not know who he is, I shall not be able to find him out.

15. TO RALPH IZARD[1]

Dear Sir   *Paris Sep. 26. 1785.*
I received a few days ago your favor of the 10th. of June and am to
thank you for the trouble you have given yourself to procure me information on the subject of the commerce of your state. I pray you
also to take the trouble of expressing my acknolegements to the Governor and Chamber of Commerce as well as to Mr. Hall for the very
precise details on this subject with which they have been pleased to
honour me. Your letter of last January, of which you make mention,
never came to my hands. Of course the papers now received are the
first and only ones which have come safe. The infidelities of the post-
offices both of England and France are not unknown to you. The former is the most rascally because they retain one's letters, not chusing
to take the trouble of copying them. The latter when they have taken
copies, are so civil as to send the originals, re-sealed clumsily with a
composition on which they have previously taken the impression of
the seal. England shews no dispositions to enter into friendly connections with us. On the contrary their detention of our posts seems to be
the speck which is to produce a storm. I judge that a war with America would be a popular war in England. Perhaps the situation of Ire-
land may deter the ministry from hastening it on. Peace is at length
made between the emperor and Dutch. The terms are not published,
but it is said he gets 10. millions of florins and the navigation of the
Scheld not quite to Antwerp, and two forts. However this is not to be
absolutely relied on. The league formed by the K. of Prussia against
the Emperor is a most formidable obstacle to his ambitious designs. It
has certainly defeated his views on Bavaria, and will render doubtful
the election of his nephew to be king of the Romans. Matters are not
yet settled between him and the Turk. In truth he undertakes too
much. At home he has made some good regulations.
    Your present pursuit being (the wisest of all) agriculture, I am not
in a situation to be useful to it. You know that France is not the country most celebrated for this art. I went the other day to see a plough
which was to be worked by a windlass, without horses or oxen. It was
a poor affair. With a very troublesome apparatus, applicable only to a

dead level, four men could do the work of two horses. There seems a possibility that the great desideratum in the use of the baloon may be obtained. There are two persons at Javel (opposite to Auteuil) who are pushing this matter. They are able to rise and fall at will without expending their gaz, and they can deflect 45°. from the course of the wind. This and better will do. I took the liberty of asking you to order me a Charlestown newspaper. The expence of French postage is so enormous that I have been obliged to desire that my newspapers from the different states may be sent to the office for foreign affairs at New York; and I have requested of Mr. Jay to have them always packed in a box and sent by the French packets as merchandize to the care of the American Consul at l'Orient, who will send them on by the periodical waggons. In this way they will cost me livres only where they now cost guineas. Will you permit me to add this to the trouble I had before given you of ordering the printer to send them under cover to Mr. Jay by such opportunities by water as occur from time to time. This request must go to the acts of your assembly also. I shall be on the watch to send you any thing which may appear here on the subjects of agriculture or the arts, which [may] be worth your perusal. I since[rely] congratulate Mrs. [Izar]d and yourself on the double accession to your family by marriage and a new birth. My daughter values much your remembrance of her and prays to have her respects presented to the ladies and yourself. In this I join her, and shall embrace with pleasure every opportunity of assuring you of the sincere esteem with which I have the honor to be Dear Sir Your most obedient and most humble servant,

Th: Jefferson

16. TO JAMES CURRIE

Dear Sir   *Paris Sep. 27. 1785.*
Your favor of Aug. 5. came to hand on the 18th. inst. and I mark well what you say, 'that my letters shall be punctually answered.' This is encouraging, and the more so, as it proves to you that in sending your letters in time to arrive at New York the middle of the month when

the French packet sails they get to hand very speedily. The last was but six weeks from you to me. I thank you again and again for the details it contains, these being precisely of the nature I would wish. Of political correspondents I can find enough. But I can persuade nobody to beleive that the small facts which they see passing daily under their eyes are precious to me at this distance: much more interesting to the heart than events of higher rank. Fancy to yourself a being who is withdrawn from his connections of blood, of marriage, of friendship, of acquaintance in all their gradations, who for years should hear nothing of what has passed among them, who returns again to see them and finds the one half dead. This strikes him like a pestilence sweeping off the half of mankind. Events which had they come to him one by one and in detail he would have weathered as other people do, when presented to his mind all at once are overwhelming. Continue then to give me facts, little facts, such as you think every one imagines beneath notice, and your letters will be the most precious to me. They will place me in imagination in my own country, and they will place me where I am happiest: but what shall I give you in return? Political events are scarcely interesting to a man who looks on them from high ground. There is always war in one place, revolution in another, pestilence in a third interspersed with spots of quiet. These chequers shift places, but they do not vanish; so that to an eye which extends itself over the whole earth there is always an uniformity of prospect. For the moment, Europe is clear of war. The Emperor and Dutch have signed articles. These are not published: but it is beleived the Emperor gets 10. millions of florins, the navigation of the Scheld to Saptinghen, and two forts; so that your conjecture is verified and the Dutch actually pay the piper. The league formed in the Germanic body by the K. of Prussia is likely to circumscribe the ambitious views of the Emperor on that side, and there seems to be no issue for them but on the side of the Turk. Their demarcation does not advance. It is a pity the emperor would not confine himself to internal regulation. In that way he has done much good. One would think it not so difficult to discover that the improvement of the country we possess is the surest means of increasing our wealth and power. This too promotes the happiness of mankind, while the others destroy it, and are always incertain of their object. England seems not to permit our friendship to enter into her political calculations as an article of any value. Her endeavor is not how to recover our affections or to bind us to her by alliance, but by what new experiments she may keep up an existence without us. Thus leaving us to carry our full weight, present and future, into the scale of her enemy, and seeming to prefer our enmity to our neutrality. The Barbary corsairs have committed depredations on us. The Emperor of Marocco took a vessel last winter, which he has since restored with the crew and cargo. The Algerines took two vessels in July. These are the only captures which were known of at Algiers on the 24th. of Aug. I mention this because the English papers would make the world beleive we have lost an infinite number. I hope soon to be able to inform our countrymen that these dangers are ceased. There is little new to communicate in the arts and sciences. The great desideratum which is to render the discovery of the baloon useful, is not absolutely desperate. There are two artists at Javel, about 4. miles from here, who are able to rise and fall at will without expending their gaz, and to deflect 45°. from the course of the wind. The investigations of air and fire which have latterly so much occupied the Chymists, have not presented any thing very interesting for some time past. I send you four books, Roland, Sigaud de la fond, Metherie, and Scheele, which will put you in possession of whatever has been discovered as yet on that subject. They are packed in a trunk directed to J. Madison of Orange which will be carried to Richmond. They are in French, which you say you do not understand well. You lose infinitely by this, as you may be assured that the publications in that language at present far exceed those of the English in science. With respect to the Encyclopedie, it is impossible for me to judge whether to send it to you or not, as I do not know your degree of knowledge in the language nor your intentions as to increasing it. Of this you must decide for yourself and instruct me accordingly. I was unlucky as to the partridges, pheasants, hares and rabbits which I had ordered to Virginia. The vessel in which I came over was to have returned to Virginia, and to Warwick. I knew I could rely on the captain's care. A fellow passenger undertook to provide them. He did so. But the destination of the vessel was changed, and the poor colonists all died while my friend was looking out for another conveyance. If I can be useful to your circulating library, the members may be assured of my zealous services. All books except English, Latin and Greek, are bought here for about two thirds of what they cost in England. They had better distribute their invoices accordingly. I must trouble you to present assurances of my friendship to Mr. and Mrs. Randolph of Tuckahoe, Mr. Cary, and their families. My attachments to them are sincere: I wish I could render them useful to them. Tell McLurg I shall enjoy a very real pleasure whenever he shall carry his intentions of writing to me into execution; and that there is no one who more fervently wishes him well. Accept yourself assurances of the esteem with which I am Dear Sir Your friend & servant,

Th: Jefferson

17. TO CHARLES BELLINI[1]

Dear Sir   *Paris Sep. 30. 1785.*

Your estimable favour covering a letter to Mr. Mazzei came to hand on the 26th. inst. The letter to Mr. Mazzei was put into his hands in the same moment, as he happened to be present. I leave to him to convey to you all his complaints, as it will be more agreeable to me to express to you the satisfaction I received on being informed of your perfect health. Tho' I could not receive the same pleasing news of Mrs. Bellini, yet the philosophy with which I am told she bears the loss of health is a testimony the more how much she deserved the esteem I bear her.—Behold me at length on the vaunted scene of Europe! It is not necessary for your information that I should enter into details concerning it. But you are perhaps curious to know how this new scene has struck a savage of the mountains of America. Not advantageously I assure you. I find the general fate of humanity here most deplorable. The truth of Voltaire's observation offers itself perpetually, that every man here must be either the hammer or the anvil. It is a true picture of that country to which they say we shall pass hereafter, and where we are to see god and his angels in splendor, and crouds of the damned trampled under their feet. While the great mass of the people are thus suffering under physical and moral oppression, I have endeavored to examine more nearly the condition of the great, to appreciate the true value of the circumstances in their situation which dazzle the bulk of the spectators, and especially to compare it with that degree of happiness which is enjoyed in America by every class of people. Intrigues of love occupy the younger, and those of ambition the more elderly part of the great. Conjugal love having no existence among them, domestic happiness, of which that is the basis, is utterly unknown. In lieu of this are substituted pursuits which nourish and invigorate all our bad passions, and which offer only moments of extasy amidst days and months of restlessness and torment. Much, very much inferior this to the tranquil permanent felicity with which domestic society in America blesses most of it's inhabitants, leaving them to follow steadily those pursuits which health and reason approve, and rendering truly delicious the intervals of these pursuits. In science, the mass of people is two centuries behind ours, their literati half a dozen years before us. Books, really good, acquire just reputation in that time, and so become known to us and communicate to us all their advances in knowledge. Is not this delay compensated by our being placed out of the reach of that swarm of nonsense which issues daily from a thousand presses and perishes almost in issuing? With respect to what are termed polite manners, without sacrificing too much the sincerity of language, I would wish [my] countrymen to adopt just so much of European politeness as to be ready [to] make all those little sacrifices of self which really render European manners amiable, and relieve society from the disagreeable scenes to which rudeness often exposes it. Here it seems that a man might pass a life without encountering a single rudeness. In the pleasures of the table they are far before us, because with good taste they unite temperance. They do not terminate the most sociable meals by transforming themselves into brutes. I have never yet seen a man drunk in France, even among the lowest of the people. Were I to proceed to tell you how much I enjoy their architecture, sculpture, painting, music, I should want words. It is in these arts they shine. The last of them particularly is an enjoiment, the deprivation of which with us cannot be calculated. I am almost ready to say it is the only thing which from my heart I envy them, and which in spight of all the authority of the decalogue I do covet.—But I am running on in an estimate of things infinitely better known to you than to me, and which will only serve to convince you that I have brought with me all the prejudices of country, habit and age. But whatever I may allow to be charged to me as prejudice, in every other instance, I have one sentiment at least founded on reality: it is that of the perfect esteem which your merit and that of Mrs. Bellini have produced, and which will for ever enable me to assure you of the sincere regard with which I am Dear Sir Your friend & servant,

Th: Jefferson

18. TO REV. JAMES MADISON

Dear Sir   *Paris Oct. 2. 1785.*
I have duly received your favor of April 10. by Mr. Mazzei. You therein speak of a new method of raising water by steam which you suppose will come into general use. I know of no new method of that kind and suppose (as you say that the account you have received of it is very imperfect) that some person has represented to you as new a fire engine erected at Paris and which supplies the greater part of the town with water. But this is nothing more than the fire engine you have seen described in the books of Hydraulics and particularly in the dictionary of arts and sciences published in 8vo. by Owen, the idea of which was first taken from Papin's digester. It would have been better called the Steam engine. The force of the steam of water you know is immense. In this engine it is made to exert itself towards the working of pumps. That of Paris is I believe the largest known, raising 400,000 cubic feet (French) of water in 24 hours: or rather, I should have said, *those* of Paris, for there are two under one roof, each raising that quantity.

The Abbé Rochon not living at Paris, I have not had an opportunity of seeing him and of asking him the questions you desire relative to the Chrystal of which I wrote you. I shall avail myself of the earliest opportunity I can of doing it.—I shall chearfully execute your commands as to the Encyclopedie when I receive them. The price will be only 30. guineas. About half the work is out. The volumes of your Buffon which are spoiled can be replaced here.

I expect that this letter will be carried by the Mr. Fitzhughs in a ship from Havre to Portsmouth. I have therefore sent to Havre some books which I expected would be acceptable to you. These are the Bibliotheque physico-œconomique which will give you most of the late improvements in the arts; the Connoissance des tems for 1786. and 1787. which is as late as they are published, and some peices on air and fire wherein you will find all the discoveries hitherto made on these subjects. These books are made into a packet with your address on them and are put into a trunk wherein is a small packet for Mr. Wythe, another for Mr. Page, and a parcel of books without direction for Peter Carr. I have taken the liberty of directing the trunk to you as the surest means of it's getting safe. I pay the freight of it here, so that there will be no new demands but for the transportation from the ships side to Wmsburg. which I will pray you to pay, and as much the greatest part is for my nephew I will take care to repay it to you.

In the last volume of the Connoissance des tems you will find the tables for the planet Herschel.[1] It is a curious circumstance that this planet was seen 30 years ago by Mayer, and supposed by him to be a fixed star. He accordingly determined a place for it in his catalogue of the Zodiacal stars, making it the 964th. of that catalogue. Bode of Berlin observed in 1781 that this star was missing. Subsequent calculations of the motion of the planet Herschel shew that it must have been, at the time of Mayer's observation, where he had placed his 964th. star.

Herschell has pushed his discoveries of double stars now to upwards of 900. being twice the number of those communicated in the Philosophical transactions. You have probably seen that a Mr. Pigott had discovered periodical variations of light in the star Algol. He has observed the same in the η of Antinous, and makes the period of variation 7D. 4H. 30′, the duration of the increase 63.H. and of the decrease 36H. What are we to conclude from this? That there are suns which have their orbits of revolution too? But this would suppose a wonderful harmony in their planets, and present a new scene where the attracting powers should be without and not within the orbit. The motion of our sun would be a miniature of this. But this must be left to you Astronomers.

We were told some time ago of a cheap method of extricating inflammable air from pit-coal. This would facilitate the experiments with baloons. Two artists are employing themselves in the means of directing their course. They can ascend and descend at will without expending their gaz, and have been able to deflect from the course of the wind 45°.

I went sometime ago to see a machine which offers something new. A man had applied to a light boat a very large screw, the thread of which was a thin plate two feet broad applied by it's edge spirally round a small axis. It somewhat resembled a bottle brush if you will suppose the hairs of the bottle brush joining together and forming a spiral plane. This, turned on it's axis in the air, carried the vessel across the Seine. It is in fact a screw which takes hold of the air and draws itself along by it: losing indeed much of it's effort by the yeilding nature of the body it lays hold of to pull itself on by. I think it may be applied in the water with much greater effect and to very useful purposes. Perhaps it may be used also for the baloon.

It is impossible but you must have heard long ago of the machine for copying letters at a single stroke, as we had received them in America before I left it. I have written a long letter to my nephew, in whose education I feel myself extremely interested. I shall rely much on your friendship for conducting him in the plan I mark out for him, and for guarding him against those shoals on which youth sometimes shipwreck. I trouble you to present to Mr. Wythe my affectionate remembrance of him and am with very great esteem Dear Sir Your friend & servant,

Th: Jefferson

19. TO G. K. VAN HOGENDORP[1]

Dear Sir   *Paris Oct. 13. 1785.*
Having been much engaged lately, I have been unable sooner to acknolege the receipt of your favor of Sep. 8. What you are pleased to say

on the subject of my Notes is more than they deserve. The condition in which you first saw them would prove to you how hastily they had been originally written; as you may remember the numerous insertions I had made in them from time to time, when I could find a moment for turning to them from other occupations. I have never yet seen Monsr. de Buffon.[2] He has been in the country all the summer. I sent him a copy of the book, and I have only heard his sentiments on one particular of it, that of the identity of the Mammoth and Elephant. As to this he retains his opinion that they are the same.—If you had formed any considerable expectations from our Revised code of laws you will be much disappointed. It contains not more than three or four laws which could strike the attention of a foreigner. Had it been a digest of all our laws, it would not have been comprehensible or instructive but to a native. But it is still less so, as it digests only the British statutes and our own acts of assembly, which are but a supplementory part of our law. The great basis of it is anterior to the date of the Magna charta, which is the oldest statute extant. The only merit of this work is that it may remove from our book shelves about twenty folio volumes of statutes, retaining all the parts of them which either their own merit or the established system of laws required.

You ask me what are those operations of the British nation which are likely to befriend us, and how they will produce this effect? The British government, as you may naturally suppose, have it much at heart to reconcile their nation to the loss of America. This is essential to the repose, perhaps even to the safety of the king and his ministers. The most effectual engines for this purpose are the public papers. You know well that that government always kept a kind of standing army of newswriters who without any regard to truth, or to what should be like truth, invented and put into the papers whatever might serve the minister. This suffices with the mass of the people who have no means of distinguishing the false from the true paragraphs of a newspaper. When forced to acknolege our independance they were forced to redouble their efforts to keep the nation quiet. Instead of a few of the papers formerly engaged, they now engaged every one. No paper therefore comes out without a dose of paragraphs against America. These are calculated for a secondary purpose also, that of preventing the emigrations of their people to America. They dwell very much on American bankruptcies. To explain these would require a long detail, but would shew you that nine tenths of these bankruptcies are truly English bankruptcies in no wise chargeable on America. However they have produced effects the most desireable of all others for us. They have destroyed our credit, and thus checked our disposition to luxury; and forcing our merchants to buy no more than they have ready money to pay for, they force them to go to those markets where that ready money will buy most. Thus you see they check our luxury, they force us to connect ourselves with all the world, and they prevent foreign emigrations to our country all of which I consider as advantageous to us. They are doing us another good turn. They attempt without disguise to possess themselves of the carriage of our produce, and to prohibit our own vessels from participating of it. This has raised a general indignation in America. The states see however that their constitutions have provided no means of counteracting it. They are therefore beginning to vest Congress with the absolute power of regulating their commerce, only reserving all revenue arising from it to the state in which it is levied. This will consolidate our federal building very much, and for this we shall be indebted to the British.

You ask what I think on the expediency of encouraging our states to be commercial? Were I to indulge my own theory, I should wish them to practice neither commerce nor navigation, but to stand with respect to Europe precisely on the footing of China. We should thus avoid wars, and all our citizens would be husbandmen. Whenever indeed our numbers should so increase as that our produce would overstock the markets of those nations who should come to seek it, the farmers must either employ the surplus of their time in manufactures, or the surplus of our hands must be employed in manufactures, or in navigation. But that day would, I think be distant, and we should long keep our workmen in Europe, while Europe should be drawing rough materials and even subsistence from America. But this is theory only, and a theory which the servants of America are not at liberty to follow. Our people have a decided taste for navigation and commerce. They take this from their mother country: and their servants are in duty bound to calculate all their measures on this datum: we wish to do it by throwing open all the doors of commerce and knocking off it's shackles. But as this cannot be done for others, unless they will do it to us, and there is no great probability that Europe will do this, I suppose we shall be obliged to adopt a system which may shackle them in our ports as they do us in theirs.

With respect to the sale of our lands, that cannot begin till a considerable portion shall have been surveyed. They cannot begin to survey till the fall of the leaf of this year, nor to sell probably till the ensuing spring. So that it will be yet a twelvemonth before we shall be able to judge of the efficacy of our land office to sink our national debt. It is made a fundamental that the proceeds shall be solely and sacredly applied as a sinking fund to discharge the capital only of the debt.

It is true that the tobaccos of Virginia go almost entirely to England. The reason is that they owe a great debt there which they are paying as fast as they can. I think I have now answered your several queries, and shall be happy to receive your reflections on the same subjects, and at all times to hear of your welfare and to give you assurances of the esteem with which I have the honor to be Dear Sir your most obedient & most humble servant,

Th: Jefferson

20. TO JOHN BANISTER, JR.[1]

Dear Sir   *Paris Oct. 15. 1785.*
I should sooner have answered the paragraph in your favor of Sep. 19. respecting the best seminary for the education of youth in Europe, but that it was necessary for me to make enquiries on the subject. The result of these has been to consider the competition as resting between Geneva and Rome. They are equally cheap, and probably are equal in the course of education pursued. The advantage of Geneva is that students acquire there the habits of speaking French. The advantages of Rome are the acquiring a local knowlege of a spot so classical and so celebrated; the acquiring the true pronuntiation of the Latin language; the acquiring a just taste in the fine arts, more particularly

those of painting, sculpture, Architecture, and Music; a familiarity with those objects and processes of agriculture which experience has shewn best adapted to a climate like ours; and lastly the advantage of a fine climate for health. It is probable too that by being boarded in a French family the habit of speaking that language may be obtained. I do not count on any advantage to be derived in Geneva from a familiar acquaintance with the principles of it's government. The late revolution has rendered it a tyrannical aristocracy more likely to give ill than good ideas to an American. I think the balance in favor of Rome. Pisa is sometimes spoken of as a place of education. But it does not offer the 1st. and 3d. of the advantages of Rome. But why send an American youth to Europe for education? What are the objects of an useful American education? Classical knowledge, modern languages and chiefly French, Spanish, and Italian; Mathematics; Natural philosophy; Natural History; Civil History; Ethics. In Natural philosophy I mean to include Chemistry and Agriculture, and in Natural history to include Botany as well as the other branches of those departments. It is true that the habit of speaking the modern languages cannot be so well acquired in America, but every other article can be as well acquired at William and Mary College as at any place in Europe. When College education is done with and a young man is to prepare himself for public life, he must cast his eyes (for America) either on Law or Physic. For the former where can he apply so advantageously as to Mr. Wythe? For the latter he must come to Europe; the medical class of students therefore is the only one which need come to Europe. Let us view the disadvantages of sending a youth to Europe. To enumerate them all would require a volume. I will select a few. If he goes to England he learns drinking, horse-racing and boxing. These are the peculiarities of English education. The following circumstances are common to education in that and the other countries of Europe. He acquires a fondness for European luxury and dissipation and a contempt for the simplicity of his own country; he is fascinated with the privileges of the European aristocrats, and sees with abhorrence the lovely equality which the poor enjoys with the rich in his own country: he contracts a partiality for aristocracy or monarchy; he forms foreign friendships which will never be useful to him, and loses the season of life for forming in his own country those friendships which of all others are the most faithful and permanent: he is led by the strongest of all the human passions into a spirit for female intrigue destructive of his own and others happiness, or a passion for whores destructive of his health, and in both cases learns to consider fidelity to the marriage bed as an ungentlemanly practice and inconsistent with happiness: he recollects the voluptuary dress and arts of the European women and pities and despises the chaste affections and simplicity of those of his own country; he retains thro' life a fond recollection and a hankering after those places which were the scenes of his first pleasures and of his first connections; he returns to his own country, a foreigner, unacquainted with the practices of domestic œconomy necessary to preserve him from ruin; speaking and writing his native tongue as a foreigner, and therefore unqualified to obtain those distinctions which eloquence of the pen and tongue ensures in a free country; for I would observe to you that what is called style in writing or speaking is formed very early in life while the imagination is warm, and impressions are permanent. I am of opinion that there never was an instance of a man's writing or speaking his native tongue with elegance who passed from 15. to 20. years of age out of the country where it was spoken. Thus no instance exists of a person writing two languages perfectly. That will always appear to be his native language which was most familiar to him in his youth. It appears to me then that an American coming to Europe for education loses in his knowledge, in his morals, in his health, in his habits, and in his happiness. I had entertained only doubts on this head before I came to Europe: what I see and hear since I come here proves more than I had even suspected. Cast your eye over America: who are the men of most learning, of most eloquence, most beloved by their country and most trusted and promoted by them? They are those who have been educated among them, and whose manners, morals and habits are perfectly homogeneous with those of the country.—Did you expect by so short a question to draw such a sermon on yourself? I dare say you did not. But the consequences of foreign education are alarming to me as an American. I sin therefore through zeal whenever I enter on the subject. You are sufficiently American to pardon me for it. Let me hear of

your health and be assured of the esteem with which I am Dear Sir
Your friend & servant,

Th: Jefferson

21. TO JAMES MADISON

Dear Sir   *Fontainebleau Oct. 28. 1785.*
Seven o'clock, and retired to my fireside, I have determined to enter
into conversation with you; this is a village of about 5,000 inhabitants
when the court is not here and 20,000 when they are, occupying a valley thro' which runs a brook, and on each side of it a ridge of small
mountains most of which are naked rock. The king comes here in the
fall always, to hunt. His court attend him, as do also the foreign diplomatic corps. But as this is not indispensably required, and my finances
do not admit the expence of a continued residence here, I propose to
come occasionally to attend the king's levees, returning again to Paris,
distant 40 miles. This being the first trip, I set out yesterday morning
to take a view of the place. For this purpose I shaped my course towards the highest of the mountains in sight, to the top of which was
about a league. As soon as I had got clear of the town I fell in with a
poor woman walking at the same rate with myself and going the same
course. Wishing to know the condition of the labouring poor I entered
into conversation with her, which I began by enquiries for the path
which would lead me into the mountain: and thence proceeded to enquiries into her vocation, condition and circumstance. She told me she
was a day labourer, at 8. sous or 4 d. sterling the day; that she had two
children to maintain, and to pay a rent of 30 livres for her house
(which would consume the hire of 75 days), that often she could get
no emploiment, and of course was without bread. As we had walked
together near a mile and she had so far served me as a guide, I gave
her, on parting 24 sous. She burst into tears of a gratitude which I
could perceive was unfeigned, because she was unable to utter a word.
She had probably never before received so great an aid. This little at-
tendrissement, with the solitude of my walk led me into a train of reflections on that unequal division of property which occasions the

numberless instances of wretchedness which I had observed in this country and is to be observed all over Europe. The property of this country is absolutely concentered in a very few hands, having revenues of from half a million of guineas a year downwards. These employ the flower of the country as servants, some of them having as many as 200 domestics, not labouring. They employ also a great number of manufacturers, and tradesmen, and lastly the class of labouring husbandmen. But after all these comes the most numerous of all the classes, that is, the poor who cannot find work. I asked myself what could be the reason that so many should be permitted to beg who are willing to work, in a country where there is a very considerable proportion of uncultivated lands? These lands are kept idle mostly for the sake of game. It should seem then that it must be because of the enormous wealth of the proprietors which places them above attention to the increase of their revenues by permitting these lands to be laboured. I am conscious that an equal division of property is impracticable. But the consequences of this enormous inequality producing so much misery to the bulk of mankind, legislators cannot invent too many devices for subdividing property, only taking care to let their subdivisions go hand in hand with the natural affections of the human mind. The descent of property of every kind therefore to all the children, or to all the brothers and sisters, or other relations in equal degree is a politic measure, and a practicable one. Another means of silently lessening the inequality of property is to exempt all from taxation below a certain point, and to tax the higher portions of property in geometrical progression as they rise. Whenever there is in any country, uncultivated lands and unemployed poor, it is clear that the laws of property have been so far extended as to violate natural right. The earth is given as a common stock for man to labour and live on. If, for the encouragement of industry we allow it to be appropriated, we must take care that other employment be furnished to those excluded from the appropriation. If we do not the fundamental right to labour the earth returns to the unemployed. It is too soon yet in our country to say that every man who cannot find employment but who can find uncultivated land, shall be at liberty to cultivate it, paying a moderate rent. But it is not too soon to provide by every possible means that as few as possible shall be without a little portion of land. The small landholders are the most precious part of a state.—The next object which struck my attention in my walk was the deer with which the wood abounded. They were of the kind called 'Cerfs' and are certainly of the same species with ours. They are blackish indeed under the belly, and not white as ours, and they are more of the chestnut red: but these are such small differences as would be sure to happen in two races from the same stock, breeding separately a number of ages.— Their hares are totally different from the animal we call by that name: but their rabbit is almost exactly like him. The only difference is in their manners; the land on which I walked for some time being absolutely reduced to a honeycomb by their burrowing. I think there is no instance of ours burrowing.—After descending the hill again I saw a man cutting fern. I went to him under the pretence of asking the shortest road to the town, and afterwards asked for what use he was cutting fern. He told me that this part of the country furnished a great deal of fruit to Paris. That when packed in straw it acquired an ill taste, but that dry fern preserved it perfectly without communicating any taste at all. I treasured this observation for the preservation of my apples on my return to my own country. They have no apple here to compare with our Newtown pipping. They have nothing which deserves the name of a peach; there being not sun enough to ripen the plumbpeach and the best of their soft peaches being like our autumn peaches. Their cherries and strawberries are fair, but I think less flavoured. Their plumbs I think are better; so also the gooseberries, and the pears infinitely beyond any thing we possess. They have no grape better than our sweet-water. But they have a succession of as good from very early in the summer till frost. I am tomorrow to go to Mr. Malsherbes (an uncle of the Chevalr. Luzerne's) about 7. leagues from hence, who is the most curious man in France as to his trees. He is making for me a collection of the vines from which the Burgundy, Champagne, Bourdeaux, Frontignac, and other the most valuable wines of this country are made. Another gentleman is collecting for me the best eating grapes, including what we call the raisin. I propose also to endeavor to colonize their hare, rabbit, red and grey partridge, pheasants of different kinds, and some other birds. But I find that I am wandering beyond the limits of my walk and will therefore bid you Adieu. Yours affectionately,

Th: Jefferson

22. TO ARCHIBALD CARY[1]

Dear Sir   *Paris Jan. 7. 1786.*
It will be a misfortune to the few of my countrymen (and very very few they are indeed) who happen to be punctual. Of this I shall give you a proof by the present application, which I should not make to you if I did not know you to be superior to the torpidity of our climate. In my conversations with the Count de Buffon on the subjects of Natural history, I find him absolutely unacquainted with our Elk and our deer. He has hitherto beleived that our deer never had horns more than a foot long; and has therefore classed them with the roe-buck, which I am sure you know them to be different from. I have examined some of the red deer of this country at the distance of about 60. yards, and I find no other difference between them and ours, but a shade or two in the colour. Will you take the trouble to procure for me the largest pair of bucks horns you can, and a large skin of each colour, that is to say a red and a blue? If it were possible to take these from a buck just killed, to leave all the bones of the head in the skin, with the horns on, to leave the bones and hoofs of the legs and feet in the skin, so that having only made an incision all along the belly and neck, to take the animal out at, we could by sewing up that incision and stuffing the skin, present the true size and form of the animal, it would be a most precious present. Our deer have been often sent to England and Scotland. Do you know (with certainty) whether they have ever bred with the red deer of those countries? With respect to the Elk, I despair of your being able to get for me any thing but the horns of it. David Ross I know has a pair; perhaps he would give them to us. It is useless to ask for the skin and skeleton, because I think it not in your power to get them, otherwise they would be most desirable. A gentleman, fellow passenger with me from Boston to England, promised to send to you in my name some hares, rabbets, pheasants and partridges,

by the return of the ship which was to go to Virginia, and the captain promised great care of them. My friend procured the animals, and, the ship changing her destination, he kept them in hopes of finding some other conveyance, till they all perished. I do not despair however of finding some opportunity still of sending a colony of useful animals. I am making a collection of vines for wine and for the table, some trees also, such as the Cork oak, &c. &c.

Every thing is absolutely quiet in Europe. There is not therefore a word of news to communicate. I pray you to present me affectionately to your family and that of Tuckahoe.[2] Whatever expence is necessary for procuring me the articles abovementioned I will instantly replace either in cash or in any thing you may wish from hence. I am with very sincere esteem Dear Sir your most obedient humble servant,

Th: Jefferson

23. TO ARCHIBALD STUART[1]

Dear Sir   *Paris Jan. 25. 1786.*
I have received your favor of the 17th. of October, which though you mention as the third you have written me, is the first which has come to hand. I sincerely thank you for the communications it contains. Nothing is so grateful to me at this distance as details both great and small of what is passing in my own country. Of the latter we receive little here, because they either escape my correspondents or are thought unworthy notice. This however is a very mistaken opinion, as every one may observe by recollecting that when he has been long absent from his neighborhood the small news of that is the most pleasing and occupies his first attention either when he meets with a person from thence, or returns thither himself. I still hope therefore that the letter in which you have been so good as to give me the minute occurrences in the neighborhood of Monticello may yet come to hand, and I venture to rely on the many proofs of friendship I have received from you, for a continuance of your favors. This will be the more meritorious as I have nothing to give you in exchange. The quiet of Europe at this moment furnishes little which can attract your notice, nor

will that quiet be soon disturbed, at least for the current year. Perhaps it hangs on the life of the K. of Prussia, and that hangs by a very slender thread. American reputation in Europe is not such as to be flattering to it's citizens. Two circumstances are particularly objected to us, the nonpaiment of our debts, and the want of energy in our government. These discourage a connection with us. I own it to be my opinion that good will arise from the destruction of our credit. I see nothing else which can restrain our disposition to luxury, and the loss of those manners which alone can preserve republican government. As it is impossible to prevent credit, the best way would be to cure it's ill effects by giving an instantaneous recovery to the creditor. This would be reducing purchases on credit to purchases for ready money. A man would then see a prison painted on every thing he wished but had not ready money to pay for.—I fear from an expression in your letter that the people of Kentucké think of separating not only from Virginia (in which they are right) but also from the confederacy. I own I should think this a most calamitous event, and such an one as every good citizen on both sides should set himself against. Our present federal limits are not too large for good government, nor will the increase of votes in Congress produce any ill effect. On the contrary it will drown the little divisions at present existing there. Our confederacy must be viewed as the nest from which all America, North and South is to be peopled. We should take care too not to think it for the interest of that great continent to press too soon on the Spaniards. Those countries cannot be in better hands. My fear is that they are too feeble to hold them till our population can be sufficiently advanced to gain it from them peice by peice. The navigation of the Mississippi we must have. This is all we are as yet ready to receive. I have made acquaintance with a very sensible candid gentleman here who was in South America during the revolt which took place there while our revolution was working. He says that those disturbances (of which we scarcely heard any thing) cost on both sides an hundred thousand lives.—I have made a particular acquaintance here with Monsieur de Buffon, and have a great desire to give him the best idea I can of our elk. Perhaps your situation may enable you to aid me in this. Were it possible, you could not oblige me more than by sending me the horns, skeleton, and skin of an elk. The most desireable form of receiving them would be to have the skin slit from the under jaw along the belly to the tail, and down the thighs to the knee, to take the animal out, leaving the legs and hoofs, the bones of the head, and the horns attached to the skin. By sewing up the belly &c. and stuffing the skin it would present the form of the animal. However as an opportunity of doing this is scarcely to be expected, I shall be glad to receive them detached, packed in a box, and sent to Richmond to the care of Doctor Currie. Every thing of this kind is precious here, and to prevent my adding to your trouble I must close my letter with assurances of the esteem and attachment with which I am Dr. Sir your friend & servt.,

Th: Jefferson

P.S. I must add a prayer for some Paccan nuts, 100. if possible, to be packed in a box of sand and sent me. They might come either directly or viâ N. York.

24. TO JAMES BUCHANAN AND WILLIAM HAY[1]

Gentlemen   *Paris Jan. 26. 1786.*

I had the honour of writing to you on the receipt of your orders to procure draughts for the public buildings, and again on the 13th. of August. In the execution of those orders two methods of proceeding presented themselves to my mind. The one was to leave to some architect to draw an external according to his fancy, in which way experience shews that about once in a thousand times a pleasing form is hit upon; the other was to take some model already devised and approved by the general suffrage of the world. I had no hesitation in deciding that the latter was best, nor after the decision was there any doubt what model to take. There is at Nismes in the South of France a building, called the Maison quarrée, erected in the time of the Caesars, and which is allowed without contradiction to be the most perfect and precious remain of antiquity in existence. It's superiority over any thing at Rome, in Greece, at Balbec or Palmyra is allowed on all hands; and this single object has placed Nismes in the general tour of travellers. Having not yet had leisure to visit it, I could only judge of it from drawings, and from the relation of numbers who had been to see it. I determined therefore to adopt this model, and to have all it's proportions justly observed. As it was impossible for a foreign artist to know what number and sizes of apartments would suit the different corps of our government, nor how they should be connected with one another, I undertook to form that arrangement, and this being done, I committed them to an Architect (Monsieur Clerisseau) who had studied this art 20. years in Rome, who had particularly studied and measured the Maison quarrée of Nismes, and had published a book containing 4 most excellent plans, descriptions, and observations on it. He was too well acquainted with the merit of that building to find himself restrained by my injunctions not to depart from his model. In one instance only he persuaded me to admit of this. That was to make the Portico two columns deep only, instead of three as the original is. His reason was that this latter depth would too much darken the apartments. Œconomy might be added as a second reason. I consented to it to satisfy him, and the plans are so drawn. I knew that it would still be easy to execute the building with a depth of three columns, and it is what I would certainly recommend. We know that the Maison quarrée has pleased universally for near 2000 years. By leaving out a column, the proportions will be changed and perhaps the effect may be injured more than is expected. What is good is often spoiled by trying to make it better.

The present is the first opportunity which has occurred of sending the plans. You will accordingly receive herewith the ground plan, the elevation of the front, and the elevation of the side. The architect having been much busied, and knowing that this was all which would be necessary in the beginning, has not yet finished the Sections of the building. They must go by some future occas[ion] as well as the models of the front and side which are making in plaister of Paris. These were absolutely necessary for the guide of workmen not very expert in their art. It will add considerably to the expence, and I would not have incurred it but that I was sensible of it's necessity. The price of the model will be 15 guineas. I shall know in a few days the cost of the drawings which probably will be the triple of the model; however this is but my conjecture. I will make it as small as possible, pay it, and render you an account in my next letter. You will find on examination that the body of this building covers an area but two fifths of that which is proposed and begun; of course it will take but about one half the bricks; and of course this circumstance will enlist all the workmen, and people of the art against the plan. Again the building begun is to have 4 porticos; this but one. It is true that this will be deeper than those were probably proposed, but even if it be made three columns deep, it will not take half the number of columns. The beauty of this is ensured by experience and by the suffrage of the whole world; the beauty of that is problematical, as is every drawing, however well it looks on paper, till it be actually executed; and tho I suppose there is more room in the plan begun, than in that now sent, yet there is enough in this for all the three branches of government and more than enough is not wanted. This contains 16. rooms, to wit, 4. on the first floor, for the General court, Delegates, Lobby, and Conference; eight on the 2d. floor for the Executive, the Senate, and 6 rooms for committees and [juri]es, and over 4. of these smaller rooms of the 2d floor are 4. Mezzanines or Entresoles, serving as offices for the clerks of the Executive, the Senate, the Delegates and the court in actual session. It will be an objection that the work is begun on the other plan. But the whole of this need not be taken to peices, and of what shall be taken to peices the bricks will do for inner work. Mortar never becomes so hard and adhesive to the bricks in a few months but that it may easily be chipped off. And upon the whole the plan now sent will save a great proportion of the expence.

Hitherto I have spoken of the Capitol only. The plans for the prison also accompany this. They will explain themselves. I send also the plan of the prison proposed at Lyons which was sent me by the architect, and to which we are indebted for the fundamental idea of ours. You will see that of a great thing a very small one is made. Perhaps you may find it convenient to build at first only two sides, forming an L. But of this you are the judges. It has been suggested to me that fine gravel mixed in the mortar prevents the prisoners from cutting themselves out, as that will destroy their tool. In my letter of Aug. 13. I mentioned that I could send workmen from hence. As I am in hopes of receiving your orders precisely in answer to that letter I shall defer actually engaging any till I receive them. In like manner I shall defer having plans drawn for a Governor's house &c. till further orders, only assuring you that the receiving and executing these orders will always give me a very great pleasure, and the more should I find that what I have done meets your approbation. I have the honour to be, with sentiments of the most perfect esteem, Gentlemen your most obedient and most humble servant,

Th: Jefferson

25. TO JAMES MADISON

Dear Sir   *Paris Feb. 8. 1786.*
My last letters have been of the 1st. and 20th. of Sep. and the 28th. of Oct. Yours unacknoleged are of Aug. 20. Oct. 3. and Nov. 15. I take this the first safe opportunity of inclosing you the bills of lading for your books, and two others for your name sake of Williamsburgh and for the attorney which I will pray you to forward. I thank you for the communication of the remonstrance against the assessment. Mazzei who is now in Holland promised me to have it published in the Leyden gazette. It will do us great honour. I wish it may be as much approved by our assembly as by the wisest part of Europe. I have heard with great pleasure that our assembly have come to the resolution of giving the regulation of their commerce to the federal head. I will venture to assert that there is not one of it's opposers who, placed on this ground, would not see the wisdom of this measure. The politics of Europe render it indispensably necessary that with respect to every thing external we be one nation only, firmly hooped together. Interior government is what each state should keep to itself. If it could be seen in Europe that all our states could be brought to concur in what the Virginia assembly has done, it would produce a total revolution in their opinion of us, and respect for us. And it should ever be held in mind that insult and war are the consequences of a want of respectability in the national character. As long as the states exercise separately those acts of power which respect foreign nations, so long will there con-

tinue to be irregularities committing by some one or other of them which will constantly keep us on an ill footing with foreign nations.

I thank you for your information as to my Notes. The copies I have remaining shall be sent over to be given to some of my friends and to select subjects in the college. I have been unfortunate here with this trifle. I gave out a few copies only, and to confidential persons, writing in every copy a restraint against it's publication. Among others I gave a copy to a Mr. Williamos. He died. I immediately took every precaution I could to recover this copy. But by some means or other a book seller had got hold of it. He had employed a hireling translator and was about publishing it in the most injurious form possible. An Abbé Morellet, a man of letters here to whom I had given a copy, got notice of this. He had translated some passages for a particular purpose: and he compounded with the bookseller to translate and give him the whole, on his declining the first publication. I found it necessary to confirm this, and it will be published in French, still mutilated however in it's freest parts. I am now at a loss what to do as to England. Every thing, good or bad, is thought worth publishing there; and I apprehend a translation back from the French and publication there. I rather believe it will be most eligible to let the original come out in that country: but am not yet decided.

I have purchased little for you in the book way since I sent the catalogue of my former purchases. I wish first to have your answer to that, and your information what parts of those purchases went out of your plan. You can easily say buy more of this kind, less of that &c. My wish is to conform myself to yours. I can get for you the original Paris edition in folio of the Encyclopedie[1] for 620 livres, 35. vols: a good edition in 39. vols 4to, for 380^{tt} and a good one in 39. vols. 8vo. for 280^{tt}. The new one will be superior in far the greater number of articles: but not in all. And the possession of the ancient one has more over the advantage of supplying present use. I have bought one for myself, but wait your orders as to you. I remember your purchase of a watch in Philadelphia. If she should not have proved good, you can probably sell her. In that case I can get for you here, one made as perfect as human art can make it for about 24. louis. I have had such a one made by the best and most faithful hand in Paris. She has a second hand, but no repeating, no day of the month, nor other useless thing to impede and injure the movements which are necessary. For 12. louis more you can have in the same cover, but on the backside, and absolutely unconnected with the movements of the watch, a pedometer which shall render you an exact account of the distances you walk. Your pleasure hereon shall be awaited.

Houdon is returned.[2] He called on me the other day to remonstrate against the inscription proposed for Genl. W's statue. He says it is too long to be put on the pedestal. I told him I was not at liberty to permit any alteration, but I would represent his objection to a friend who could judge of it's validity, and whether a change could be authorized. This has been the subject of conversations here, and various devices and inscriptions have been suggested. The one which has appeared best to me may be translated as follows: 'Behold, Reader, the form of George Washington. For his worth, ask History: that will tell it, when this stone shall have yeilded to the decays of time. His country erects this monument: Houdon makes it.' This for one side. On the 2d. represent the evacuation of Boston with the motto 'hostibus primum fugatis.' On the 3d. the capture of the Hessians with 'hostibus iterum devictis.' On the 4th. the surrender of York, with 'hostibus ultimum debellatis.' This is seising the three most brilliant actions of his military life. By giving out here a wish of receiving mottos for this statue, we might have thousands offered, of which still better might be chosen. The artist made the same objection of *length* to the inscription for the bust of the M. de la fayette. An alteration of that might come in time still, if an alteration was wished. However I am not certain that it is desireable in either case. The state of Georgia has given 20,000 acres of land to the Count d'Estaing. This gift is considered here as very honourable to him, and it has gratified him much. I am persuaded that a gift of lands by the state of Virginia to the Marquis de la fayette would give a good opinion here of our character, and would reflect honour on the Marquis. Nor am I sure that the day will not come when it might be an useful asylum to him. The time of life at which he visited America was too well adapted to receive good and lasting impressions to permit him ever to accommodate himself to the principles of monarchical government; and it will need all his own prudence and that of his friends to make this country a safe residence for him. How glorious, how comfortable in reflection will it be to have prepared a refuge for him in case of a reverse. In the mean time he could settle it with tenants from the freest part of this country, Bretagny. I have never suggested the smallest idea of this kind to him: because the execution of it should convey the first notice. If the state has not a right to give him lands with their own officers, they could buy up at cheap prices the shares of others.—I am not certain however whether in the public or private opinion, a similar gift to Count Rochambeau could be dispensed with. If the state could give to both, it would be better: but in any event I think they should to the Marquis. C. Rochambeau too has really deserved more attention than he has received. Why not set up his bust, that of Gates, Greene, Franklin in your new Capitol? à propos of the Capitol, do my dear friend exert yourself to get the plan begun or set aside, and that adopted which was drawn here. It was taken from a model which has been the admiration of 16. centuries, which has been the object of as many pilgrimages as the tomb of Mahomet; which will give unrivalled honour to our state, and furnish a model whereon to form the taste of our young men. It will cost much less too than the one begun, because it does not cover one half the Area. Ask if you please, a sight of my letter of Jan. 26. to Messrs. Buchanan and Hay, which will spare me the repeating it's substance here.

Every thing is quiet in Europe. I recollect but one new invention in the arts which is worth mentioning. It is a mixture of the arts of engraving and printing, rendering both cheaper. Write or draw any thing on a plate of brass with the ink of the inventor,[3] and in half an hour he gives you copies of it so perfectly like the original that they could not be suspected to be copies. His types for printing a whole page are all in one solid peice. An author therefore only prints a few copies of his work from time to time as they are called for. This saves the loss of printing more copies than may possibly be sold, and prevents an edition from being ever exhausted.

I am with a lively esteem Dear Sir your sincere friend & servant,

Th: Jefferson

P.S. Could you procure and send me an hundred or two nuts of the Paccan? They would enable me to oblige some characters here whom I should be much gratified to oblige. They should come packed in sand. The seeds of the sugar maple too would be a great present.

26. NOTES OF A TOUR OF ENGLISH GARDENS

Memorandums made on a tour to some of the gardens in England described by Whateley in his book on gardening.[1] While his descriptions in point of style are models of perfect elegance and classical correctness, they are as remarkeable for their exactness. I always walked over the gardens with his book in my hand, examined with attention the particular spots he described, found them so justly characterised by him as to be easily recognised, and saw with wonder, that his fine imagination had never been able to seduce him from the truth. My enquiries were directed chiefly to such practical things as might enable me to estimate the expence of making and maintaining a garden in that style. My journey was in the months of March and April 1786.

Cheswick.[2] Belongs to D. of Devonshire. Garden about 6. acres. The Octagonal dome has an ill effect, both within and without; the garden shews still too much of art; an obelisk of very ill effect. Another in the middle of a pond useless.

Hampton court. Old fashioned. Clipt yews grown wild.

Twickenham. Pope's original garden 3½ as. Sr. Wm. Stanhope added 1½ acre. This is a long narrow slope, grass and trees in the middle, walk all round. Now Sr. Wellbore Ellis's. Obelisk at bottom of Pope's garden as monument to his mother. Inscription. Ah! Edithe matrum optuma, mulierum amantissima, Vale.[3] The house about 30. yds. from the Thames; the ground shelves gently to the water side. On the back of the house passes the street, and beyond that the garden. The grotto is under the street, and goes out level to the water. In the center of the garden a mound with a spiral walk round it. A rookery.

Esher place. The house in a bottom near the river. On the other side the ground rises pretty much. The road by which we come to the house forms a dividing line in the middle of the front. On the right are heights, rising one beyond and above another, with clumps of trees. On the farthest a temple. A hollow filled up with a clump of trees, the tallest in the bottom, so that the top is quite flat. On the left the ground descends. Clumps of trees. The clumps on each hand balance finely. A most lovely mixture of concave and convex. The garden is of about 45. as. besides the park which joins. Belongs to Lady Francis Pelham.

Claremont. Ld. Clive. Nothing remarkeable.

Paynshill. Mr. Hopkins. 323. as. garden and park all in one. Well described by Whateley. Grotto said to have cost 7000.£. Whateley says one of the bridges is of stone. But both are now of wood. The lower 60. f. high. There is too much evergreen. The Dwelling house built by Hopkins. Ill situated. He has not been there in 5. years. He lived there 4. years while building the present house. It is not finished. It's architecture is incorrect. A Doric temple beautiful.

Woburn. Belongs to Ld. Peters. Ld. Loughborough is the present tenant for 2. lives. 4. people to the farm. 4. to the pleasure garden. 4. to the kitchen garden. All are intermixed, the pleasure garden being merely a highly ornamented walk through and round the divisions of the farm and kitchen garden.

Caversham.[4] Sold by Ld. Cadogan to Majr. Marsac. 25. as. of garden, 400. as. of park, 6 as. of kitchen garden. A large lawn, separated by a sunk fence from the garden, appears to be part of it. A straight broad gravel walk passes before the front and parallel to it, terminated on the right by a Doric temple, and opening at the other end on a fine prospect. This straight walk has an ill effect. The lawn in front, which is pasture, well disposed with clumps of trees.

Wotton. Now belongs to the M. of Buckingham, son of George Grenville. The lake covers 50. as. the river 5. as. the bason 15. as. the little river 2. as. = 72. as. of water. The lake and great river are on a level. They fall into the bason 5. f. below, and that again into the little river 5. f. lower. These waters lie in form of an L. The house is in middle of open side, forming the angle. A walk goes round the whole, 3. miles in circumference, and containing within it about 300. as. Sometimes it passes close to the water, sometimes so far off as to leave large pasture ground between it and water. But 2. hands to keep the pleasure grounds in order. Much neglected. The water affords 2000. brace of carp a year. There is a Palladian bridge of which I think Whateley does not speak.

Stowe. Belongs to the M. of Buckingham, son of G. Grenville, and who takes it from Ld. Temple. 15. men and 18. boys employed in keeping pleasure grounds. Within the Walk are considerable portions separated by inclosures and used for pasture. The Egyptian pyramid is almost entirely taken down by the late Ld. Temple to erect a building there, in commemoration of Mr. Pitt, but he died before beginning it, and nothing is done to it yet. The grotto, and two rotundas are taken away. There are 4. levels of water, receiving it one from the other. The bason contains 7. as. the lake below that 10. as. Kent's building is called the temple of Venus. The inclosure is entirely by ha! ha! At each end of the front line there is a recess like the bastion of a fort. In one of these is the temple of Friendship, in the other the temple of Venus. They are seen the one from the other, the line of sight passing, not thro' the garden, but through the country parallel to the line of the garden. This has a good effect. In the approach to Stowe, you are brought a mile through a straight avenue, pointing to the Corinthian arch and to the house, till you get to the Arch. Then you turn short to the right. The straight approach is very ill. The Corinthian arch has a very useless appearance, inasmuch as it has no pretension to any destination. Instead of being an object from the house, it is an obstacle to a very pleasing distant prospect. The Graecian valley being clear of trees, while the hill on each side is covered with them, is much deepened to appearance.

Leasowes. In Shropshire. Now the property of Mr. Horne by purchase. 150. as. within the walk. The waters small. This is not even an ornamented farm. It is only a grazing farm with a path round it. Here and there a seat of board, rarely any thing better. Architecture has contributed nothing. The obelisk is of brick. Shenstone had but 300£ a year, and ruined himself by what he did to this farm. It is said that he died of the heartaches which his debts occasioned him. The part next the road is of red earth, that on the further part grey. The 1st. and 2d. cascades are beautiful. The landscape at No. 18. and prospect at 32. are fine. The Walk through the wood is umbrageous and pleasing. The whole arch of prospect may be of 90°. Many of the inscriptions are lost.

Hagley. Now Ld. Wescot. 1000. as. No distinction between park and garden. Both blended, but more of the character of garden. 8. or 9. labourers keep it in order. Between 2. and 300. deer in it, some few of them red deer. They breed sometimes with the fallow. This garden occupying a descending hollow between the Clent and Witchbury hills, with the spurs from those hills, there is no level in it for a spacious water. There are therefore only some small ponds. From one of these there is a fine cascade; but it can only be occasionally, by opening the sluice. This is in a small, dark, deep hollow, with recesses of stone in the banks on every side. In one of these is a Venus pudique,[5] turned half round as if inviting you with her into the recess. There is another cascade seen from the Portico on the bridge. The castle is triangular, with a round tower at each angle, one only entire; it seems to be between 40. and 50. f. high. The ponds yield a great deal of trout. The walks are scarcely gravelled.

Blenheim. 2500. as. of which 200. is garden, 150. water, 12. kitchen garden, and the rest park. 200. people employed to keep it in order, and to make alterations and additions. About 50. of these employed in pleasure grounds. The turf is mowed once in 10. days, in summer. About 2000. fallow deer in the park, and 2. or 3000. sheep. The palace of H.2.[6] was remaining till taken down by Sarah, widow of the 1st. D. of Marlborough. It was on a round spot levelled by art, near what is now water, and but a little above it. The island was a part of the high road leading to the palace. Rosamond's bower was near where is now a little grove about 200. yards from the palace. The well is near where the bower was. The water here is very beautiful, and very grand. The cascade from the lake a fine one. Except this the garden has no great beauties. It is not laid out in fine lawns and woods, but the trees are scattered thinly over the ground, and every here and there small thickets of shrubs, in oval raised beds, cultivated, and flowers among the shrubs. The gravelled walks are broad. Art appears too much. There are but a few seats in it, and nothing of architecture more dignified. There is no one striking position in it. There has been a great addition to the length of the river since Whateley wrote.

Enfield chase.[7] One of the 4. lodges. Garden about 60. as. originally by Ld. Chatham, now in the tenure of Dr. Beaver, who married the daughter of Mr. Sharpe. The lease lately renewed. Not in good repair. The water very fine. Would admit of great improvement by extending walks &c. to the principal water at the bottom of the lawn.

[Moor-Park] Lawn about 30. as. A piece of ground up the hill of 6. as. A small lake. Clumps of Spruce firs. Surrounded by walk separately inclosed. Destroys unity. The property of Mr. Rous, who bought of Sr. Thomas Dundas. The building superb. The principal front a Corinthian portico of 4. columns. In front of the wings a colonnade, Ionic, subordinate. Back front a terras, 4. Corinthian pilasters. Pulling down wings of building. Removing deer. Wants water.

Kew. Archimedes' screw for raising water. A horizontal shaft made to turn the oblique one of the screw by a patent machinery of this form.

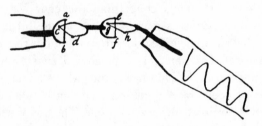

The pieces separate.

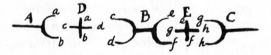

A. is driven by it's shank into the horizontal axis of the wheel which turns the [whole machine.]

B. is an intermediate iron to connect the motion of A. and C.

C. is driven by it's shank, into the axis of the screw.

D. is a cross axis, the ends a. and b. going into the corresponding holes a. and b. of the iron A. [and the ends c. and d. going into the corresponding holes c. and d. of the iron B.]

E. is another cross axis, the ends e. and f. going into the corresponding holes [e. and f.] of the iron B. and the ends g. and h. going into the corresponding holes g. and h. of the iron C.

JOHN ADAMS'S DIARY ENTRY FOR THE SAME TOUR

London, April. Mr. Jefferson and myself went in a postchaise to Woburn farm, Caversham, Wotton, Stowe, Edgehill, Stratford upon Avon, Birmingham, the Leasowes, Hagley, Stourbridge, Worcester, Woodstock, Blenheim, Oxford, High Wycombe, and back to Grosvenor Square.—Edgehill and Worcester were curious and interesting to us, as scenes where freemen had fought for their rights. The people in the neighborhood appeared so ignorant and careless at Worcester, that I was provoked, and asked, 'And do Englishmen so soon forget the ground where liberty was fought for? Tell your neighbors and your children that this is holy ground; much holier than that on which your churches stand. All England should come in pilgrimage to this hill once a year.'—This animated them, and they seemed much pleased with it. Perhaps their awkwardness before might arise from their uncertainty of our sentiments concerning the civil wars.—Stratford upon Avon is interesting, as it is the scene of the birth, death, and sepulture of Shakspeare. Three doors from the inn is the house where he was born, as small and mean as you can conceive. They showed us an old wooden chair in the chimney corner where he sat. We cut off a chip according to custom. A mulberry tree that he planted has been cut down, and is carefully preserved for sale. The house where he died has been taken down, and the spot is now only yard or garden. The curse upon him who should remove his bones, which is written on his gravestone, alludes to a pile of some thousands of human bones which lie exposed in that church. There is nothing preserved of this great genius which is worth knowing; nothing which might inform us what education, what company, what accident, turned his mind to letters and the drama. His name is not even on his gravestone. An ill-sculptured head is set up by his wife, by the side of his grave in the church. But paintings and sculpture would be thrown away on his fame. His wit, fancy, his taste and judgment, his knowledge of nature, of life and character, are immortal.—At Birmingham we only walked round the town, and viewed a manufactory of paintings upon paper. The gentlemen's seats were the highest entertainment we met with. Stowe, Hagley, and Blenheim, are superb; Woburn, Caversham, and the Leasowes are beautiful. Wotton is both great and elegant, though neglected. Architecture, painting, statuary, poetry, are all employed in the embellishment of these residences of greatness and luxury. A national debt of two hundred and seventy-four millions sterling, accumulated by jobs, contracts, salaries, and pensions, in the course of a century might easily produce all this magnificence. The pillars, obelisks, &c., erected in honor of kings, queens, and princesses, might procure the means.—The temples to Bacchus and Venus are quite unnecessary, as mankind have no need of artificial incitement to such amusements. The temples of ancient Virtue, of the British worthies, of Friendship, of Concord and Victory, are in higher taste. I mounted Lord Cobham's Pillar, one hundred and twenty feet high, with pleasure, as his Lordship's name was familiar to me from Pope's works.— Lord Littleton's seat interested me, from a recollection of his works, as well as the grandeur and beauty of the scenes. Pope's pavilion and Thomson's seat made the excursion poetical. Shenstone's Leasowes is the simplest and plainest, but the most rural of all. I saw no spot so small that exhibited such a variety of beauties.—It will be long, I hope, before ridings, parks, pleasure grounds, gardens, and ornamented farms, grow so much in fashion in America; but nature has done greater things and furnished nobler materials there; the oceans, islands, rivers, mountains, valleys, are all laid out upon a larger scale. If any man should hereafter arise to embellish the rugged grandeur of Pen's Hill he might make something to boast of, although there are many situations capable of better improvement.—Since my return I have been over Blackfriar's Bridge to see Viny's manufacture of patent wheels made of bent timber. (Adams, *Works,* ed. C. F. Adams, III, 394–6)

27. TO JOHN PAGE[1]

Dear Sir   *Paris May 4. 1786.*
Your two favours of Mar. 15, and Aug. 23. 1785. by Monsieur de la Croix came to hand on the 15th. of November. His return gives me an opportunity of sending you a copy of the Nautical almanacs for 1786.

7. 8. 9. There is no late and interesting publication here or I would send it by the same conveiance. With these almanacs I pack a copy of some notes I wrote for Monsr. de Marbois in the year 1781. of which I had a few printed here. They were written in haste and for his private inspection. A few friends having asked copies I found it cheaper to print than to write them. One of these got into the hands of a bookseller who getting a bad translation of them made, obliged me to consent that they should appear on condition of their being translated by a better hand. I apprehend therefore they will get further than I intended; tho' as yet they are in few hands. They will offer nothing new to you, not even as an oblation of my friendship for you which is as old almost as we are ourselves. Mazzei brought me your favor of Apr. 28. I thank you much for your communications. Nothing can be more grateful at such a distance. It is unfortunate that most people think the occurrences passing daily under their eyes, are either known to all the world, or not worth being known. They therefore do not give them place in their letters. I hope you will be so good as to continue your friendly information. The proceedings of our public bodies, the progress of the public mind on interesting questions, the casualties which happen among our private friends, and whatever is interesting to yourself and family will always be anxiously received by me. There is one circumstance in the work you were concerned in which has not yet come to my knowledge. To wit How far Westward from Fort Pitt does the Western boundary of Pennsylvania pass, and where does it strike the Ohio? The proposition you mention from Mr. Anderson on the purchase of tobacco, I would have made use of, but that I have engaged the abuses of the tobacco trade on a more general scale. I confess their redress does not appear with any certainty; but till I see all hope of removing the evil by the roots, I cannot propose to prune it's branches. I returned but three or four days ago from a two months trip to England. I traversed that country much, and own both town and country fell short of my expectations. Comparing it with this, I found a much greater proportion of barrens, a soil in other parts not naturally so good as this, not better cultivated, but better manured, and therefore more productive. This proceeds from the practice of long leases there, and short ones here. The labouring people here are

poorer than in England. They pay about one half their produce in rent, the English in general about a third. The gardening in that country is the article in which it surpasses all the earth. I mean their pleasure gardening. This indeed went far beyond my ideas. The city of London, tho' handsomer than Paris, is not so handsome as Philadelphia. Their architecture is in the most wretched stile I ever saw, not meaning to except America where it is bad, nor even Virginia where it is worse than in any other part of America, which I have seen. The mechanical arts in London are carried to a wonderful perfection. But of these I need not speak, because of them my countrymen have unfortunately too many samples before their eyes. I consider the extravagance which has seized them as a more baneful evil than toryism was during the war. It is the more so as the example is set by the best and most amiable characters among us. Would a missionary appear who would make frugality the basis of his religious system, and go thro the land preaching it up as the only road to salvation, I would join his school tho' not generally disposed to seek my religion out of the dictates of my own reason and feelings of my own heart. These things have been more deeply impressed on my mind by what I have heard and seen in England. That nation hates us, their ministers hate us, and their king more than all other men. They have the impudence to avow this, tho' they acknolege our trade important to them. But they say we cannot prevent our countrymen from bringing that into their laps. A conviction of this determines them to make no terms of commerce with us. They say they will pocket our carrying trade as well as their own. Our overtures of commercial arrangement have been treated with a derision which shew their firm persuasion that we shall never unite to suppress their commerce or even to impede it. I think their hostility towards us is much more deeply rooted at present than during the war. In the arts the most striking thing I saw there, new, was the application of the principle of the steam-engine to grist mills. I saw 8. pr. of stones which are worked by steam and they are to set up 30 pair in the same house. A hundred bushels of coal a day are consumed at present. I do not know in what proportion the consumption will be increased by the additional geer. Be so good as to present my respects to Mrs. Page and your family, to W. Lewis, F. Willis and their families and to accept yourself assurances of the sincere regard with which I am Dr. Sir your affectionate friend & servt,

Th: Jefferson

P.S. Mazzei is still here and will publish soon a book on the subject of America.

28. FROM JEFFERSON'S OBSERVATIONS ON DÉMEUNIER'S MANUSCRIPT[1]

[June 22, 1786]

... Pa. 240. 'Les officiers Americains' &c., to pa. 264. 'qui le meritoient.' I would propose to new-model this Section in the following manner. 1. Give a succinct history of the origin and establishment of the Cincinnati. 2. Examine whether in it's present form it threatens any dangers to the state. 3. Propose the most practicable method of preventing them. Having been in America during the period in which this institution was formed, and being then in a situation which gave me opportunities of seeing it in all it's stages, I may venture to give M. de Meusnier materials for the 1st. branch of the preceding distribution of the subject. The 2d. and 3d. he will best execute himself. I should write it's history in the following form.

When on the close of that war which established the independance of America, it's army was about to be disbanded, the officers, who during the course of it had gone thro the most trying scenes together, who by mutual aids and good offices had become dear to one another, felt with great oppression of mind the approach of that moment which was to separate them never perhaps to meet again. They were from different states and from distant parts of the same state. Hazard alone could therefore give them but rare and partial occasions of seeing each other. They were of course to abandon altogether the hope of ever meeting again, or to devise some occasion which might bring them together. And why not come together on purpose at stated times? Would not the trouble of such a journey be greatly overpaid by the pleasure of seeing each other again, by the sweetest of all consolations, the talking over the scenes of difficulty and of endearment they had gone through? This too would enable them to know who of them should succeed in the world, who should be unsuccessful, and to open the purses of all to every labouring brother. This idea was too soothing not to be cherished in conversation. It was improved into that of a regular association, with an organised administration, with periodical meetings general and particular, fixed contributions for those who should be in distress, and a badge by which not only those who had not had occasion to become personally known should be able to recognise one another, but which should be worne by their descendants to perpetuate among them the friendships which had bound their ancestors together.   Genl. Washington was at that moment oppressed with the operation of disbanding an army which was not paid, and the difficulty of this operation was increased by some two or three of the states having expressed sentiments which did not indicate a sufficient attention to their paiment. He was sometimes present when his officers were fashioning in their conversations their newly proposed society. He saw the innocence of it's origin, and foresaw no effects less innocent. He was at that time writing his valedictory letter to the states, which has been so deservedly applauded by the world. Far from thinking it a moment to multiply the causes of irritation, by thwarting a proposition which had absolutely no other basis but of benevolence and friendship, he was rather satisfied to find himself aided in his difficulties by this new incident, which occupied, and at the same time soothed the minds of the officers. He thought too that this institution would be one instrument the more for strengthening the federal band, and for promoting federal ideas. The institution was formed. They incorporated into it the officers of the French army and navy by whose sides they had fought, and with whose aid they had finally prevailed extending it to such grades as they were told might be permitted to enter into it. They sent an officer to France to make the proposition to them, and to procure the badges which they had devised for their order. The moment of disbanding the army having come on before they could have a full meeting to appoint their president, the General was prayed to act in that office till their first general meeting, which was to be held at Philadelphia in the month of May following. The laws of the society were published. Men who read them in their closets, unwarmed by those sentiments of friendship which had produced them, inattentive to those pains which an approaching separation had excited in the minds of the institutors, Politicians, who see in every thing only the dangers with which it threatens civil society, in fine, the labouring people, who, shielded by equal laws, had never seen any difference between man and man, but had read of terrible oppressions which people of their description experience in other countries from those who are distinguished by titles and badges, began to be alarmed at this new institution. A remarkeable silence however was observed. Their sollicitudes were long confined within the circles of private conversation. At length however a Mr. Burke, chief justice of South Carolina, broke that silence. He wrote against the new institution; foreboding it's dangers. Very imperfectly indeed, because he had nothing but his imagination to aid him. An American could do no more: for to detail the real evils of aristocracy they must be seen in Europe. Burke's fears were thought exaggerations in America; while in Europe it is known that even Mirabeau has but faintly sketched the curses of hereditary aristocracy as they are experienced here, and as they would have followed in America had this institution remained. The epigraph of Burke's pamphlet was 'Blow ye the trumpet in Zion.' It's effect corresponded with it's epigraph. This institution became first the subject of general conversation. Next it was made the subject of deliberation in the legislative assemblies of some of the states. The governor of South Carolina censured it in an address to his assembly. The assemblies of Massachusets, Rhode island and Pennsylvania condemned it's principles. No circumstance indeed brought the consideration of it expressly before Congress, yet it had sunk deep into their minds. An offer having been made to them on the part of the Polish order of divine providence to receive some of their distinguished citizens into that order, they made that an occasion to declare that these distinctions were contrary to the principles of their confederation.   The uneasiness excited by this institution had very early caught the notice of General Washington. Still recollecting all the purity of the motives which gave it birth, he became sensible that it might produce political evils which the warmth of these motives had masked. Add to this that it was disapproved by the mass of the citizens of the Union. This alone was reason strong enough in a country where the will of the majority is the law, and ought to be the law. He saw that the objects of the institution were too light to be opposed to considerations as serious as these; and that it was become necessary to annihilate it absolutely. On this therefore he was decided. The first annual meeting at Philadelphia was now at hand. He went to that, determined to exert all his influence for it's suppression. He proposed it to his fellow officers, and urged it with all his powers. It met an opposition which was observed to cloud his face with an anxiety that the most distressful scenes of the war had scarcely ever produced. It was canvassed for several days, and at length it was no more a doubt what would be it's ultimate fate. The order was on the point of receiving it's annihilation by the vote of a very great majority of it's members. In this moment their envoy arrived from France, charged with letters from the French officers accepting with cordiality the proposed badges of union, with sollicitations from others to be received into the order, and with notice that their respectable sovereign had been pleased to recognise it, and to permit his officers to wear it's badge. The prospect was now changed. The question assumed a new form. After the offer made by them, and accepted by their friends, in what words could they clothe a proposition to retract it which would not cover themselves with the reproaches of levity and ingratitude? Which would not appear an insult to those whom they loved? Federal principles, popular discontent, were considerations whose weight was known and felt by themselves. But would foreigners know and feel them equally? Would they so far acknolege their cogency as to permit without any indignation the eagle and ribbon to be torn from their breasts by the very hands which had placed them there? The idea revolted the whole society. They found it necessary then to preserve so much of their institution as might continue to support this foreign branch, while they should prune off every other which could give offence to their fellow citizens; thus sacrificing on each hand to their friends and to their country. The society was to retain it's existence, it's name, it's meetings, and it's charitable funds; but these last were to be deposited with their respective legislatures; the order was to be no longer hereditary, a reformation which had been even pressed from this side the Atlantic; it was to be communicated to no new members; the general meetings instead of annual were to be triennial only. The eagle and ribbon indeed were retained; because they were worn, and they wished them to be worn, by their friends who were in a country where they would not be objects of offence; but themselves never wore them. They laid them up in their bureaus with the medals of American independance, with those of the trophies they had taken and the battles they had won. But through all the United states no officer is seen to offend the public eye with the display of this badge. These changes have tranquilised the American states. Their citizens do justice to the circumstance which prevented a total annihilation of the order. They feel too much interest in the reputation of their officers, and value too much whatever may serve to recall to the memory of their allies the moments wherein they formed but one people. Tho they are obliged by a prudent foresight to keep out every thing from among themselves which might pretend to divide them into orders, and to degrade one description of men below another, yet they hear with pleasure that their allies whom circumstances have already placed under these distinctions, are willing to consider it as one to have aided them in the establishment of their liberties, and to wear a badge which may recall them to their remembrance; and it would be an extreme affliction to them if the domestic reformation which has been found necessary, if the censures of individual writers, or if any other circumstances should discourage the wearing their badge, or lessen it's reputation.

This short but true history of the order of the Cincinnati, taken from the mouths of persons on the spot who were privy to it's origin, and progress, and who know it's present state, is the best apology which can be made for an institution which appeared to be, and was really, so heterogeneous to the governments in which it was erected. It should be further considered that, in America, no other distinction between man and man had ever been known, but that of persons in office exercising powers by authority of the laws, and private individuals. Among these last the poorest labourer stood on equal ground with the wealthiest Millionary, and generally on a more favoured one whenever their rights seemed to jar. It has been seen that a shoemaker, or other artisan, removed by the voice of his country from his work bench into a chair of office, has instantly commanded all the respect and obedience which the laws ascribe to his office. But of distinctions by birth or badge they had no more idea than they had of the mode of existence in the moon or planets. They had heard only that there were such, and knew that they must be wrong. A due horror of the evils which flow from these distinctions could be excited in Europe only, where the dignity of man is lost in arbitrary distinctions, where the human species is classed into several stages of degradation, where the many are crouched under the weight of the few, and where the order established can present to the contemplation of a thinking being no other picture than that of God almighty and his angels trampling under foot the hosts of the damned. No wonder then that the institution of the Cincinnati could be innocently conceived by one order of American citizens, could raise in the other orders only a slow, temperate, and rational opposition, and could be viewed in Europe as a detestable parricide.

The 2d. and 3d. branches of this subject, nobody can better execute than M. de Meusnier. Perhaps it may be curious to him to see how they strike an American mind at present. He shall therefore have the ideas of one who was an enemy to the institution from the first moment of it's conception, but who was always sensible that the officers neither foresaw, nor intended the injury they were doing to their country.

As to the question then, Whether any evil can proceed from the institution as it stands at present, I am of opinion there may. 1. From the meetings. These will keep the officers formed into a body; will continue a distinction between civil and military which it would be for the good of the whole to obliterate as soon as possible; and military assemblies will not only keep alive the jealousies and the fears of the civil government, but give ground for these fears and jealousies. For when men meet together, they will make business if they have none; they will collate their grievances, some real, some imaginary, all highly painted; they will communicate to each other the sparks of discontent; and these may engender a flame which will consume their particular, as well as the general, happiness. 2. The charitable part of the institution is still more likely to do mischeif, as it perpetuates the dangers apprehended in the preceding clause. For here is a fund provided of permanent existence. To whom will it belong? To the descendants of American officers of a certain description. These descendants then will form a body, having a sufficient interest to keep up an attention to their description, to continue meetings, and perhaps, in some moment, when the political eye shall be slumbering, or the firmness of their fellow-citizens relaxed, to replace the insignia of the order, and revive all it's pretentions. What good can the officers propose which may weigh against these possible evils? The securing their descendants against want? Why afraid to trust them to the same fertile soil, and the same genial climate which will secure from want the descendants of their other fellow-citizens? Are they afraid they will be reduced to labour the earth for their sustenance? They will be rendered thereby both honester and happier. An industrious farmer occupies a more dignified place in the scale of beings, whether moral or political, than a lazy lounger, valuing himself on his family, too proud to work, and drawing out a miserable existence by eating on that surplus of other mens' labour which is the sacred fund of the helpless poor. A pitiful annuity will only prevent them from exerting that industry and those talents which would soon lead them to better fortune.

How are these evils to be prevented? 1. At their first general meeting let them distribute the funds on hand to the existing objects of their destination, and discontinue all further contributions. 2. Let them declare at the same time that their meetings general and particular shall thenceforth cease. And 3. let them melt up their eagles and add the mass to the distributable fund that their descendants may have no temptation to hang them in their button holes.

These reflections are not proposed as worthy the notice of M. de Meusnier. He will be so good as to treat the subject in his own way, and no body has a better. I will only pray him to avail us of his forcible manner to evince that there is evil to be apprehended even from the ashes of this institution, and to exhort the society in America to make their reformation complete; bearing in mind that we must keep the passions of men on our side even when we are persuading them to do what they ought to do....

28A. TO JEAN NICOLAS DÉMEUNIER

[June 26, 1786]

Mr. Jefferson presents his compliments to M. de Meusnier and sends him copies of the 13th. 23d. and 24th. articles of the treaty between the K. of Prussia and the United States. In the negociation with the minister of Portugal at London, the latter objected to the 13th. article. The observations which were made in answer to his objections, Mr. Jefferson incloses. They are a commentary on the 13th. article. Mr. de Meusnier will be so good as to return the sheet on which these observations are, as Mr. Jefferson does not retain a copy of it.

If M. de Meusnier proposes to mention the facts of cruelty of which he and Mr. Jefferson spoke yesterday, the 24th. article will introduce them properly, because they produced a sense of the necessity of that article. These facts are 1. the death of upwards of 11,000 American prisoners in one prison ship (the Jersey) and in the space of 3. years. 2. General Howe's permitting our prisoners taken at the battle of Germantown and placed under a guard in the yard of the Statehouse of Philadelphia to be so long without any food furnished them that many perished with hunger. Where the bodies laid, it was seen that they had eaten all the grass round them within their reach, after they had lost the power of rising or moving from their place. 3. The 2d. fact was the act of a commanding officer: the 1st. of several commanding officers and for so long a time as must suppose the approbation of government. But the following was the act of government itself. During the periods that our affairs seemed unfavourable and theirs succesful, that is to say after the evacuation of New York, and again after the taking of Charlestown in South Carolina, they regularly sent our prisoners taken on the seas and carried to England to the E. Indies. This is so certain, that in the month of Novemb. or Decemb. 1785. Mr. Adams having officially demanded a delivery of the American prisoners sent to the East Indies, Ld. Carmarthaen answered officially 'that orders were immediately issued for their discharge.' M. de Meusnier is at liberty to quote this fact. 4. A fact not only of the Government but of the parliament, who passed an act for that purpose in the beginning of the war, was the obliging our prisoners taken at sea to join them and fight against their countrymen. This they effected by starving and whipping them. The insult on Capt. Stanhope, which happened at Boston last year, was a consequence of this. Two persons, Dunbar and Lorthrope, whom Stanhope had treated in this manner (having particularly inflicted 24 lashes on Dunbar) meeting him at Boston, attempted to beat him. But the people interposed and saved him. The fact is referred to in that paragraph of the declaration of independance which sais 'he has constrained our fellow citizens taken captive on the high seas, to bear arms against their country, to become the executioners of their friends and brethren, or to fall themselves by their hands.' This was the most afflicting to our prisoners of all the cruelties exercised on them. The others affected the body only, but this the mind. They were haunted by the horror of having perhaps themselves shot the ball by which a father or a brother fell. Some of them had constancy enough to hold out against half allowance of food and repeated whippings. These were generally sent to England and from thence to the East Indies. One of these escaped from the East Indies and got back to Paris, where he gave an account of his sufferings to Mr. Adams who happened to be then at Paris.

M. de Meusnier, where he mentions that the slave-law has been passed in Virginia, without the clause of emancipation, is pleased to mention that neither Mr. Wythe nor Mr. Jefferson were present to make the proposition they had meditated; from which people, who do not give themselves the trouble to reflect or enquire, might conclude hastily that their absence was the cause why the proposition was not made; and of course that there were not in the assembly persons of virtue and firmness enough to propose the clause for emancipation. This supposition would not be true. There were persons there who wanted neither the virtue to propose, nor talents to enforce the proposition had they seen that the disposition of the legislature was ripe for it. These worthy characters would feel themselves wounded, degraded, and discouraged by this idea. Mr. Jefferson would therefore be obliged to M. de Meusnier to mention it in some such manner as this. 'Of the two commissioners who had concerted the amendatory clause for the gradual emancipation of slaves Mr. Wythe could not be present as being a member of the judiciary department, and Mr. Jefferson was absent on the legation to France. But there wanted not in that assembly men of virtue enough to propose, and talents to vindicate this clause. But they saw that the moment of doing it with success was not yet arrived, and that an unsuccesful effort, as too often happens, would only rivet still closer the chains of bondage, and retard the moment of delivery to this oppressed description of men. What a stupendous, what an incomprehensible machine is man! Who can endure toil, famine, stripes, imprisonment or death itself in vindication of his own liberty, and the next moment be deaf to all those motives whose power supported him thro' his trial, and inflict on his fellow men a bondage, one hour of which is fraught with more misery than ages of that which he rose in rebellion to oppose. But we must await with patience the workings of an overruling providence, and hope that that is preparing the deliverance of these our suffering brethren. When the measure of their tears shall be full, when their groans shall have involved heaven itself in darkness, doubtless a god of justice will awaken to their distress, and by diffusing light and liberality among their oppressors, or at length by his exterminating thunder, manifest his attention to the things of this world, and that they are not left to the guidance of a blind fatality....

29. TO WILLIAM STEPHENS SMITH

Dear Sir   *Paris July 9. 1786.*
I wrote you last on the 16th. of June. Since that your favors of May 21. and June 12. have come to hand. The accounts of the K. of Prussia are such that we may expect his exit soon. He is like the snuff of a candle; sometimes seeming to be out; then blazing up again for a moment. It is thought that his death will not be followed by any immediate disturbance of the public tranquillity; that his kingdom may be considered as a machine which will go of itself a considerable time with the winding up he has given it. Besides this he has for some time employed his successor in his councils, who is endeavoring to possess himself of and to pursue his uncle's plan of policy. The connection which has long subsisted between the Van Staphorsts, the Grands,[1] and this court

is known to you. I think it probable that private sollicitations first suggested the late appointment and might be the real efficient cause of it. The ostensible one, and which has some reality too, is the accomodation of the lenders in Holland. It will doubtless facilitate the borrowing money there for this country, and multiply the partisans of the new alliance. The policy of this country is indeed wise. What would have been said a dozen years ago had any one pretended to foretell that in that short space of time France would get Holland, America and even England under her wing?

We have had here some strong altercations between the court and the parliament of Bourdeaux. The latter used a language which a British parliament would not have dared to use. The court was in the wrong and will have the wisdom and moderation to recede. The question is whether lands called Alluvions, on the river Garonne belong to the king or to the proprietors to whose soil they have been added.

I have received by Dr. Bancroft the portable copying press.[2] It is perfectly well made. Be so good as to present my compliments and thanks to Mr. Cavallo for his attention to it. To yourself I suppose you would rather I should present the money. This I will do the moment you will inform me of the sum. In your letter of May 21. you mention that you had paid the maker £5-10. But a former letter gave me reason to believe you had to pay something to another person for a board or the box or something else. I will beg the favor of you at the same time to inform me what a pair of chariot harness will cost in London, plated, not foppish but genteel, and I will add the price, or not add it to the bill I shall send you, according as I shall find it when compared with prices here. Cannot you invent some commissions for me here, by way of reprisal for the vexations I give you? Silk stockings, gillets, &c. for yourself, gewgaws and contrivances for Madame? à propos, All hail, Madame! May your nights and days be many and full of joy! May their fruits be such as to make you feel the sweet union of parent and lover, but not so many as that you may feel their weight! May they be handsome and good as their mother, wise and honest as their father, but more milky!—For your old age I will compose a prayer thirty years hence.

To return to business (for I am never tempted to pray but when a warm feeling for my friends comes athwart my heart) they tell me that they are about altering Dr. Ramsay's book in London in order to accomodate it to the English palate and pride. I hope this will not be done without the consent of the author, and I do not believe that will be obtained. If the booksellers of London are afraid to sell it I think it can be sold here. Even the English themselves will apply for it here. It is very much esteemed by those who have read it. The French translation will be out in a short time. There is no gutting in that. All Europe will read the English transactions in America, as they really happened. To what purpose then hoodwink themselves? Like the foolish Ostrich who when it has hid it's head, thinks it's body cannot be seen. I will beg the favor of you to prevail on Mr. Dilly to send me 50. copies by the Diligence. We shall see by the sale of these what further number we may call for. I will undertake to justify this to the author. They must come unbound. It will be necessary at the same time to put into some of the English papers the following advertisement. 'The bookseller, to whom Dr. Ramsay's history of the revolution of S. Carolina was addressed for sale, having been advised that the executing that commission would expose him to the actions of certain persons whose conduct in America, as therein represented, is not in their favor, the public are hereby notified that they may be furnished with the said work either in the original English, or well translated into French, by writing to Froullé, libraire au quai des Augustins à Paris, and franking their letters. An opportunity of sending it to London occurs every week by the Diligence.' Send me a paper or two with this advertisement in it.

To put an end to your trouble I will wish you a good night. I beg your pardon, I had forgot that you would have it without my wishes: I bid you therefore a simple Adieu, with assurances of my friendship & esteem,

Th: Jefferson

30. TO GEORGE WYTHE[1]

Dear Sir   *Paris Aug. 13. 1786.*
Your favors of Jan. 10. and Feb. 10. came to hand on the 20th. and 23d
of May. I availed myself of the first opportunity which occurred, by a
gentleman going to England, of sending to Mr. Joddrel a copy of the
Notes on our country, with a line informing him that it was you who
had emboldened me to take that liberty. Madison, no doubt, informed
you of the reason why I had sent only a single copy to Virginia. Being
assured by him that they will not do the harm I had apprehended, but
on the contrary may do some good, I propose to send thither the
copies remaining on hand, which are fewer than I had intended, but of
the numerous corrections they need, there are one or two so essential
that I must have them made, by printing a few new leaves and substi-
tuting them for the old. This will be done while they are engraving a
map which I have constructed of the country from Albemarle sound
to Lake Erie, and which will be inserted in the book. A bad French
translation which is getting out here, will probably oblige me to publish the original more freely, which it neither deserved nor was ever
intended. Your wishes, which are laws to me, will justify my destining
a copy for you. Otherwise I should as soon have thought of sending
you a horn-book; for there is no truth there that is not familiar to you,
and it's errors I should hardly have proposed to treat you with.

Immediately on the receipt of your letter, I wrote to a correspondent at Florence to enquire after the family of Tagliaferro as you desired. I received his answer two days ago, a copy of which I now
inclose. The original shall be sent by some other occasion. I will have
the copper plate immediately engraved. This may be ready within a
few days, but the probability is that I shall be long getting an opportunity of sending it to you, as these rarely occur. You do not mention the
size of the plate but, presuming it is intended for labels for the inside
of books, I shall have it made of a proper size for that. I shall omit the
word αριsos,[2] according to the license you allow me, because I think
the beauty of a motto is to condense much matter in as few words as
possible. The word omitted will be supplied by every reader.

The European papers have announced that the assembly of Virginia were occupied on the revisal of their Code of laws. This, with some other similar intelligence, has contributed much to convince the people of Europe, that what the English papers are constantly publishing of our anarchy, is false; as they are sensible that such a work is that of a people only who are in perfect tranquillity. Our act for freedom of religion is extremely applauded. The Ambassadors and ministers of the several nations of Europe resident at this court have asked of me copies of it to send to their sovereigns, and it is inserted at full length in several books now in the press; among others, in the new Encyclopedie. I think it will produce considerable good even in these countries where ignorance, superstition, poverty and oppression of body and mind in every form, are so firmly settled on the mass of the people, that their redemption from them can never be hoped. If the almighty had begotten a thousand sons, instead of one, they would not have sufficed for this task. If all the sovereigns of Europe were to set themselves to work to emancipate the minds of their subjects from their present ignorance and prejudices, and that as zealously as they now endeavor the contrary, a thousand years would not place them on that high ground on which our common people are now setting out. Ours could not have been so fairly put into the hands of their own common sense, had they not been separated from their parent stock and been kept from contamination, either from them, or the other people of the old world, by the intervention of so wide an ocean. To know the worth of this, one must see the want of it here. I think by far the most important bill in our whole code is that for the diffusion of knowlege among the people. No other sure foundation can be devised for the preservation of freedom, and happiness. If any body thinks that kings, nobles, or priests are good conservators of the public happiness, send them here. It is the best school in the universe to cure them of that folly. They will see here with their own eyes that these descriptions of men are an abandoned confederacy against the happiness of the mass of people. The omnipotence of their effect cannot be better proved than in this country particularly, where notwithstanding the finest soil upon earth, the finest climate under heaven, and a people of the most benevolent, the most gay, and amiable character of which the human form is susceptible, where such a people I say, surrounded by so many blessings from nature, are yet loaded with misery by kings, nobles and priests, and by them alone. Preach, my dear Sir, a crusade against ignorance; establish and improve the law for educating the common people. Let our countrymen know that the people alone can protect us against these evils, and that the tax which will be paid for this purpose is not more than the thousandth part of what will be paid to kings, priests and nobles who will rise up among us if we leave the people in ignorance.—The people of England, I think, are less oppressed than here. But it needs but half an eye to see, when among them, that the foundation is laid in their dispositions, for the establishment of a despotism. Nobility, wealth, and pomp are the objects of their adoration. They are by no means the free-minded people we suppose them in America. Their learned men too are few in number, and are less learned and infinitely less emancipated from prejudice than those of this country. An event too seems to be prospering, in the order of things, which will probably decide the fate of that country. It is no longer doubtful that the harbour of Cherbourg will be completed, that it will be a most excellent one, and capacious enough to hold the whole navy of France. Nothing has ever been wanting to enable this country to invade that, but a naval force conveniently stationed to protect the transports. This change of situation, must oblige the English to keep up a great standing army, and there is no king, who, with a sufficient force, is not always ready to make himself absolute.—My paper warns me it is time to recommend myself to the friendly recollection of Mrs. Wythe, of Colo. Taliaferro and his family and particularly of Mr. R. T. and to assure you of the affectionate esteem with which I am Dear Sir your friend & servt.,

Th: Jefferson

31. TO JOHN ADAMS

Dear Sir   *Paris Aug. 27. 1786.*
...I inclose you the article 'Etats Unis' of one of the volumes of the Encyclopedie, lately published. The author, M. de Meusnier, was introduced to me by the D. de la Rochefoucault. He asked of me infor-

mation on the subject of our states, and left with me a number of queries to answer. Knowing the importance of setting to rights a book so universally diffused and which will go down to late ages, I answered his queries as fully as I was able, went into a great many calculations for him, and offered to give further explanations where necessary. He then put his work into my hands. I read it, and was led by that into a still greater number of details by way of correcting what he had at first written, which was indeed a mass of errors and misconceptions from beginning to end. I returned him his work and my details; but he did not communicate it to me after he had corrected it. It has therefore come out with many errors which I would have advised him to correct, and the rather as he was very well disposed. He has still left in a great deal of the Abbé Raynal, that is to say a great deal of falsehood, and he has stated other things on bad information. I am sorry I had not another correction of it. He has paid me for my trouble, in the true coin of his country, most unmerciful compliment. This, with his other errors, I should surely have struck out had he sent me the work, as I expected, before it went to the press. I find in fact that he is happiest of whom the world sais least, good or bad.—I think if I had had a little more warning, my desire to see Holland, as well as to meet again Mrs. Adams and yourself, would have tempted me to take a flying trip there. I wish you may be tempted to take Paris in your return. You will find many very happy to see you here, and none more so than, Dear Sir, your friend and servant,

Th: Jefferson

32. TO THOMAS MANN RANDOLPH, JR.

Dear Sir   *Paris Aug. 27. 1786.*

I am honoured with your favour of the 16th. instant, and desirous, without delay, of manifesting my wishes to be useful to you, I shall venture to you some thoughts on the course of your studies which must be submitted to the better advice with which you are surrounded. A longer race through life may have enabled me to seise some truths which have not yet been presented to your observation. A more intimate knowlege of the country in which you are to live and of the circumstances in which you will be placed, may enable me to point your attention to the branches of science which will administer the most to your happiness there. The foundations which you have laid in languages and mathematics are proper for every superstructure. The former exercises our memory while that and no other faculty is yet matured, and prevents our acquiring habits of idleness; the latter gives exercise to our reason, as soon as that has acquired a certain degree of strength, and stores the mind with truths which are useful in other branches of science. At this moment then a second order of preparation is to commence. I shall propose to you that it be extensive, comprehending Astronomy, Natural philosophy (or Physics) Natural history, Anatomy, Botany and Chemistry. No inquisitive mind will be content to be ignorant of any one of these branches. But I would advise you to be contented with a course of lectures in most of them, without attempting to make yourself completely master of the whole. This is more than any genius, joined to any length of life is equal to. You will find among them some one study to which your mind will more particularly attach itself. This then I would pursue and propose to attain eminence in. Your own country furnishes the most aliment for Natural history, Botany and Physics, and as you express a fondness for the former you might make it your principal object, endeavouring however to make myself more acquainted with the two latter than with other branches likely to be less useful. In fact you will find botany offering it's charms to you at every step, during summer, and Physics in every season. All these branches of science will be better attained by attending courses of lectures in them; you are now in a place where the best courses upon earth are within your reach, and being delivered in your native language, you lose no part of their benefit. Such an opportunity you will never again have. I would therefore strongly press on you to fix no other limitation to your stay in Edinburgh, than your having got thro this whole circle. The omission of any one part of it will be an affliction and a loss to you as long as you live. Besides the comfort of knowlege, every science is auxiliary to every other. While you are attending these courses you can proceed by yourself in a regular series of historical reading. It would be a waste of time to attend a professor of this. It is to be acquired from books, and if you pursue it by yourself, you can accomodate it to your other reading so as to fill up those chasms of time not otherwise appropriated. There are portions of the day too when the mind should be eased. Particularly after dinner it should be applied to lighter occupations. History is of this kind. It exercises principally the memory. Reflection also indeed is necessary, but not generally in a laborious degree. To conduct yourself in this branch of science you have only to consider what aeras of it merit a general and what a particular attention, and in each aera also to distinguish between the countries the knowlege of whose history will be useful, and those where it suffices only to be not altogether ignorant. Having laid down your plan as to the branches of history you would pursue, the order of time will be your sufficient guide. After what you have read in Antient history, I should suppose Millot's digest would be useful and sufficient. The histories of Greece and Rome are worthy a good degree of attention. They should be read in the original authors. The transition from Antient to modern history will be best effected by reading Gibbons, then a general history of the principal states of Europe, but particular ones of England. Here too the original writers are to be preferred. Kennet published a considerable collection of these in 3. vols. folio but there are some others, not in his collection, well worth being read. After the history of England, that of America will claim your attention. Here too original authors, and not compilers, are best. An author who writes of his own times, or of times near his own, presents in his own ideas and manner the best picture of the moment of which he writes. History need not be hurried, but may give way to the other sciences; because history can be pursued after you shall have left your present situation, as well as while you remain in it.

When you shall have got thro' this second order of preparation, the study of the law is to be begun. This, like history, is to be acquired from books. All the aid you will want will be a catalogue of the books to be read, and the order in which they are to be read. It being absolutely indifferent in what place you carry on this reading, I should propose your doing it in France. The advantages of this will be that you will at the same time acquire the habit of speaking French which is the object of a year or two, you may be giving attention to such of the fine arts as your taste may lead you to, and you will be forming an acquaintance with the individuals and character of a nation with whom we must long remain in the closest intimacy, and to whom we are bound by the strong ties of gratitude and policy; a nation in short of the most amiable dispositions on earth, the whole mass of which is penetrated with an affection for us. You might, before your return to your own country, make a visit to Italy also.

I should have performed the office of but half a friend were I to confine myself to the improvement of the mind only. Knowlege indeed is a desireable, a lovely possession, but I do not scruple to say that health is more so. It is of little consequence to store the mind with science if the body be permitted to become debilitated. If the body be feeble, the mind will not be strong. The sovereign invigorator of the body is exercise, and of all the exercises walking is best. A horse gives but a kind of half exercise, and a carriage is no better than a cradle. No one knows, till he tries, how easily a habit of walking is acquired. A person who never walked three miles will in the course of a month become able to walk 15. or 20. without fatigue. I have known some great walkers and had particular accounts of many more; and I never knew or heard of one who was not healthy and long lived. This species of exercise therefore is much to be advised. Should you be disposed to try it, as your health has been feeble, it will be necessary for you to begin with a little, and to increase it by degrees. For the same reason you must probably at first ascribe to it hours the most precious for study, I mean those about the middle of the day. But when you shall find yourself strong, you may venture to take your walks in the evening after the digestion of the dinner is pretty well over. This is making a composition between health and study. The latter would be too much interrupted were you to take from it the early hours of the day, and habit will soon render the evening's exercise as salutary as that of the morning. I speak this from my own experience, having, from an attachment to study, very early in life, made this arrangement of my time, having ever observed it, and still observing it, and always with perfect success. Not less than two hours a day should be devoted to exercise, and the weather should be little regarded. A person not sick will not be injured by getting wet. It is but taking a cold bath, which never gives a cold to any one. Brute animals are the most healthy, and they are exposed to all weather, and of men, those are healthiest who are the most exposed. The recipe of those two descriptions of beings is simple diet, exercise and the open air, be it's state what it will; and we may venture to say that this recipe will give health and vigor to every other description.—By this time I am sure you will think I have sermonized enough. I have given you indeed a lengthy lecture. I have been led through it by my zeal to serve you; if in the whole you find one useful counsel, that will be my reward and a sufficient one. Few persons in your own country have started from as advantageous ground as that whereon you will be placed. Nature and fortune have been liberal to you. Every thing honourable or profitable there is placed within your own reach, and will depend on your own efforts. If these are exerted with assiduity, and guided by unswerving honesty, your success is infallible: and that it may be as great as you wish is the sincere desire of, Dear Sir, your most affectionate humble servant,

Th: Jefferson

33. TO EZRA STILES[1]

Sir   *Paris Sep. 1. 1786.*

I am honoured with your letter of May 8. That which you mention to have written in the winter preceding never came to hand. I return you my thanks for the communications relative to the Western country. When we reflect how long we have inhabited those parts of America which lie between the Alleghaney and the ocean, that no monument has ever been found in them which indicated the use of iron among it's aboriginal inhabitants, that they were as far advanced in arts, at least, as the inhabitants on the other side the Alleghaney, a good degree of infidelity may be excused as to the new discoveries which suppose regular fortifications of brick work to have been in use among the Indians on the waters of the Ohio. Intrenchments of earth they might indeed make; but brick is more difficult. The art of making it may have preceded the use of iron, but it would suppose a greater degree of industry than men in the hunter state usually possess. I should like to know whether General Parsons himself saw actual bricks among the remains of fortification. I suppose the settlement of our continent is of the most remote antiquity. The similitude between it's inhabitants and those of the Eastern parts of Asia renders it probable that ours are descended from them, or they from ours. The latter is my opinion, founded on this single fact. Among the red inhabitants of Asia there are but a few languages radically different. But among our Indians the number of languages is infinite which are so radically different as to exhibit at present no appearance of their having been derived from a common source. The time necessary for the generation of so many languages must be immense.—A countryman of yours, a Mr. Lediard who was with Capt. Cook on his last voiage, proposes either to go to Kamschatka, cross from thence to the Western side of America, and penetrate through the Continent to our side of it, or to go to Kentucke, and thence penetrate Westwardly to the South sea. He went from hence lately to London, where if he found a passage to Kamschatka or the Western coast of America he would avail himself of it; otherwise he proposed to return to our side of America to attempt that route. I think him well calculated for such an enterprize, and wish he may undertake it. Another countryman of yours, Mr. Trumbul, has paid us a visit here, and brought with him two pictures which are the admiration of the Connoisseurs. His natural talents for this art seem almost unparalleled. I send you the 5th. and 6th. vols. of the Bibliotheque physico-oeconomique, erroneously lettered as the 7th. and 8th. which are not yet come out. I inclose with them the article 'Etats unis' of the new Encyclopedie. This article is recently published, and a few copies have been printed separate. For this twelvemonth past little new and excellent has appeared either in literature or the arts. An Abbé Rochon has applied the metal called platina to the telescope instead of the mixed metal of which the specula were formerly composed. It is insusceptible of rust, as gold is, and he thinks it's reflective power equal to that of the mixed metal. He has observed a very curious effect of the natural chrystals, and especially of those of Iceland; which is that lenses made of them have two distinct focuses, and present you the object distinctly at two different distances. This I have seen myself. A new method of copying has been invented here. I called on the inventor,[2] and he presented me a plate of copper, a pen and ink. I wrote a note on the plate, and in about three quarters of an hour he brought me an hundred copies, as perfect as the imagination can conceive. Had I written my name, he could have put it to so many bonds, so that I should have acknoleged the signature to be my own. The copying of paintings in England is very inconceivable. Any number may be taken, which shall give you the true lineaments and colouring of the original without injuring that. This is so like creation, that had I not seen it, I should have doubted it.—The death of the K. of Prussia, which happened on the 17th. inst. will probably employ the pens, if not the swords of politicians. We had exchanged the ratifications of our treaty with him. The articles of this which were intended to prevent or mitigate wars, by lessening their aliment, are so much applauded in Europe that I think the example will be followed. I have the honour to be with very sincere esteem, Dear Sir, your most obedt. humble servt.,

Th: Jefferson

34. TO MARIA COSWAY

Th: Jefferson to Mrs. Cosway   *Thursday [Oct. 5, 1786]*
I have passed the night in so much pain that I have not closed my eyes.[1] It is with infinite regret therefore that I must relinquish your charming company for that of the Surgeon whom I have sent for to examine into the cause of this change. I am in hopes it is only the having rattled a little too freely over the pavement yesterday. If you do not go to day I shall still have the pleasure of seeing you again. If you do, god bless you wherever you go. Present me in the most friendly terms to Mr. Cosway, and let me hear of your safe arrival in England. Addio Addio.

Let me know if you do not go to day.

35. TO MARIA COSWAY

[My Dear] Madam   *Paris Octob. 12. 1786.*

Having performed the last sad office of handing you into your carriage at the Pavillon de St. Denis, and seen the wheels get actually into motion, I turned on my heel and walked, more dead than alive, to the opposite door, where my own was awaiting me. Mr. Danquerville was missing. He was sought for, found, and dragged down stairs. [We] were crammed into the carriage, like recruits for the Bastille, and not having [sou]l enough to give orders to the coachman, he presumed Paris our destination, [and] drove off. After a considerable interval, silence was broke with a 'je suis vraiment affligé du depart de ces bons gens.' This was the signal for a mutual confession [of dist]ress. We began immediately to talk of Mr. and Mrs. Cosway, of their goodness, their [talents], their amability, and tho we spoke of nothing else, we seemed hardly to have entered into matter when the coachman announced the rue St. Denis, and that we were opposite Mr. Danquerville's. He insisted on descending there and traversing a short passage to his lodgings. I was carried home. Seated by my fire side, solitary and sad, the following dialogue took place between my Head and my Heart.

Head. Well, friend, you seem to be in a pretty trim.

Heart. I am indeed the most wretched of all earthly beings. Overwhelmed with grief, every fibre of my frame distended beyond it's natural powers to bear, I would willingly meet whatever catastrophe should leave me no more to feel or to fear.

Head. These are the eternal consequences of your warmth and precipitation. This is one of the scrapes into which you are ever leading us. You confess your follies indeed: but still you hug and cherish them, and no reformation can be hoped, where there is no repentance.

Heart. Oh my friend! This is no moment to upbraid my foibles. I am rent into fragments by the force of my grief! If you have any balm, pour it into my wounds: if none, do not harrow them by new torments. Spare me in this awful moment! At any other I will attend with patience to your admonitions.

Head. On the contrary I never found that the moment of triumph with you was the moment of attention to my admonitions. While suffering under your follies you may perhaps be made sensible of them, but, the paroxysm over, you fancy it can never return. Harsh therefore as the medecine may be, it is my office to administer it. You will be pleased to remember that when our friend Trumbull used to be telling us of the merits and talents of these good people, I never ceased whispering to you that we had no occasion for new acquaintance; that the greater their merit and talents, the more dangerous their friendship to our tranquillity, because the regret at parting would be greater.

Heart. Accordingly, Sir, this acquaintance was not the consequence of my doings. It was one of your projects which threw us in the way of it. It was you, remember, and not I, who desired the meeting, at Legrand & Molinos. I never trouble myself with domes nor arches. The Halle aux bleds[1] might have rotted down before I should have gone to see it. But you, forsooth, who are eternally getting us to sleep with your diagrams and crotchets, must go and examine this wonderful piece of architecture. And when you had seen it, oh! it was the most superb thing on earth! What you had seen there was worth all you had yet seen in Paris! I thought so too. But I meant it of the lady and gentleman to whom we had been presented, and not of a parcel of sticks and chips put together in pens. You then, Sir, and not I, have been the cause of the present distress.

Head. It would have been happy for you if my diagrams and crotchets had gotten you to sleep on that day, as you are pleased to say they eternally do. My visit to Legrand & Molinos had publick utility for it's object. A market is to be built in Richmond. What a commodious plan is that of Legrand & Molinos: especially if we put on it the noble dome of the Halle aux bleds. If such a bridge as they shewed us can be thrown across the Schuylkill at Philadelphia, the floating bridges taken up, and the navigation of that river opened, what a copious resource will be added, of wood and provisions, to warm and feed the poor of that city. While I was occupied with these objects, you were dilating with your new acquaintances, and contriving how to prevent a separation from them. Every soul of you had an engagement for the day. Yet all these were to be sacrificed, that you might dine together. Lying messengers were to be dispatched into every quarter of the city with apologies for your breach of engagement. You particularly had the effrontery [to] send word to the Dutchess Danville that, in the moment we were setting out to d[ine] with her, dispatches came to hand which required immediate attention. You [wanted] me to invent a more ingenious excuse; but I knew you were getting into a scrape, and I would have nothing to do with it. Well, after dinner to St. Cloud, from St. Cloud to Ruggieri's, from Ruggieri to Krumfoltz, and if the day had been as long as a Lapland summer day, you would still have contrived means, among you, to have filled it.

Heart. Oh! my dear friend, how you have revived me by recalling to my mind the transactions of that day! How well I remember them all, and that when I came home at night and looked back to the morning, it seemed to have been a month agone. Go on then, like a kind comforter, and paint to me the day we went to St. Germains. How beautiful was every object! the Port de Neuilly, the hills along the Seine, the rainbows of the machine of Marly, the terras of St. Germains, the chateaux, the gardens, the [statues] of Marly, the pavillon of Lucienne. Recollect too Madrid, Bagatelle, the King's garden, the Dessert.[2] How grand the idea excited by the remains of such a column! The spiral staircase too was beautiful. Every moment was filled with something agreeable. The wheels of time moved on with a rapidity of which those of our carriage gave but a faint idea, and yet in the evening, when one took a retrospect of the day, what a mass of happiness had we travelled over! Retrace all those scenes to me, my good companion, and I will forgive the unkindness with which you were chiding me. The day we went to St. Germains was a little too warm, I think, was not it?

Head. Thou art the most incorrigible of all the beings that ever sinned! I reminded you of the follies of the first day, intending to deduce from thence some useful lessons for you, but instead of listening to these, you kindle at the recollection, you retrace the whole series with a fondness which shews you want nothing but the opportunity to act it over again. I often told you during it's course that you were imprudently engaging your affections under circumstances that must cost you a great deal of pain: that the persons indeed were of the greatest merit, possessing good sense, good humour, honest hearts, honest manners, and eminence in a lovely art: that the lady had moreover qualities and accomplishments, belonging to her sex, which might form a chapter apart for her: such as music, modesty, beauty, and that softness of disposition which is the ornament of her sex and charm of ours. But that all these considerations would increase the pang of separation: that their stay here was to be short: that you rack our whole system when you are parted from those you love, complaining that such a separation is worse than death, inasmuch as this ends our sufferings, whereas that only begins them: and that the separation would in this instance be the more severe as you would probably never see them again.

Heart. But they told me they would come back again the next year.

Head. But in the mean time see what you suffer: and their return too depends on so many circumstances that if you had a grain of prudence you would not count upon it. Upon the whole it is improbable and therefore you should abandon the idea of ever seeing them again.

Heart. May heaven abandon me if I do!

Head. Very well. Suppose then they come back. They are to stay here two months, and when these are expired, what is to follow? Perhaps you flatter yourself they may come to America?

Heart. God only knows what is to happen. I see nothing impossible in that supposition, and I see things wonderfully contrived sometimes to make us happy. Where could they find such objects as in America for the exercise of their enchanting art? especially the lady, who paints landscape so inimitably. She wants only subjects worthy of immortality to render her pencil immortal. The Falling spring, the Cascade of Niagara, the Passage of the Potowmac thro the Blue mountains, the Natural bridge. It is worth a voiage across the Atlantic to see these objects; much more to paint, and make them, and thereby ourselves, known to all ages. And our own dear Monticello, where has nature spread so rich a mantle under the eye? mountains, forests, rocks, rivers. With what majesty do we there ride above the storms! How sublime to look down into the workhouse of nature, to see her clouds, hail, snow, rain, thunder, all fabricated at our feet! And the glorious Sun, when rising as if out of a distant water, just gilding the tops of the mountains, and giving life to all nature!——I hope in god no circumstance may ever make either seek an asylum from grief! With what sincere sympathy I would open every cell of my composition to receive the effusion of their woes! I would pour my tears into their wounds: and if a drop of balm could be found at the top of the Cordilleras, or at the remotest sources of the Missouri, I would go thither myself to seek and to bring it. Deeply practised in the school of affliction, the human heart knows no joy which I have not lost, no sorrow of which I have not drank! Fortune can present no grief of unknown form to me! Who then can so softly bind up the wound of another as he who has felt the same wound himself? But Heaven forbid they should ever know a sorrow!—Let us turn over another leaf, for this has distracted me.

Head. Well. Let us put this possibility to trial then on another point. When you consider the character which is given of our country by the lying newspapers of London, and their credulous copyers in other countries; when you reflect that all Europe is made to believe we are a lawless banditti, in a state of absolute anarchy, cutting one another's throats, and plundering without distinction, how can you expect that any reasonable creature would venture among us?

Heart. But you and I know that all this is false: that there is not a country on earth where there is greater tranquillity, where the laws are milder, or better obeyed: where every one is more attentive to his own business, or meddles less with that of others: where strangers are better received, more hospitably treated, and with a more sacred respect.

Head. True, you and I know this, but your friends do not know it.

Heart. But they are sensible people who think for themselves. They will ask of impartial foreigners who have been among us, whether they saw or heard on the spot any instances of anarchy. They will judge too that a people occupied as we are in opening rivers, digging navigable canals, making roads, building public schools, establishing academies, erecting busts and statues to our great men, protecting religious freedom, abolishing sanguinary punishments, reforming and improving our laws in general, they will judge I say for themselves whether these are not the occupations of a people at their ease, whether this is not better evidence of our true state than a London newspaper, hired to lie, and from which no truth can ever be extracted but by reversing everything it says.

Head. I did not begin this lecture my friend with a view to learn from you what America is doing. Let us return then to our point. I wished to make you sensible how imprudent it is to place your affections, without reserve, on objects you must so soon lose, and whose loss when it comes must cost you such severe pangs. Remember the last night. You knew your friends were to leave Paris to-day. This was enough to throw you into agonies. All night you tossed us from one side of the bed to the other. No sleep, no rest. The poor crippled wrist too, never left one moment in the same position, now up, now down, now here, now there; was it to be wondered at if all it's pains returned? The Surgeon then was to be called, and to be rated as an ignoramus because he could not devine the cause of this extraordinary change.— In fine, my friend, you must mend your manners. This is not a world to live at random in as you do. To avoid these eternal distresses, to which you are for ever exposing us, you must learn to look forward before you take a step which may interest our peace. Everything in this world is matter of calculation. Advance then with caution, the balance in your hand. Put into one scale the pleasures which any object may offer; but put fairly into the other the pains which are to follow, and see which preponderates. The making an acquaintance is not a matter of indifference. When a new one is proposed to you, view it all round. Consider what advantages it presents, and to what inconveniencies it may expose you. Do not bite at the bait of pleasure till you know there is no hook beneath it. The art of life is the art of avoiding pain: and he is the best pilot who steers clearest of the rocks and shoals with which it is beset. Pleasure is always before us; but misfortune is at our side: while running after that, this arrests us. The most effectual means of being secure against pain is to retire within ourselves, and to suffice for our own happiness. Those, which depend on ourselves, are the only pleasures a wise man will count on: for nothing is ours which another may deprive us of. Hence the inestimable value of intellectual pleasures. Ever in our power, always leading us to something new, never cloying, we ride, serene and sublime, above the concerns of this mortal world, contemplating truth and nature, matter and motion, the laws which bind up their existence, and that eternal being who made and bound them up by these laws. Let this be our employ. Leave the bustle and tumult of society to those who have not talents to occupy themselves without them. Friendship is but another name for an alliance with the follies and the misfortunes of others. Our own share of miseries is sufficient: why enter then as volunteers into those of another? Is there so little gall poured into our own cup that we must needs help to drink that of our neighbor? A friend dies or leaves us: we feel as if a limb was cut off. He is sick: we must watch over him, and participate of his pains. His fortune is shipwrecked: ours must be laid under contribution. He loses a child, a parent or a partner: we must mourn the loss as if it was our own.

Heart. And what more sublime delight than to mingle tears with one whom the hand of heaven hath smitten! To watch over the bed of sickness, and to beguile it's tedious and it's painful moments! To share our bread with one to whom misfortune has left none! This world abounds indeed with misery: to lighten it's burthen we must divide it with one another. But let us now try the virtues of your mathematical balance, and as you have put into one scale the burthens of friendship, let me put it's comforts into the other. When languishing then under disease, how grateful is the solace of our friends! How are we penetrated with their assiduities and attentions! How much are we supported by their encouragements and kind offices! When Heaven has taken from us some object of our love, how sweet is it to have a bosom whereon to recline our heads, and into which we may pour the torrent of our tears! Grief, with such a comfort, is almost a luxury! In a life where we are perpetually exposed to want and accident, yours is a wonderful proposition, to insulate ourselves, to retire from all aid, and to wrap ourselves in the mantle of self-sufficiency! For assuredly nobody will care for him who cares for nobody. But friendship is precious not only in the shade but in the sunshine of life: and thanks to a benevolent arrangement of things, the greater part of life is sunshine. I will recur for proof to the days we have lately passed. On these indeed the sun shone brightly! How gay did the face of nature appear! Hills, vallies, chateaux, gardens, rivers, every object wore it's liveliest hue! Whence did they borrow it? From the presence of our charming companion. They were pleasing, because she seemed pleased. Alone, the scene would have been dull and insipid: the participation of it with her gave it relish. Let the gloomy Monk, sequestered from the world, seek unsocial pleasures in the bottom of his cell! Let the sublimated philosopher grasp visionary happiness while pursuing phantoms dressed in the garb of truth! Their supreme wisdom is supreme folly: and they mistake for happiness the mere absence of pain. Had they ever felt the solid pleasure of one generous spasm of the heart, they would exchange for it all the frigid speculations of their lives, which you have been vaunting in such elevated terms. Believe me then, my friend, that that is a miserable arithmetic which would estimate friendship at nothing, or at less than nothing. Respect for you has induced me to enter into this discussion, and to hear principles uttered which I detest and abjure. Respect for myself now obliges me to recall you into the proper limits of your office. When nature assigned us the same habitation, she gave us over it a divided empire. To you she allotted the field of science, to me that of morals. When the circle is to be squared, or the orbit of a comet to be traced; when the arch of greatest strength, or the solid of least resistance is to be investigated, take you the problem: it is yours: nature has given me no cognisance of it. In like manner in denying to you the feelings of sympathy, of benevolence, of gratitude, of justice, of love, of friendship, she has excluded you from their controul. To these she has adapted the mechanism of the heart. Morals were too essential to the happiness of man to be risked on the incertain combinations of the head. She laid their foundation therefore in sentiment, not in science. That she gave to all, as necessary to all: this to a few only, as sufficing with a few. I know indeed that you pretend authority to the sovereign controul of our conduct in all it's parts: and a respect for your grave saws and maxims, a desire to do what is right, has sometimes induced me to conform to your counsels. A few facts however which I can readily recall to your memory, will suffice to prove to you that nature has not organised you for our moral direction. When the poor wearied souldier, whom we overtook at Chickahominy with his pack on his back, begged us to let him get up behind our chariot, you began to calculate that the road was full of souldiers, and that if all should be taken up our horses would fail in their journey. We drove on therefore. But soon becoming sensible you had made me do wrong, that tho we cannot relieve all the distressed we should relieve as many as we can, I turned about to take up the souldier; but he had entered a bye path, and was no more to be found: and from that moment to this I could never find him out to ask his forgiveness. Again, when the poor woman came to ask a charity in Philadelphia, you whispered that she looked like a drunkard, and that half a dollar was enough to give her for the ale-house. Those who want the dispositions to give, easily find reasons why they ought not to give. When I sought her out afterwards, and did what I should have done at first, you know that she employed the money immediately towards placing her child at school. If our country, when pressed with wrongs at the point of the bayonet, had been governed by it's heads instead of it's hearts, where should we have been now? hanging on a gallows as high as Haman's.[3] You began to calculate and to compare wealth and numbers: we threw up a few pulsations of our warmest blood: we supplied enthusiasm against wealth and numbers: we put our existence to the hazard, when the hazard seemed against us, and we saved our country: justifying at the same time the ways of Providence, whose precept is to do always what is right, and leave the issue to him. In short, my friend, as far as my recollection serves me, I do not know that I ever did a good thing on your suggestion, or a dirty one without it. I do for ever then disclaim your interference in my province. Fill paper as you please with triangles and squares: try how many ways you can hang and combine them together. I shall never envy nor controul your sublime delights. But leave me to decide when and where friendships are to be contracted. You say I contract them at random, so you said the woman at Philadelphia was a drunkard. I receive no one into my esteem till I know they are worthy of it. Wealth, title, office, are no recommendations to my friendship. On the contrary great good qualities are requisite to make amends for their having wealth, title and office. You confess that in the present case I could not have made a worthier choice. You only object that I was so soon to lose them. We are not immortal ourselves, my friend; how can we expect our enjoiments to be so? We have no rose without it's thorn; no pleasure without alloy. It is the law of our existence; and we must acquiesce. It is the condition annexed to all our pleasures, not by us who receive, but by him who gives them. True, this condition is pressing cruelly on me at this moment. I feel more fit for death than life. But when I look back on the pleasures of which it is the consequence, I am conscious they were worth the price I am paying. Notwithstanding your endeavors too to damp my hopes, I comfort myself with expectations of their promised return. Hope is sweeter than despair, and they were too good to mean to deceive me. In the summer, said the gentleman; but in the spring, said the lady: and I should love her forever, were it only for that! Know then, my friend, that I have taken these good people into my bosom: that I have lodged them in the warmest cell I could find: that I love them, and will continue to love them thro life: that if fortune should dispose them on one side the globe, and me on the other, my affections shall pervade it's whole mass to reach them. Knowing then my determination, attempt not to disturb it. If you can at any time furnish matter for their amusement, it will be the office of a good neighbor to do it. I will in like manner seize any occasion which may offer to do the like good turn for you with Condorcet, Rittenhouse, Madison, La Cretelle, or any other of those worthy sons of science whom you so justly prize.'

———

I thought this a favorable proposition whereon to rest the issue of the dialogue. So I put an end to it by calling for my nightcap. Methinks I hear you wish to heaven I had called a little sooner, and so spared you the ennui of such a tedious sermon. I did not interrupt them sooner because I was in a mood for hearing sermons. You too were the subject; and on such a thesis I never think the theme long; not even if I am to write it, and that slowly and awkwardly, as now, with the left hand. But that you may not be discoraged from a correspondence which begins so formidably, I will promise you on my honour that my future letters shall be of a reasonable length. I will even agree to express but half my esteem for you, for fear of cloying you with too full a dose. But, on your part, no curtailing. If your letters are as long as the bible, they will appear short to me. Only let them be brim full of affection. I shall read them with the dispositions with which Arlequin in les deux billets[4] spelt the words 'je t'aime' and wished that the whole alphabet had entered into their composition.

We have had incessant rains since your departure. These make me fear for your health, as well as that you have had an uncomfortable journey. The same cause has prevented me from being able to give you any account of your friends here. This voiage to Fontainbleau will probably send the Count de Moutier and the Marquise de Brehan to America. Danquerville promised to visit me, but has not done it as yet. De latude comes sometimes to take family soupe with me, and entertains me with anecdotes of his five and thirty years imprisonment. How fertile is the mind of man which can make the Bastille and Dungeon of Vincennes yeild interesting anecdotes. You know this was for making four verses on Mme. de Pompadour. But I think you told me you did not know the verses. They were these. 'Sans esprit, sans sentiment, Sans etre belle, ni neuve, En France on peut avoir le premier amant: Pompadour en est l'epreuve.'[5] I have read the memoir of his three escapes. As to myself my health is good, except my wrist which mends slowly, and my mind which mends not at all, but broods constantly over your departure. The lateness of the season obliges me to decline my journey into the South of France. Present me in the most friendly terms to Mr. Cosway, and receive me into your own recollection with a partiality and a warmth, proportioned, not to my own poor merit, but to the sentiments of sincere affection and esteem with which I have the honour to be, my dear Madam, your most obedient humble servant,

Th: Jefferson

36. TO MARIA COSWAY

My Dear Madam   *Paris Octob. 13. 1786*
Just as I had sealed the inclosed I received a letter of a good length, dated Antwerp, with your name at the bottom. I prepared myself for a feast. I read two or three sentences: looked again at the signature to see if I had not mistaken it. It was visibly yours. Read a sentence or two more. Diable! Spelt your name distinctly. There was not a letter of it omitted. Began to read again. In fine after reading a little and examining the signature, alternately, half a dozen times, I found that your name was to four lines only instead of four pages. I thank you for the

four lines however because they prove you think of me. Little indeed, but better a little than none. To shew how much I think of you I send you the inclosed letter of three sheets of paper, being a history of the evening I parted with you. But how expect you should read a letter of three mortal sheets of paper? I will tell you. Divide it into six doses of half a sheet each, and every day, when the toilette begins, take a dose, that is to say, read half a sheet. By this means it will have the only merit it's length and dulness can aspire to, that of assisting your coëffeuse to procure you six good naps of sleep. I will even allow you twelve days to get through it, holding you rigorously to one condition only, that is, that at whatever hour you receive this, you do not break the seal of the inclosed till the next toilette. Of this injunction I require a sacred execution. I rest it on your friendship, and that in your first letter you tell me honestly whether you have honestly performed it.—I send you the song I promised. Bring me in return it's subject, *Jours heureux!* Were I a songster I should sing it all to these words 'Dans ces lieux qu'elle tarde à se rendre'!¹ Learn it I pray you, and sing it with feeling.—My right hand presents it's devoirs to you, and sees with great indignation the left supplanting it in a correspondence so much valued. You will know the first moment it can resume it's rights. The first exercise of them shall be addressed to you, as you had the first essay of it's rival. It will yet, however, be many a day. Present my esteem to Mr. Cosway, and believe me to be yours very affectionately,

Th: Jefferson

37. TO WILLIAM STEPHENS SMITH

Dear Sir   *Paris Oct. 22. 1786.*
How the right hand became disabled would be a long story for the left to tell. It was by one of those follies from which good cannot come, but ill may. As yet I have no use of that hand, and as the other is an awkward scribe, I must be sententious and not waste words. Yours of Sep. 18 and 22. and Oct. 1. and 4. have been duly received, as have been also the books from Lackington and Stockdale, and the second parcel from Dilly. The harness is at the Douane of Paris, not yet delivered to me.

Dilly's first parcel of books, and the first copying press are arrived at Rouen. You see how much reason I have to say 'well done thou good and faithful servant.' With Chastellux' voiages and Latré's map I took a great deal more trouble than was necessary, such as going myself to the book shop when a servant might as well have gone &c. merely from a desire to do something in return for you, and that I might feel as if I had done something. You desire to know whether the 2d. order for copying paper and ink was meant to be additional to the former? It was, but I had now rather not receive the paper because I have found a better kind here. The ink I shall be glad of. The twelve sheet map I shall send by the first good opportunity: and hope ere long to receive the plate of mine from Mr. Neele.[1] I will trouble you to have the inclosed note to Jones delivered. Will you undertake to prevail on Mr. Adams to set for his picture and on Mr. Brown to draw it for me? I wish to add it to those of other principal American characters which I have or shall have: and I had rather it should be original than a copy. We saw a picture of Sr. W. Raleigh at Birmingham, and I do not know whether it was of Mr. Adams or yourself I asked the favor to get it for me. I must pray your taylor to send me a buff Casimir waistcoat and breeches with those of cotton, and of my shoemaker to send me two pr. of thin waxed leather slippers. Things of this kind come better by private hands if any such should be coming within any reasonable time. The accident to my wrist has defeated my views of visiting the South of France this fall. Present me very affectionately to Mrs. Adams and Mrs. Smith. I hope the former is very well, and that the latter is, or has been very sick, otherwise I would observe to you that it is high time. Adieu. Yours affectionately,

Th: Jefferson

38. TO GEORGE WASHINGTON

Sir   *Paris Nov. 14. 1786.*
... The author of the Political part of the Encyclopedie methodique desired me to examine his article 'Etats unis.' I did so. I found it a tissue of errors. For in truth they know nothing about us here. Particu-

larly however the article 'Cincinnati' was a mere Philippic against that institution: in which it appeared that there was an utter ignorance of facts and motives. I gave him notes on it. He reformed it as he supposed and sent it again to me to revise. In this reformed state Colo. Humphreys saw it. I found it necessary to write that article for him. Before I gave it to him I shewed it to the Marq. de la fayette who made a correction or two. I then sent it to the author. He used the materials, mixing a great deal of his own with them. In a work which is sure of going down to the latest posterity I thought it material to set facts to rights as much as possible. The author was well disposed: but could not entirely get the better of his original bias. I send you the Article as ultimately published. If you find any material errors in it and will be so good as to inform me of them, I shall probably have opportunities of setting this author to rights. What has heretofore passed between us on this institution, makes it my duty to mention to you that I have never heard a person in Europe, learned or unlearned, express his thoughts on this institution, who did not consider it as dishonourable and destructive to our governments, and that every writing which has come out since my arrival here, in which it is mentioned, considers it, even as now reformed, as the germ whose developement is one day to destroy the fabric we have reared. I did not apprehend this while I had American ideas only. But I confess that what I have seen in Europe has brought me over to that opinion: and that tho' the day may be at some distance, beyond the reach of our lives perhaps, yet it will certainly come, when, a single fibre left of this institution, will produce an hereditary aristocracy which will change the form of our governments from the best to the worst in the world. To know the mass of evil which flows from this fatal source, a person must be in France, he must see the finest soil, the finest climate, the most compact state, the most benevolent character of people, and every earthly advantage combined, insufficient to prevent this scourge from rendering existence a curse to 24 out of 25 parts of the inhabitants of this country. With us the branches of this institution cover all the states. The Southern ones at this time are aristocratical in their disposition: and that that spirit should grow and extend itself is within the natural order of things. I do not flatter myself with the immortality of our governments: but I shall think little also of their longevity unless this germ of destruction be taken out. When the society themselves shall weigh the possibility of evil against the impossibility of any good to proceed from this institution, I cannot help hoping they will eradicate it. I know they wish the permanence of our governments as much as any individuals composing them.—An interruption here and the departure of the gentleman by whom I send this obliges me to conclude it, with assurances of the sincere respect and esteem with which I have the honor to be Dear Sir Your most obedt. & most humble servt.,

Th: Jefferson

39. TO MARIA COSWAY

Paris Nov. 19. 1786

I begin, my dear Madam, to write a little with the right hand, and you are by promise, as well as by inclination entitled to it's first homage. But I write with pain and must be short. This is good news for you; for were the hand able to follow the effusions of the heart, that would cease to write only when this shall cease to beat. My first letter warned you of this danger. I became sensible myself of my transgression and promised to offend no more. Your goodness seems to have induced you to forgive, and even to flatter me. That was a great error. When sins are dear to us we are but too prone to slide into them again. The act of repentance itself is often sweetened with the thought that it clears our account for a repetition of the same sin. The friendly letter I have received from you might have been taken as a release from my promise: but you are saved by a cruel cramp in my hand which admonishes me in every line to condense my thoughts and words.

I made your excuses to Madame de Corny. She was as uneasy, as you had been, under the appearance of a failure in point of civility and respect. I knew the key to the riddle, and asked her on what day she had returned to town. She said on the 6th. of October. I told her you had left it on the 5th. Thus each stands excused in the eye of the other, and she will have the pleasure of seeing you in London. Nothing more will be necessary, for good people naturally grow together. I wish she could put me into her pocket, when she goes, or you, when she comes back.—Mercy, cramp! that twitch was too much. I am done, I am done.—Adieu ma chere madame: je ne suis plus à moi. Faites mes compliments à Monsieur Cosway, assurez le de mon amitié, et daignez d'agreer vous meme l'hommage d'un sincere & tendre attachement. Encore adieu.

40. TO MADAME DE TOTT

Paris Nov. 28. 1786

I profit, Madam, of the permission which your goodness has induced you to give me, and commence the pleasing office of studying with you the rythm of Homer. For this purpose I have committed to writing the few rules of Greek prosody which must be indispensably known. Those in the first page should be fixed in the memory: what follows need only be read once. If you do not find them sufficiently intelligible, I will have the honor of explaining them to you when I shall do myself that of waiting on you in Paris.

If from the nature of my office I may assume to myself just so much merit as to claim your acceptance of the best edition extant of your divine countryman Homer, which is sent me from London, I shall be extremely gratified. Permit me then, Madam, to ask this favour in his name as well as my own. Besides the beauty of the type, it has the particular merit of being without a single typographical error. To so perfect an edition then of so charming a poet, allow me to add so charming a reader, and oblige by this further proof of your goodness him who has the honour to be with sentiments of the most perfect esteem and respect, Madam, your most obedient & most humble servant,

Th: Jefferson

41. TO MARIA COSWAY

Paris Nov. 29. 1786.

My letters which pass thro' the post office either of this country or of England being all opened, I send thro' that channel only such as are very indifferent in their nature. This is not the character, my dear madam of those I write to you. The breathings of a pure affection would be profaned by the eye of a Commis of the poste. I am obliged then to wait for private conveiances. I wrote to you so long ago as the 19th. of this month by a gentleman who was to go to London immediately. But he is not yet gone. Hence the delay of which you express yourself kindly sensible in yours of the 17th. instant. Could I write by the post, I should trouble you too often: for I am never happier than when I commit myself into dialogue with you, tho' it be but in imagination.   Heaven has submitted our being to some unkind laws. When those charming moments were present which I passed with you, they were clouded with the prospect that I was soon to lose you: and now, when I pass the same moments in review, I recollect nothing but the agreeable passages, and they fill me with regret. Thus, present joys are damped by a consciousness that they are passing from us; and past ones are only the subjects of sorrow and regret. I am determined when you come next not to admit the idea that we are ever to part again. But are you to come again? I dread the answer to this question, and that my poor heart has been duped by the fondness of it's wishes. What a triumph for the head! God bless you! May your days be many and filled with sunshine! May your heart glow with warm affections, and all of them be gratified! Write to me often. Write affectionately, and freely, as I do to you. Say many kind things, and say them without reserve. They will be food for my soul. Adieu my dear friend!

P.S. No private conveiance occurring I must trust this thro' the post-office, disguising my seal and superscription.

42. TO ELIZABETH HOUSE TRIST

Dear Madam   *Paris Dec. 15. 1786.*

I have duly received your friendly letter of July 24. and received it with great pleasure as I do all those you do me the favor to write me. If I have been long in acknowleging the receipt, the last cause to which it should be ascribed would be want of inclination. Unable to converse with my friends in person, I am happy when I do it in black and white. The true cause of the delay has been an unlucky dislocation of my wrist which has disabled me from writing three months. I only begin to write a little now, but with pain. I wish, while in Virginia, your curiosity had led you on to James river. At Richmond you would have seen your old friends Mr. and Mrs. Randolph, and a little further you would have become acquainted with my friend Mrs. Eppes whom you would have found among the most amiable women on earth. I doubt whether you would ever have got away from her. This trip would have made you better acquainted too with my lazy and hospitable countrymen, and you would have found that their character has some good traits mixed with some feeble ones. I often wish myself among them, as I am burning the candle of life without present pleasure, or future object. A dozen or twenty years ago this scene would have amused me. But I am past the age for changing habits. I take all the fault on myself, as it is impossible to be among a people who wish more to make one happy, a people of the very best character it is possible for one to have. We have no idea in America of the real French character. With some true samples, we have had many false ones.—I am very, very sorry I did not receive your letter three or four months sooner. It would have been absolutely convenient for me while in England to have seen Browse's relations, and I should have done it with infinite pleasure. At present I have no particular expectation of returning there. Yet it is among possible events, and the desire of being useful to him would render it a pleasing one. The former journey thither was made at a week's warning without the least previous expectation. Living from day to day, without a plan for four and twenty hours to come, I form no catalogue of impossible events. Laid up in port, for life, as I thought myself at one time, I am thrown out to sea, and an unknown one to me. By so slender a thread do all our plans of life hang!—My hand denies itself further, every letter admonishing me, by a pain, that it is time to finish, but my heart would go on in expressing to you all it's friendship. The happiest moments it knows are those in which it is pouring forth it's affections to a few esteemed characters. I will pray you to write to me often. I wish to know that you enjoy health and that you are happy. Present me in the most friendly terms to your mother and brother, and be assured of the sincerity of the esteem with which I am, Dear Madam, your affectionate friend & humble servant,

Th: Jefferson

43. TO MARIA COSWAY

Paris Dec. 24. 1786.

Yes, my dear Madam, I have received your three letters, and I am sure you must have thought hardly of me, when at the date of the last, you had not yet received one from me. But I had written two. The second, by the post, I hope you got about the beginning of this month: the first has been detained by the gentleman who was to have carried it. I suppose you will receive it with this.

I wish they had formed us like the birds of the air, able to fly where we please. I would have exchanged for this many of the boasted pre-eminencies of man. I was so unlucky when very young, as to read the history of Fortunatus. He had a cap of such virtues that when he put it on his head, and wished himself anywhere, he was there. I have been all my life sighing for this cap. Yet if I had it, I question if I should use it but once. I should wish myself with you, and not wish myself away again. En attendant the cap, I am always thinking of you. If I cannot be with you in reality, I will in imagination. But you say not a word of coming to Paris. Yet you were to come in the spring, and here is winter. It is time therefore you should be making your arrangements, packing your baggage &c. unless you really mean to disappoint us. If you do, I am determined not to suppose I am never to see you again. I will believe you intend to go to America, to draw the Natural bridge, the Peaks of Otter &c., that I shall meet you there, and visit with you all those grand scenes. I had rather be deceived, than live without hope. It is so sweet! It makes us ride so smoothly over the roughnesses of life. When clambering a mountain, we always hope the hill we are on is the last. But it is the next, and the next, and still the next.   Think of me much, and warmly. Place me in your breast with those who you love most: and comfort me with your letters. Addio la mia cara ed amabile amica!

  After finishing my letter, the gentleman who brought yours sent me a roll he had overlooked, which contained songs of your composition. I am sure they are charming, and I thank you for them. The first words which met my eye on opening them, are I fear, ominous. 'Qua l'attendo, e mai non viene.'[1]

44. TO ST. JOHN DE CRÈVECOEUR[1]

Dear Sir   *Paris Jan. 15. 1787.*
I see by the Journal of this morning that they are robbing us of another of our inventions to give it to the English. The writer indeed only admits them to have revived what he thinks was known to the Greeks, that is the making the circumference of a wheel of one single peice. The farmers in New Jersey were the first who practised it, and they practised it commonly. Dr. Franklin, in one of his trips to London, mentioned this practice to the man, now in London, who has the patent for making those wheels (I forget his name.[2]) The idea struck him. The Doctor promised to go to his shop and assist him in trying to make the wheel of one peice. The Jersey farmers did it by cutting a young sapling, and bending it, while green and juicy, into a circle; and leaving it so till it became perfectly seasoned. But in London there are no saplings. The difficulty was then to give to old wood the pliancy of young. The Doctor and the workman laboured together some weeks, and succeeded, and the man obtained a patent for it which has made his fortune. I was in his shop in London, he told me the whole story himself, and acknowleged, not only the origin of the idea, but how much the assistance of Dr. Franklin had contributed to perform the

operation on dry wood. He spoke of him with love and gratitude. I think I have had a similar account from Dr. Franklin, but cannot be certain quite. I know that being in Philadelphia when the first set of patent wheels arrived from London, and were spoken of by the gentleman (an Englishman) who brought them as a wonderful discovery. The idea of it's being a new discovery was laughed at by the Philadelphians, who in their Sunday parties across the Delaware had seen every farmer's cart mounted on such wheels. The writer in the paper supposes the English workman got his idea from Homer. But it is more likely that the Jersey farmer got the idea from thence, because ours are the only farmers who can read Homer: because too the Jersey practice is precisely that stated by Homer; the English practice very different. Homer's words are (comparing a young hero killed by Ajax to a poplar felled by a workman)———

ὁ δ᾽ εν κονιησι, χαμαι πεϛεν, αιγειρος ὡς,
Ἡ ρα τ᾽εν ειαμενη ελεος μεγαλοιο πεφυκε
Λειη αταρ τε ὁι οζοι επ᾽ ακροτατη πεφυαϛι
Τὴν μεν θάρματοπηγος ανηρ αιθωνι ϛιδηρῳ
Εξεταμ᾽ οφρα ιτυν καμψη περικαλλέι διφρῳ,
Ἡ μεν τ᾽αζομενη κειται ποταμοιο παρ οχθας   4. Il. 482.

literally thus 'he fell on the ground, like a poplar, which has grown, smooth, in the wet part of a great meadow; with it's branches shooting from it's summit. But the Chariot-maker with his sharp axe, has felled it, that he may bend a wheel for a beautiful chariot. It lies drying on the banks of the river.' Observe the circumstances which coincide with the Jersey practice. 1. It is a tree growing in a moist place, full of juices, and easily bent. 2. It is cut while green. 3. It is bent into the circumference of a wheel. 4. It is left to dry in that form. You, who write French well and readily, should write a line for the Journal to reclaim the honour of our farmers. Adieu. Your's affectionately,

Th: Jefferson

45. TO ABIGAIL ADAMS SMITH

Paris Jan. 15. 1787.

Mr. Jefferson has the honour to present his compliments to Mrs. Smith and to send her the two pair of Corsets she desired. He wishes they may be suitable, as Mrs. Smith omitted to send her measure. Times are altered since Mademoiselle de Sanson had the honour of knowing her. Should they be too small however, she will be so good as to lay them by a while. There are ebbs as well as flows in this world. When the mountain refused to come to Mahomet, he went to the mountain. Mr. Jefferson wishes Mrs. Smith a happy new year, and abundance of happier ones still to follow it. He begs leave to assure her of his esteem and respect, and that he shall always be happy to be rendered useful to her by being charged with her commands.

46. TO EDWARD CARRINGTON[1]

Dear Sir   *Paris Jan. 16. 1787.*

Incertain whether you might be at New York at the moment of Colo. Franks's arrival, I have inclosed my private letters for Virginia under cover to our delegation in general, which otherwise I would have taken the liberty to inclose particularly to you, as best acquainted with the situation of the persons to whom they are addressed. Should this find you at New York, I will still ask your attention to them. The two large packages addressed to Colo. N. Lewis contain seeds, not valuable enough to pay postage, but which I would wish to be sent by the stage, or any similar quick conveyance. The letters to Colo. Lewis and Mr. Eppes (who take care of my affairs) are particularly interesting to me. The package for Colo. Richd. Cary our judge of Admiralty near Hampton, contains seeds and roots, not to be sent by post. Whether they had better go by the stage, or by water, you will be the best judge. I beg your pardon for giving you this trouble. But my situation and your goodness will I hope excuse it.

In my letter to Mr. Jay I have mentioned the meeting of the Notables appointed for the 29th. inst. It is now put off to the 7th. or 8th. of next month. This event, which will hardly excite any attention in America, is deemed here the most important one which has taken place in their civil line during the present century. Some promise their country great things from it, some nothing. Our friend de la fayette was placed on the list originally. Afterwards his name disappeared: but finally was reinstated. This shews that his character here is not considered as an indifferent one; and that it excites agitation. His education in our school has drawn on him a very jealous eye from a court whose principles are the most absolute despotism. But I hope he has nearly passed his crisis. The king, who is a good man, is favorably disposed towards him: and he is supported by powerful family connections, and by the public good will. He is the youngest man of the Notables, except one whose office placed him on the list.

The Count de Vergennes has within these ten days had a very severe attack of what is deemed an unfixed gout. He has been well enough however to do business to-day. But anxieties for him are not yet quieted. He is a great and good minister, and an accident to him might endanger the peace of Europe.

The tumults in America,[2] I expected would have produced in Europe an unfavorable opinion of our political state. But it has not. On the contrary, the small effect of those tumults seems to have given more confidence in the firmness of our governments. The interposition of the people themselves on the side of government has had a great effect on the opinion here. I am persuaded myself that the good sense of the people will always be found to be the best army. They may be led astray for a moment, but will soon correct themselves. The people are the only censors of their governors: and even their errors will tend to keep these to the true principles of their institution. To punish these errors too severely would be to suppress the only safeguard of the public liberty. The way to prevent these irregular interpositions of the people is to give them full information of their affairs thro' the channel of the public papers, and to contrive that those papers should penetrate the whole mass of the people. The basis of our governments being the opinion of the people, the very first object should be to keep that right; and were it left to me to decide whether we should have a government without newspapers, or newspapers without a government, I should not hesitate a moment to prefer the latter. But I should mean that every man should receive those papers and be capable of reading them. I am convinced that those societies (as the Indians) which live without government enjoy in their general mass an infinitely greater degree of happiness than those who live under European governments. Among the former, public opinion is in the place of law, and restrains morals as powerfully as laws ever did any where. Among the latter, under pretence of governing they have divided their nations into two classes, wolves and sheep. I do not exaggerate. This is a true picture of Europe. Cherish therefore the spirit of our people, and keep alive their attention. Do not be too severe upon their errors, but reclaim them by enlightening them. If once they become inattentive to the public affairs, you and I, and Congress, and Assemblies, judges and governors shall all become wolves. It seems to be the law of our general nature, in spite of individual exceptions; and experience declares that man is the only animal which devours his own kind, for I can apply no milder term to the governments of Europe, and to the general prey of the rich on the poor.— The want of news has led me into disquisition instead of narration, forgetting you have every day enough of that. I shall be happy to hear from you some times, only observing that whatever passes thro' the post is read, and that when you write what should be read by myself only, you must be so good as to confide your letter to some passenger or officer of the packet. I will ask your permission to write to you sometimes, and to assure you of the esteem & respect with which I have the honour to be Dear Sir your most obedient & most humble servt.,

Th: Jefferson

47. TO JAMES MADISON

Dear Sir   *Paris Jan. 30. 1787.*
My last to you was of the 16th of Dec. since which I have received yours of Nov. 25. and Dec. 4. which afforded me, as your letters always do, a treat on matters public, individual and oeconomical. I am impa-

tient to learn your sentiments on the late troubles in the Eastern states. So far as I have yet seen, they do not appear to threaten serious consequences. Those states have suffered by the stoppage of the channels of their commerce, which have not yet found other issues. This must render money scarce, and make the people uneasy. This uneasiness has produced acts absolutely unjustifiable: but I hope they will provoke no severities from their governments. A consciousness of those in power that their administration of the public affairs has been honest, may perhaps produce too great a degree of indignation: and those characters wherein fear predominates over hope may apprehend too much from these instances of irregularity. They may conclude too hastily that nature has formed man insusceptible of any other government but that of force, a conclusion not founded in truth, nor experience. Societies exist under three forms sufficiently distinguishable. 1. Without government, as among our Indians. 2. Under governments wherein the will of every one has a just influence, as is the case in England in a slight degree, and in our states in a great one. 3. Under governments of force: as is the case in all other monarchies and in most of the other republics. To have an idea of the curse of existence under these last, they must be seen. It is a government of wolves over sheep. It is a problem, not clear in my mind, that the 1st. condition is not the best. But I believe it to be inconsistent with any great degree of population. The second state has a great deal of good in it. The mass of mankind under that enjoys a precious degree of liberty and happiness. It has it's evils too: the principal of which is the turbulence to which it is subject. But weigh this against the oppressions of monarchy, and it becomes nothing. Malo periculosam, libertatem quam quietam servitutem.[1] Even this evil is productive of good. It prevents the degeneracy of government, and nourishes a general attention to the public affairs. I hold it that a little rebellion now and then is a good thing, and as necessary in the political world as storms in the physical. Unsuccesful rebellions indeed generally establish the incroachments on the rights of the people which have produced them. An observation of this truth should render honest republican governors so mild in their punishment of rebellions, as not to discourage them too much. It is a medecine necessary for the sound health of government. If these transactions give me no uneasiness, I feel very differently at another peice of intelligence, to wit, the possibility that the navigation of the Missisipi may be abandoned to Spain. I never had any interest Westward of the Alleghaney; and I never will have any. But I have had great opportunities of knowing the character of the people who inhabit that country. And I will venture to say that the act which abandons the navigation of the Missisipi is an act of separation between the Eastern and Western country. It is a relinquishment of five parts out of eight of the territory of the United States, an abandonment of the fairest subject for the paiment of our public debts, and the chaining those debts on our own necks in perpetuum. I have the utmost confidence in the honest intentions of those who concur in this measure; but I lament their want of acquaintance with the character and physical advantages of the people who, right or wrong, will suppose their interests sacrificed on this occasion to the contrary interests of that part of the confederacy in possession of present power. If they declare themselves a separate people, we are incapable of a single effort to retain them. Our citizens can never be induced, either as militia or as souldiers, to go there to cut the throats of their own brothers and sons, or rather to be themselves the subjects instead of the perpetrators of the parricide. Nor would that country quit the cost of being retained against the will of it's inhabitants, could it be done. But it cannot be done. They are able already to rescue the navigation of the Missisipi out of the hands of Spain, and to add New Orleans to their own territory. They will be joined by the inhabitants of Louisiana. This will bring on a war between them and Spain; and that will produce the question with us whether it will not be worth our while to become parties with them in the war, in order to reunite them with us, and thus correct our error? And were I to permit my forebodings to go one step further, I should predict that the inhabitants of the U.S. would force their rulers to take the affirmative of that question. I wish I may be mistaken in all these opinions.

We have for some time expected that the Chevalier de la Luzerne would obtain a promotion in the diplomatic line, by being appointed to some of the courts where this country keeps an Ambassador. But none of the vacancies taking place which had been counted on, I think the present disposition is to require his return to his station in America. He told me himself lately, that he should return in the spring. I have never pressed this matter on the court, tho' I knew it to be desireable and desired on our part: because if the compulsion on him to return had been the work of Congress, he would have returned in such ill temper with them as to disappoint them in the good they expected from it. He would for ever have laid at their door his failure of promotion. I did not press it for another reason, which is that I have great reason to beleive that the character of the Count de Moutier, who would go were the Chevalier to be otherwise provided for, would give the most perfect satisfaction in America.—As you are now returned into Congress it will become of importance that you should form a just estimate of certain public characters; on which therefore I will give you such notes as my knowlege of them has furnished me with.[2] You will compare them with the materials you are otherwise possessed of, and decide on a view of the whole. You know the opinion I *formerly* entertained of *my friend Mr. Adams.* Yourself and the governor were the first who *shook* that opinion. I afterwards saw proofs which *convicted* him of a degree of *vanity,* and of a *blindness* to it, of which no germ *had appeared* in Congress. A *7-months'* intimacy with him *here* and *as* many *weeks* in *London* have given me opportunities of studying him closely. *He is vain, irritable and a bad calculator of* the force and probable effect of the motives which govern men. This is *all* the *ill* which can possibly be *said of him.* He is as disinterested as the being which made him: he is profound in his views: and accurate in his judgment *except where knowledge of the world* is necessary to form a judgment. He is so amiable, that I pronounce you will love him if ever you become acquainted with him. He would be, as he was, a great man in *Congress. Mr. Carmichael*[3] is I think very little *known* in *America.* I never *saw him* and while I was *in Congress I* formed rather a *disadvantageous idea* of him. His letters, received then, shewed him *vain* and more attentive to *ceremony* and *etiquette* than we suppose men *of sense* should be. I have now a constant correspondence with him, and find *him* a little *hypocondriac* and *discontented.* He possesses very *good understanding* tho' not of the *first order. I have* had great opportunities of *searching into* his *character* and have availed myself *of it.* Many persons of different nations *coming* from *Madrid* to *Paris* all speak of *him as* in *high esteem* and *I think* it certain that he has more of the *Count de Florid. B's friendship* than any *diplomatic* character at *that court.* As long as this *minister* is in *office Carmichael* can do *more than* any other *person who* could be *sent there.* You will see *Franks*⁴ *and* doubtless he will be *asking some appointment.* I wish there may be any one for *which* he is *fit.* He is *light, indiscreet, [act]ive, honest, affectionate.* Tho' *Bingham*⁵ is not in *diplomatic office* yet as he wishes to be so I will mention such circumstances of *him as you might* otherwise be *deceived in. He* will make *you believe he* was on the most intimate footing with the first *characters in Europe* and versed in the *secrets* of every *cabinet.* Not a word of this *is true. He* had a rage for being *presented* to *great men* and had no *modesty* in the methods by which he could effect it. If *he obtained access* afterwards, it was with such as who were susceptible of impression from the *beauty of his wife.* I must *except* the *Marquis de Bouilli* who had been an *old acquaintance.* The *Marquis de Lafayette* is a most valuable *auxiliary to me.* His *zeal* is unbounded, and his *we[ight]* with those in *power great.* His *education* having been merely *military, commerce* was an unknown feild to him. But his good sense enabling him to *comprehend* perfectly whatever is *explained to him, his agency* has been very *efficacious. He* has a great deal of *sound genius,* is well *remarked* by the *king* and rising in *popularity. He* has nothing against *him but* the *suspicion of republican principles.* I think he will one day *be of* the *ministry.* His *foible* is a *canine appetite for popularity and fame.* But he will get *above* this. *The Count de Vergennes*⁶ is *ill.* The possibility of his *recovery* renders it dangerous for *us to express a doubt but* he is *in danger.* He is *a great Minister* in *European affairs* but has very *imperfect ideas* of *ours* [and] *no confidence in* them. His *devotion to* the principles of *pure despotism* render him *unaffectionate to our governments* but *his fear* of *England makes him value us* as a *make weight.* He is *cool, reserved in political conversation, free* and *familiar* on other *subjects,* and a very *attentive, aggreeable person* to *do business with.* It is impossible to have a clearer, better *organised head* but *age* has *chilled his heart.* Nothing should be spared on our part to attach this country to us. It is the only one on which we can rely for support under every event. It's inhabitants love us more I think than they do any other nation on earth. This is very much the effect of the good dispositions with which the French officers returned.

In a former letter I mentioned to you the dislocation of my wrist. I can make not the least use of it, except for the single article of writing, tho' it is going on five months since the accident happened. I have great anxieties lest I should never recover any considerable use of it. I shall, by the advice of my Surgeons, set out in a fortnight for the waters of Aix in Provence. I chose these out of several they proposed to me, because if they fail to be effectual, my journey will not be useless altogether. It will give me an opportunity of examining the canal of Languedoc and of acquiring knowlege of that species of navigation which may be useful hereafter: but more immediately it will enable me to take the tour of the ports concerned in commerce with us, to examine on the spot the defects of the late regulations respecting our commerce, to learn the further improvements which may be made on it, and, on my return, to get this business finished. I shall be absent between two and three months, unless any thing happens to recall me here sooner, which may always be effected in ten days, in whatever part of my route I may be. In speaking of *characters* I omitted *those of Reyneval and Henin,* the *two eyes* of *M. de Vergennes.* The *former* is the most important *character because possessing* the most of the *confidence* of the *Count, he* is rather *cunning* than *wise. His* views of things being neither *great* nor *liberal he governs* himself by *principles* which he has *learnt* by *rote* and is *fit only* for the *details* of *execution. His heart* is susceptible of *little passions* but not of *good ones. He* is *brother* in *law* to *M. Gerard* from whom he received *disadvantageous impressions* of *us which* cannot be *effaced. He* has much *duplicity. Henin* is a *philosopher sincere, friendly, liberal, learned, beloved* by every *body,* the *other* by *nobody. I think* it a great *misfortune* that the *United States* are in the *department* of the *former.* As particulars of this kind may be useful to you in your present situation, I may hereafter continue the chapter. I know it safely lodged in your discretion.

Feb. 5.

Since writing thus far *Franks* is *returned* from *England.* I *learn* that *Mr. Adams* desires to be *recalled* and that *Smith* should be *appointed charge des affairs* there. It is not for me to decide whether any *diplomatic character* should be *kept* at a *court* which *keeps* none with *us.* You can judge of *Smith's abilities* by *his letters.* They are not of the *first order* but they are *good.* For his *honesty* he is like our friend *Monroe.* Turn his *soul* wrong side outwards and there is not a speck on it. *He* has one *foible,* an *excessive inflammability* of *temper,* but he feels it when it comes on, and has *resolution enough* to *suppress* it, and to *remain silent* till it *passes* over.

I send you by Colo. Franks your pocket telescope, walking stick, and chemical box. The two former could not be combined together. The latter could not be had in the form you referred to. Having a great desire to have a portable copying machine, and being satisfied from some experiments that the principle of the large machine might be applied in a small one, I planned one when in England and had it made. It answers perfectly. I have since set a workman to making them here, and they are in such demand that he has his hands full. Being assured that you will be pleased to have one, when you shall have tried it's convenience, I send you one by Colo. Franks. The machine costs 96 livres, the appendages 24. livres, and I send you paper and ink for 12 livres, in all 132 livres. There is a printed paper of directions: but you must expect to make many essays before you succeed perfectly. A soft brush, like a shaving brush, is more convenient than the sponge. You can get as much ink and paper as you please from London. The paper costs a guinea a ream.

48. TO ANNE WILLING BINGHAM

Paris Feb. 7. 1787.

I know, Madam, that the twelvemonth is not yet expired; but it will be, nearly, before this will have the honour of being put into your hands. You are then engaged to tell me truly and honestly whether you do not find the tranquil pleasures of America preferable to the empty bustle of Paris. For to what does that bustle tend? At eleven o'clock it is day chez Madame. The curtains are drawn. Propped on bolsters and pillows, and her head scratched into a little order, the bulletins of the sick are read, and the billets of the well. She writes to some of her acquaintance and receives the visits of others. If the morning is not very thronged, she is able to get out and hobble round the cage of the Palais royal: but she must hobble quickly, for the Coeffeur's turn is come; and a tremendous turn it is! Happy, if he does not make her arrive when dinner is half over! The torpitude of digestion a little passed, she flutters half an hour thro' the streets by way of paying visits, and then to the Spectacles.[1] These finished, another half hour is devoted to dodging in and out of the doors of her very sincere friends, and away to supper. After supper cards; and after cards bed, to rise at noon the next day, and to tread, like a mill-horse, the same trodden circle over again. Thus the days of life are consumed, one by one, without an object beyond the present moment: ever flying from the ennui of that, yet carrying it with us; eternally in pursuit of happiness which keeps eternally before us. If death or a bankruptcy happen to trip us out of the circle, it is matter for the buz of the evening, and is completely forgotten by the next morning.

In America, on the other hand, the society of your husband, the fond cares for the children, the arrangements of the house, the improvements of the grounds fill every moment with a healthy and an useful activity. Every exertion is encouraging, because to present amusement it joins the promise of some future good. The intervals of leisure are filled by the society of real friends, whose affections are not thinned to cob-web by being spread over a thousand objects.—This is the picture in the light it is presented to my mind; now let me have it in yours. If we do not concur this year, we shall the next: or if not then, in a year or two more. You see I am determined not to suppose myself mistaken. To let you see that Paris is not changed in it's pursuits since it was honoured with your presence, I send you it's monthly history.[2] But this relating only to the embellishments of their persons I must add that those of the city go on well also. A new bridge, for example, is begun at the Place Louis Quinze; the old ones are clearing of the rubbish which encumbered them in the form of houses; new hospitals erecting; magnificent walls of inclosure and Custom houses at their entrance &c. &c. &c.—I know of no interesting change among those whom you honoured with your acquaintance, unless Monsr. de Saint James was of that number. His bankruptcy and taking asylum in the Bastile have furnished matter of astonishment. His garden at the Pont de Neuilly, where, on seventeen acres of ground he had laid out fifty thousand Louis, will probably sell for somewhat less money.—The workmen of Paris are making rapid strides towards English perfection. Would you believe that in the course of the last two years they have learnt even to surpass their London rivals in some articles? Commission me to have you a Phaeton made, and if it is not as much handsomer than a London one, as that is than a Fiacre, send it back to me. Shall I fill the box with caps, bonnets &c? not of my own chusing, but—I was going to say of Mademoiselle Bertin's, forgetting for the moment that she too is bankrupt. They shall be chosen then by whom you please; or, if you are altogether non plus-ed by her eclipse, we will call an assembleé des Notables to help you out of the difficulty, as is now the fashion. In short, honour me with your commands of any kind, and they shall be faithfully executed. The packets, now established from Havre to New York, furnish good opportunities of sending whatever you wish.

I shall end where I began, like a Paris day, reminding you of your engagement to write me a letter of respectable length, an engagement the more precious to me as it has furnished me the occasion, after presenting my respects to Mr. Bingham, of assuring you of the sincerity of those sentiments of esteem & respect with which I have the honour to be, dear Madam, your most obedient & most humble servt.,

Th: Jefferson

49. TO ABIGAIL ADAMS

Dear Madam   *Paris Feb. 22. 1787.*
I am to acknolege the honor of your letter of Jan. 29. and of the papers you were so good as to send me. They were the latest I had seen or have yet seen. They left off too in a critical moment; just at the point where the Malcontents make their submission on condition of pardon, and before the answer of government was known. I hope they pardoned them. The spirit of resistance to government is so valuable on certain occasions, that I wish it to be always kept alive. It will often be exercised when wrong, but better so than not to be exercised at all. I like a little rebellion now and then. It is like a storm in the Atmosphere. It is wonderful that no letter or paper tells us who is president

of Congress, tho' there are letters in Paris to the beginning of January. I suppose I shall hear when I come back from my journey, which will be eight months after he will have been chosen. And yet they complain of us for not giving them intelligence. Our Notables assembled to-day, and I hope before the departure of Mr. Cairnes I shall have heard something of their proceedings worth communicating to Mr. Adams. The most remarkeable effect of this convention as yet is the number of puns and bon mots it has generated. I think were they all collected it would make a more voluminous work than the Encyclopedie. This occasion, more than any thing I have seen, convinces me that this nation is incapable of any serious effort but under the word of command. The people at large view every object only as it may furnish puns and bon mots; and I pronounce that a good punster would disarm the whole nation were they ever so seriously disposed to revolt. Indeed, Madam, they are gone. When a measure so capable of doing good as the calling the Notables is treated with so much ridicule, we may conclude the nation desperate, and in charity pray that heaven may send them good kings.—The bridge at the place Louis XV. is begun. The hotel dieu is to be abandoned and new ones to be built. The old houses on the old bridges are in a course of demolition. This is all I know of Paris. We are about to lose the Count d'Aranda, who has desired and obtained his recall. Fernand Nunnez, before destined for London is to come here. The Abbés Arnoux and Chalut are well. The Dutchess Danville somewhat recovered from the loss of her daughter. Mrs. Barrett very homesick, and fancying herself otherwise sick. They will probably remove to Honfleur. This is all our news. I have only to add then that Mr. Cairnes has taken charge of 15. aunes of black lace for you at 9 livres the aune, purchased by Petit[1] and therefore I hope better purchased than some things have been for you; and that I am with sincere esteem Dear Madam your affectionate humble servt.,

Th: Jefferson

50. TO MADAME DE TOTT

Paris Feb. 28. 1787.

Have you been, Madam, to see the superb picture now exhibiting in the rue Ste. Nicaise, No. 9. chez Mde. Drouay? It is that of Marius[1] in the moment when the souldier [ente]rs to assassinate him. It is made by her son, a student at Rome under the care of David, and is much in David's manner. All Paris is running to see it, and really it appears to me to have extraordinary merit. It fixed me like a statue a quarter of an hour, or half an hour, I do [not] know which, for I lost all ideas of time, "even the consciousness of my existence." If you have not been, let me engage you to go, for I think it will give you pleasure. Write me your judgment on it: it will serve to rectify my own, which as I have told you is a bad one, and needs a guide. It will multiply too the occasions of my hearing from you; occasions which I claim by promise, and which will strew some roses in the lengthy road I am to travel. That your road, through life, may be covered with roses, is the sincere prayer of him who has the honour to mingle his Adieus with sentiments of the most affectionate esteem and respect,

Th: Jefferson

51. TO WILLIAM SHORT

Dear Sir   *Lyons Mar. 15. 1787.*

So far all is well. No complaints; except against the weather-maker, who has pelted me with rain, hail, and snow, almost from the moment of my departure to my arrival here. Now and then a few gleamings of sunshine to chear me by the way. Such is this life: and such too will be the next, if there be another, and we may judge of the future by the past. My road led me about 60 miles through Champagne, mostly a corn country, lying in large hills of the colour and size of those in the neighborhood of Elkhill.[1] The plains of the Yonne are of the same colour, that is to say, a brownish red; a singular circumstance to me, as our plains on the water side are always black or grey. The people here were ill clothed, and looked ill, and I observed the women performing the heavy labours of husbandry; an unequivocal proof of extreme poverty. In Burgundy and Beaujolois they do only light work in the feilds, being principally occupied within doors. In these counties they were well clothed and appeared to be well fed. Here the hills become mountains, larger than those of Champagne, more abrupt, more red and stony. I passed thro about 180 miles of Burgundy; it resembles extremely our red mountainous country, but is rather more stony, all in corn and vine. I mounted a bidet,[2] put a peasant on another and rambled thro' their most celebrated vineyards, going into the houses of the labourers, cellars of the Vignerons, and mixing and conversing with them as much as I could. The same in Beaujolois, where nature has spread it's richest gifts in profusion. On the right we had fine mountain sides lying in easy slopes, in corn and vine, and on the left the rich extensive plains of the Saone in corn and pasture. This is the richest country I ever beheld. I passed some time at the Chateau de Laye Epinaye, a seignory of about 15,000 acres, in vine, corn, pasture and wood, a rich and beautiful scene. I was entertained by Madame de Laye with a hospitality, a goodness and an ease which was charming, and left her with regret. I beg of you to present to the good Abbés Chalut and Arnoud my thanks for their introduction to this family: indeed I should be obliged to you if you could see Monsr. de Laye and express to him how sensible I am of my obligation to him for the letter to Madame de Laye, and of her attention and civilities. I have been much indebted here too for the letters from the Abbés, tho' the shortness of my stay does not give me time to avail myself of all their effect. A constant tempest confined me to the house the first day: the second, I determined to see every thing within my plan before delivering my letters, that I might do as much, in as little time, as possible. The third and fourth have been filled up with all the attentions they would admit, and I am now on the wing, as soon as this letter is closed. I enter into these details because they are necessary to justify me to the Abbés for the little time I had left to profit of the good dispositions of their friends. Six or seven hundred leagues still before me, and circumscribed in time, I am obliged to hasten my movements. I have not visited at all the manufactures of this place: because a knowlege of them would be useless, and would extrude from the memory other things more worth retaining. Architecture, painting, sculpture, antiquities, agriculture, the condition of the labouring poor fill all my moments. Hitherto I have derived as much satisfaction and even delight from my journey as I could propose to myself. The plan of having servants who know nothing of me, places me perfectly at my ease. I intended to have taken a new one at every principal city, to have carried him on to serve me on the road to the next and there changed him. But the one I brought forward from Dijon is so good a one that I expect to keep him through the greater part of the journey, taking additionally a valet de place wherever I stay a day or two. You shall hear from me from Aix where I hope to meet letters from you giving me news both great and small. Present me affectionately to my friends and more particularly to Madame de Tessé and Madame de Tott: and accept assurances of my perfect esteem & friendship to yourself. Adieu.

52. TO MADAME DE TESSÉ[1]

Nismes. Mar. 20. 1787.

Here I am, Madam, gazing whole hours at the Maison quarrée, like a lover at his mistress. The stocking-weavers and silk spinners around it consider me as an hypochondriac Englishman, about to write with a pistol the last chapter of his history. This is the second time I have been in love since I left Paris. The first was with a Diana at the Chateau de Laye Epinaye in the Beaujolois, a delicious morsel of sculpture, by Michael Angelo Slodtz. This, you will say, was in rule, to fall in love with a fine woman: but, with a house! It is out of all precedent! No, madam, it is not without a precedent in my own history. While at Paris, I was violently smitten with the hotel de Salm, and used to go to the Thuileries almost daily to look at it. The loueuse des chaises, inattentive to my passion, never had the complaisance to place a chair there; so that, sitting on the parapet, and twisting my neck round to see the object of my admiration, I generally left it with a torticollis. From Lyons to Nismes I have been nourished with the remains of Roman grandeur. They have always brought you to my mind, because I know your affection for whatever is Roman and noble. At

Vienne I thought of you. But I am glad you were not there; for you would have seen me more angry than I hope you will ever see me. The Pretorian palace, as it is called, comparable for it's fine proportions to the Maison quarrée, totally defaced by the Barbarians who have converted it to it's present purpose; it's beautiful, fluted, Corinthian columns cut out in part to make space for Gothic windows, and hewed down in the residue to the plane of the building. At Orange too I thought of you. I was sure you had seen with rapture the sublime triumphal arch at the entrance into the city. I went then to the Arenas. Would you believe Madam, that in [this 18th. centur]y, in France, und[er the reign of Louis XVI, they] are [at this mo]ment pulling down the circular wall of this superb remain [to pave a ro]ad? And that too from a hill which is itself an entire mass of stone just as fit, and more accessible. A former Intendant, a Monsr. de Baville has rendered his memory dear to travellers and amateurs by the pains he took to preserve and to restore these monuments of antiquity. The present one (I do not know who he is) is demolishing the object to make a good road to it. I thought of you again, and I was then in great good humour, at the Pont du Gard, a sublime antiquity, and [well] preserved. But most of all here, where Roman taste, genius, and magnificence excite ideas analogous to yours at every step, I could no longer oppose the inclination to avail myself of your permission to write to you, a permission given with too much complaisance by you, taken advantage of with too much indiscretion by me. Madame de Tott too did me the same honour. But she being only the descendant of some of those puny heroes who boiled their own kettles before the walls of Troy, I shall write to her from a Graecian, rather than a Roman canton; when I shall find myself for example among her Phocean relations at Marseilles. Loving, as you do Madam, the precious remains of antiquity, loving architecture, gardening, a warm sun, and a clear sky, I wonder you have never thought of moving Chaville to Nismes. This is not so impracticable as you may think. The next time a Surintendant des batiments du roi, after the example of M. Colbert, sends persons to Nismes to move the Maison [Car]rée to Paris, that they may not come empty-handed, desire them to bring Chaville with them to replace it. À propos of Paris. I have now been three weeks from there without knowing any thing of what has past. I suppose I shall meet it all [at Aix, where] I have directed my letters to be lodged poste restante. My journey has given me leisure to reflect on this Assemblée des Notables. Under a good and young king as the present, I think good may be m[ade of it.] I would have the deputies then by all means so conduct themselves as [to encourage] him to repeat the calls of this assembly. Their first step should be to get th[emselves] divided into two chambers, instead of seven, the Noblesse and the commons separately. The 2d. to persuade the king, instead of chusing the deputies of the commons himself, to summon those chosen by the people for the Provincial administrations. The 3d. as the Noblesse is too numerous to be all admitted into the assemblée, to obtain permission for that body to chuse it's own deputies. The rest would follow. Two houses so elected would contain a mass of wisdom which would make the people happy, and the king great; would place him in history where no other act can possibly place him. This is my plan Madam; but I wish to know yours, which I am sure is better.

[From a correspondent at N]ismes you will not expect news. Were I [to attempt to give you news, I shoul]d tell you stories a thousand years old. [I should detail to you the intrigue]s of the courts of the Caesars, how they [affect us here, the oppressions of their] Praetors, Praefects &c. I am immersed [in antiquities from morning to night]. For me the city of Rome is actually [existing in all the splendor of it's] empire. I am filled with alarms for [the event of the irruptions dayly m]aking on us by the Goths, Ostrogoths, [Visigoths and Vandals, lest they shoul]d reconquer us to our original bar[barism. If I am sometimes ind]uced to look forward to the eighteenth [century, it is only when recalled] to it by the recollection of your goodness [and friendship, and by those sentiments of] sincere esteem and respect with which [I have the honor to be, Madam, your] most obedient & most humble servant,

Th: Jefferson

53. TO WILLIAM SHORT

Dear Sir   *Aix en Provence March. 27. 1787.*
...I am now in the land of corn, wine, oil, and sunshine. What more can man ask of heaven? If I should happen to die at Paris I will beg of you to send me here, and have me exposed to the sun. I am sure it will bring me to life again. It is wonderful to me that every free being who possesses cent ecus de rente, does not remove to the Southward of the Loire. It is true that money will carry to Paris most of the good things of this canton. But it cannot carry thither it's sunshine, nor procure any equivalent for it. This city is one of the cleanest and neatest I have ever seen in any country. The streets are streight, from 20. to 100 feet wide, and as clean as a parlour floor. Where they are of width suffi-cient they have 1. 2. or 4. rows of elms from 100 to 150 years old, which make delicious walks. There are no portes-cocheres, so that the build-ings shew themselves advantageously on the streets. It is in a valley just where it begins to open towards the mouth of the Rhone, forming in that direction a boundless plain which is an entire grove of olive trees, and is moreover in corn, lucerne, or vines, for the happiness of the olive tree is that it interferes with no superficial production. Prob-ably it draws it's nourishment from parts out of the reach of any other plant. It takes well in every soil, but best where it is poorest, or where there is none. Comparing the Beaujolois with Provence, the former is of the richest soil, the latter richest in it's productions. But the climate of Beaujolois cannot be compared with this. I expect to find the situa-tion of Marseilles still pleasanter: business will carry me thither soon, for a time at least. I can receive there daily the waters from this place, with no other loss than that of their warmth, and this can easily be re-stored to them. I computed my journey on leaving Paris to be of 1000 leagues. I am now over one fourth of it. My calculation is that I shall conclude it in the earlier half of June. Letters may come to me here till the last day of April, about which time I shall be vibrating by this place Westwardly.—In the long chain of causes and effects, it is droll sometimes to seize two distant links and to present the one as the con-sequence of the other. Of this nature are these propositions. The want of dung prevents the progress of luxury in Aix. The poverty of the soil

makes it's streets clean. These are legitimate consequences from the following chain. The preciousness of the soil prevents it's being employed in grass. Therefore no cattle, no dung. Hence the dung-gatherers (a numerous calling here) hunt it as eagerly in the streets as they would diamonds. Every one therefore can walk cleanly and commodiously. Hence few carriages. Hence few assemblies, routs, and other occasions for the display of dress.—I thank M. Pio for his anxieties on my account. My ostensible purpose of travelling without a servant was only to spare Espagnol the pain of being postponed to another, as I was quite determined to be master of my own secret, and therefore to take a servant who should not know me. At Fontainebleau I could not get one: but at Dijon I got a very excellent one who will probably go through the journey with me. Yet I must say, it is a sacrifice to opinion, and that without answering any one purpose worth a moment's consideration. They only serve to insulate me from the people among whom I am. Present me in the most friendly terms to M. Pio, M. Mazzei and other friends and believe me to be with the most sincere esteem your affectionate friend & servant,

Th: Jefferson

54. TO MARTHA JEFFERSON

Aix en Provence March. 28. 1787.

I was happy, my dear Patsy, to receive, on my arrival here, your letter informing me of your health and occupations. I have not written to you sooner because I have been almost constantly on the road. My journey hitherto has been a very pleasing one. It was undertaken with the hope that the mineral waters of this place might restore strength to my wrist. Other considerations also concurred. Instruction, amusement, and abstraction from business, of which I had too much at Paris. I am glad to learn that you are employed in things new and good in your music and drawing. You know what have been my fears for some time past; that you do not employ yourself so closely as I could wish. You have promised me a more assiduous attention, and I have great confidence in what you promise. It is your future happiness which interests me, and nothing can contribute more to it (moral rectitude always excepted) than the contracting a habit of industry and activity. Of all the cankers of human happiness, none corrodes it with so silent, yet so baneful a tooth, as indolence. Body and mind both unemployed, our being becomes a burthen, and every object about us loathsome, even the dearest. Idleness begets ennui, ennui the hypochrondria, and that a diseased body. No laborious person was ever yet hysterical. Exercise and application produce order in our affairs, health of body, chearfulness of mind, and these make us precious to our friends. It is while we are young that the habit of industry is formed. If not then, it never is afterwards. The fortune of our lives therefore depends on employing well the short period of youth. If at any moment, my dear, you catch yourself in idleness, start from it as you would from the precipice of a gulph. You are not however to consider yourself as unemployed while taking exercise. That is necessary for your health, and health is the first of all objects. For this reason if you leave your dancing master for the summer, you must increase your other exercise. I do not like your saying that you are unable to read the antient print of your Livy, but with the aid of your master. We are always equal to what we undertake with resolution. A little degree of this will enable you to decypher your Livy. If you always lean on your master, you will never be able to proceed without him. It is a part of the American character to consider nothing as desperate; to surmount every difficulty by resolution and contrivance. In Europe there are shops for every want. It's inhabitants therefore have no idea that their wants can be furnished otherwise. Remote from all other aid, we are obliged to invent and to execute; to find means within ourselves, and not to lean on others. Consider therefore the conquering your Livy as an exercise in the habit of surmounting difficulties, a habit which will be necessary to you in the country where you are to live, and without which you will be thought a very helpless animal, and less esteemed. Music, drawing, books, invention and exercise will be so many resources to you against ennui. But there are others which to this object add that of utility. These are the needle, and domestic oeconomy. The latter you cannot learn here, but the former you may. In the country life of America there are many moments when a woman can have recourse to nothing but her needle for employment. In a dull company and in dull weather for instance. It is ill manners to read; it is ill manners to leave them; no card-playing there among genteel people; that is abandoned to blackguards. The needle is then a valuable resource. Besides without knowing to use it herself, how can the mistress of a family direct the works of her servants? You ask me to write you long letters. I will do it my dear, on condition you will read them from time to time, and practice what they will inculcate. Their precepts will be dictated by experience, by a perfect knowlege of the situation in which you will be placed, and by the fondest love for you. This it is which makes me wish to see you more qualified than common. My expectations from you are high: yet not higher than you may attain. Industry and resolution are all that are wanting. No body in this world can make me so happy, or so miserable as you. Retirement from public life will ere long become necessary for me. To your sister and yourself I look to render the evening of my life serene and contented. It's morning has been clouded by loss after loss till I have nothing left but you. I do not doubt either your affection or dispositions. But great exertions are necessary, and you have little time left to make them. Be industrious then, my dear child. Think nothing unsurmountable by resolution and application, and you will be all that I wish you to be. You ask me if it is my desire you should dine at the abbess's table? It is. Propose it as such to Madame de Traubenheim with my respectful compliments and thanks for her care of you. Continue to love me with all the warmth with which you are beloved by, my dear Patsy, yours affectionately,

Th: Jefferson

55. TO WILLIAM SHORT

Dear Sir   *Aix Mar. 29. 1787.*
... I did not see Mount Cenis. My plan was to have gone to Montbard which was on the left of my road, and then to have crossed again to the right to Mount Cenis. But there were no posts on these roads, the obtaining horses was difficult and precarious, and a constant storm of

wind, hail, snow, and rain offered me little occasion of seeing any thing. I referred it therefore to some future excursion from Fontainebleau. The groupe of which M. de Laye spoke to you carries the perfection of the chissel to a degree of which I had no conception.[1] It is the only thing in sculpture which I have seen on my journey worthy of notice. In painting I have seen good things at Lyons only. In Architecture nothing any where except the remains of antiquity. These are more in number, and less injured by time than I expected, and have been to me a great treat. Those at Nismes, both in dignity and preservation, stand first. There is however at Arles an Amphitheatre as large as that of Nismes, the external walls of which from the top of the arches downwards is well preserved. Another circumstance contrary to my expectation is the change of language. I had thought the Provençale only a dialect of the French; on the contrary the French may rather be considered as a dialect of the Provençale. That is to say, the Latin is the original. Tuscan and Spanish are degeneracies in the first degree. Piedmontese (as I suppose) in the 2d. Provençale in the 3d. and Parisian French in the 4th. But the Provençale stands nearer to the Tuscan than it does to the French, and it is my Italian which enables me to understand the people here, more than my French. This language, in different shades occupies all the country South of the Loire. Formerly it took precedence of the French under the name of la langue Romans. The ballads of it's Troubadours were the delight of the several courts of Europe, and it is from thence that the novels of the English are called Romances. Every letter is pronounced, the articulation is distinct, no nasal sounds disfigure it, and on the whole it stands close to the Italian and Spanish in point of beauty. I think it a general misfortune that historical circumstances gave a final prevalence to the French instead of the Provençale language. It loses it's ground slowly, and will ultimately disappear because there are few books written in it, and because it is thought more polite to speak the language of the Capital. Yet those who learn that language here, pronounce it as the Italians do. We were last night treated with Alexis and Justine, and Mazet, in which the most celebrated actress from Marseilles came to bear a part for the advantage of her friend whose benefit night it was. She is in the stile of Mde. Dugazon, has ear, voice, taste and action. She is moreover young and handsome: and has an advantage over Mde. Dugazon and some other of the celebrated ones of Paris, in being clear of that dreadful wheeze or rather whistle in respiration which resembles the agonizing struggles for breath in a dying person.—I thank you for your information of the health of my daughter. My respects to the family of Chaville are always to be understood if not expressed. To Mr. and Mde. de la Fayette also, Messrs. Mazzei, Pio and Crevecoeur, I wish to be presented. Be assured as to yourself that no person can more sincerely wish your prosperity and happiness, nor entertain warmer sentiments of esteem than Dear Sir your affectionate humble servant.

56. TO CHASTELLUX

Marseilles Apr. 4. 1787.

I must return you many thanks, my dear friend, for your kind attention in procuring me the acquaintance of Monsr. Bergasse, from whom I have received many civilities, and, what is more precious, abundance of information. To you and to him also I am indebted for an introduction to Monsr. Audibert, in whom I saw enough to make me regret that I could not see more of him. My journey from Paris to this place has been a continued feast of new objects, and new ideas. To make the most of the little time I have for so long a circuit, I have been obliged to keep myself rather out of the way of good dinners and good company. Had they been my objects, I should not have quitted Paris. I have courted the society of gardeners, vignerons, coopers, farmers &c. and have devoted every moment of every day almost, to the business of enquiry. M. de Bergasse however united for me all objects, a good dinner, good company, and information. I was unlucky in not having called on you before you went into the country, as I should have derived from you much useful counsel for my journey. I have still a favor to ask of you, which is, a letter to some one good person at Tours in Touraine, where I shall make a short stay of a day or two on my return about the latter part of May or beginning of June. The article Coquilles in the Questions Encyclopediques de Voltaire will inform you

what is my object there.¹ I have found the Abbés in general most useful acquaintances. They are unembarrassed with families, uninvolved
in form and etiquette, frequently learned, and always obliging. If you
know such a one at Tours you will oblige me infinitely by a letter to
him: or if you know none yourself, perhaps some of your friends may.
I will only beg to be announced but as a voyageur etranger simple-
ment, and that it be addressed à Monsr. Jefferson à Tours, poste
restante. This deception keeps me clear of those polite obligations to
which I might otherwise be engaged, and leaves me the whole of the
little time I have to pursue the objects that always delight me.—I have
been concerned with the country I have passed thro hitherto. I could
not help comparing it, en passant, with England, and found the comparison much more disadvantageous to the latter than I had expected.
I shall have many interrogations to ask of you. These being too many
for a letter, they shall therefore be reserved to some future conversation, when I can have the pleasure of returning you thanks in person
for the multiplied instances of your goodness and partiality to me, and
of assuring you how sincere are those sentiments of esteem and
friendship with which I have the honor to be Dear Sir, your affectionate friend & humble servant,

Th: Jefferson

57. TO MADAME DE TOTT¹

Marseilles Apr. 5. 1787.

I thank you sincerely, Madam, for the favour of your letter on the subject of M. Drouay's picture.² It has confirmed a part of my own ideas,
given some which had escaped me, and corrected others wherein I had
been wrong. The strong expression given to the countenance of Marius had absorbed all my attention, and made me overlook the slender-
ness of his frame, which you justly recall to my mind as faulty in that
particular. Give me leave in return to rectify for you an opinion in another kind which I suppose you to entertain, because you have not yet
had time to correct all the errors of the [human] mind. I presume that
you think, as most people think, that a person cannot be in two places

at one time. Yet is there no error more palpable than this. You know, for example, that you have been in Paris and it's neighborhood, constantly since I had the pleasure of seeing you there: yet I declare you have been with me above half my journey. I could repeat to you long conversations, word for word, and on a variety of subjects. When I find you fatigued with conversation and sighing for your pallet and pencil, I permit you to return to Paris a while, and amuse myself with philosophizing on the objects which occur. The plan of my journey, as well as of my life, being to take things by the smooth handle, few occur which have not something tolerable to offer me. [The Auberge] for instance in which I am obliged to take refuge at night, presents in the first moment nothing but noise, dirt, and disorder. But the auberge is not to be too much abused. True, it has not the charming gardens of Chaville without, nor it's decorations, nor it's charming society within. I do not seek therefore for the good things which it has not, but those which it has. 'A traveller, sais I, retired at night to his chamber in an Inn, all his effects contained in a single trunk, all his cares circumscribed by the walls of his apartment, unknown to all, unheeded, and undisturbed, writes, reads, thinks, sleeps, just in the moments when nature and the movements of his body and mind require. Charmed with the tranquillity of his little cell, he finds how few are our real wants, how cheap a thing is happiness, how expensive a one pride. He views with pity the wretched rich, whom the laws of the world have submitted to the cumbrous trappings of rank: he sees him labouring through the journey of life like an ass oppressed under ingots of gold, little of which goes to feed, to clothe, or to cover himself; the rest gobbled up by harpies of various description with which he has surrounded himself. These, and not himself, are it's real masters. He wonders that a thinking mind can be so subdued by opinion, and that he does not run away from his own crouded house, and take refuge in the chamber of an Inn.' Indeed I wonder so too, unless he has a Chaville to retire to, and a family composed like that of Chaville, where quiet and friendship can both be indulged. But between the society of real friends, and the tranquillity of solitude the mind finds no middle ground.—Thus reconciled to my Auberge by night, I was still persecuted by day with the cruel whip of the postillion. How to find a smooth handle to this tremendous instrument? At length however I found it in the callous nerves of the horse, to which these terrible stripes may afford but a gentle and perhaps a pleasing irritation; like a pinch of snuff to an old snuff-taker.

Sometimes I amuse myself with physical researches. Those enormous boots, for instance, in which the postillion is incased like an Egyptian mummy, have cost me more pondering than the laws of planetary motion did to Newton. I have searched their solution in his physical, and in his moral constitution. I fancied myself in conversation with one of Newton's countrymen, and asked him what he thought could be the reason of their wearing those boots? 'Sir, says he, it is because a Frenchman's heels are so light, that, without this ballast, he would turn keel up.' 'If so, Sir, sais I, it proves at least that he has more *gravity* in his head than your nation is generally willing to allow him.' I should go on, Madam, detailing to you my dreams and speculations; but that my present situation is most unfriendly to speculation. Four thousand three hundred and fifty market-women (I have counted them one by one) brawling, squabbling, and jabbering Patois, three hundred asses braying and bewailing to each other, and to the world, their cruel oppressions, four files of mule-carts passing in constant succession, with as many bells to every mule as can be hung about him, all this in the street under my window, and the weather too hot to shut it. Judge whether in such a situation it is easy to hang one's ideas together. Besides, writing from a colony of your own country, you would rather I should say less of myself and more of that. But, just dropped among them, how can I pretend to judge them with justice? Of beauty, you will say, one may judge on a single coup d'oeil. Of beauty then, Madam, they have a good share, as far as the public walks, the Spectacles, and the assembleé of Mademlle. Conil enable me to decide. But it is not a legitimate Graecian beauty. It is not such as yours. The reason I suppose is that yours is genuine, brought from the spot; [where]as theirs has been made here, and like all fabricated wares is sophisticated with foreign mixture. Perhaps you would rather I should write you news? Les Amandes sont de 22.^{tt}, Cacao 19s, Caffé 31., Cotton 130.^{tt}, huile 22.^{tt}, riz 21.^{tt}, savon 42.^{tt}, terebenthine 17.s &c. &c. This is not in the stile of Paris news; but I write from Marseilles, and it is the news of the place. I could continue it thro' the whole table of prices current; but that I am sure you have enough, and have already in your heart wished an end to my letter. I shall therefore annex but one preliminary condition; which is a permission to express here my respectful attachment to Madame and Monsieur de Tessé, and to assure yourself of those sentiments of perfect friendship & affection with which I have the honor to be sincerely & constantly, Madam, your most obedient & most humble servant,

Th: Jefferson

58. TO LAFAYETTE

Nice, April 11, 1787.

Your head, my dear friend, is full of Notable things; and being better employed, therefore, I do not expect letters from you. I am constantly roving about, to see what I have never seen before and shall never see again. In the great cities, I go to see what travellers think alone worthy of being seen; but I make a job of it, and generally gulp it all down in a day. On the other hand, I am never satiated with rambling through the fields and farms, examining the culture and cultivators, with a degree of curiosity which makes some take me to be a fool, and others to be much wiser than I am. I have been pleased to find among the people a less degree of physical misery than I had expected. They are generally well clothed, and have a plenty of food, not animal indeed, but vegetable, which is as wholesome. Perhaps they are over worked, the excess of the rent required by the landlord, obliging them to too many hours of labor, in order to produce that, and wherewith to feed and clothe themselves. The soil of Champagne and Burgundy I have found more universally good than I had expected, and as I could not help making a comparison with England, I found that comparison more unfavorable to the latter than is generally admitted. The soil, the climate, and the productions are superior to those of England, and the husbandry as good, except in one point; that of manure. In England, long leases for twenty-one years, or three lives, to wit, that of the farmer, his wife, and son, renewed by the son as soon as he comes to the possession, for his own life, his wife's and eldest child's, and so on, render the farms there almost hereditary, make it worth the farmer's while to manure the lands highly, and give the landlord an opportunity of occasionally making his rent keep pace with the improved state of the lands. Here the leases are either during pleasure, or for three, six, or nine years, which does not give the farmer time to repay himself for the expensive operation of well manuring, and therefore, he manures ill, or not at all. I suppose, that could the practice of leasing for three lives be introduced in the whole kingdom, it would, within the term of your life, increase agricultural productions fifty per cent; or were any one proprietor to do it with his own lands, it would increase his rents fifty per cent, in the course of twenty-five years. But I am told the laws do not permit it. The laws then, in this particular, are unwise and unjust, and ought to give that permission. In the southern provinces, where the soil is poor, the climate hot and dry, and there are few animals, they would learn the art, found so precious in England, of making vegetable manure, and thus improving these provinces in the article in which nature has been least kind to them. Indeed, these provinces afford a singular spectacle. Calculating on the poverty of their soil, and their climate by its latitude only, they should have been the poorest in France. On the contrary, they are the richest, from one fortuitous circumstance. Spurs or ramifications of high mountains, making down from the Alps, and as it were, reticulating these provinces, give to the vallies the protection of a particular inclosure to each, and the benefit of a general stagnation of the northern winds produced by the whole of them, and thus countervail the advantage of several degrees of latitude. From the first olive fields of Pierrelate, to the orangeries of Hieres, has been continued rapture to me. I have often wished for you. I think you have not made this journey. It is a pleasure you have to come, and an improvement to be added to the many you have already made. It will be a great comfort to you to know, from your own inspection, the condition of all the provinces of your own country, and it will be interesting to them at some future day to be known to you. This is perhaps the only moment of your life in which you can acquire that knolege. And to do it most effectually you must be absolutely incognito, you must ferret the people out of their hovels as I have done, look into their kettles, eat their bread, loll on their beds under pretence of resting yourself, but in fact to find if they are soft. You will feel a sublime pleasure in the course of this investigation, and a sublimer one hereafter when you shall be able to apply your knolege to the softening of their beds, or the throwing a morsel of meat into the kettle of vegetables. You will not wonder at the subjects of my letter: they are the only ones which have been present to my mind for some time past, and the waters must always be what are the fountain from which they flow. According to this indeed I should have intermixed from beginning to end warm expressions of friendship to you: but according to the ideas of our country we do not permit ourselves to speak even truths when they may have the air of flattery. I content myself therefore with saying once for all that I love you, your wife and children. Tell them so and Adieu. Your's affectionately,

Th: Jefferson

59. TO MARTHA JEFFERSON

My Dear Patsy   *Marseilles May 5. 1787.*
I got back to Aix the day before yesterday, and found there your letter of the 9th. of April, from which I presume you to be well tho' you do not say so. In order to exercise your geography I will give you a detail of my journey. You must therefore take your map and trace out the following places. Dijon, Lyons, Pont St. Esprit, Nismes, Arles, St. Remis, Aix, Marseilles, Toulon, Hieres, Frejus, Antibes, Nice, Col de Tende, Coni, Turin, Vercelli, Milan, Pavia, Tortona, Novi, Genoa, by sea to Albenga, by land to Monaco, Nice, Antibes, Frejus, Brignolles, Aix, and Marseille. The day after tomorrow I set out hence for Aix, Avignon, Pont du Gard, Nismes, Montpelier, Narbonne, along the Canal of Languedoc to Toulouse, Bourdeaux, Rochefort, Rochelle, Nantes, Lorient, Nantes, Tours, Orleans and Paris where I shall arrive about the middle of June, after having travelled something upwards of a thousand leagues. From Genoa to Aix was very fatiguing, the first two days having been at sea, and mortally sick, two more clambering the cliffs of the Appennine, sometimes on foot, sometimes on a mule

according as the path was more or less difficult, and two others travelling thro' the night as well as day, without sleep. I am not yet rested, and shall therefore shortly give you rest by closing my letter, after mentioning that I have received a letter from your sister, which tho a year old, gave me great pleasure. I inclose it for your perusal, as I think it will be pleasing to you also. But take care of it, and return it to me when I shall get back to Paris, for trifling as it seems, it is precious to me. When I left Paris, I wrote to London to desire that your harpsichord might be sent during the months of April and May, so that I am in hopes it will arrive a little before I shall, and give me an opportunity of judging whether you have got the better of that want of industry which I had began to fear would be the rock on which you would split. Determine never to be idle. No person will have occasion to complain of the want of time, who never loses any. It is wonderful how much may be done, if we are always doing. And that you may be always doing good, my dear, is the ardent prayer of yours affectionately,

Th: Jefferson

60. TO MARTHA JEFFERSON

May 21. 1787.

I write to you, my dear Patsy, from the Canal of Languedoc, on which I am at present sailing, as I have been for a week past, cloudless skies above, limpid waters below, and on each hand a row of nightingales in full chorus. This delightful bird had given me a rich treat before at the fountain of Vaucluse. After visiting the tomb of Laura[1] at Avignon, I went to see this fountain, a noble one of itself, and rendered for ever famous by the songs of Petrarch who lived near it. I arrived there somewhat fatigued, and sat down by the fountain to repose myself. It gushes, of the size of a river, from a secluded valley of the mountain, the ruins of Petrarch's chateau being perched on a rock 200 feet perpendicular above. To add to the enchantment of the scene, every tree and bush was filled with nightingales in full song. I think you told me you had not yet noticed this bird. As you have trees in the garden of the convent, there must be nightingales in them, and this is the season of their song. Endeavor, my dear, to make yourself acquainted with the music of this bird, that when you return to your own country you may be able to estimate it's merit in comparison with that of the mocking bird. The latter has the advantage of singing thro' a great part of the year, whereas the nightingale sings but 5. or 6. weeks in the spring, and a still shorter term and with a more feeble voice in the fall. I expect to be at Paris about the middle of next month. By that time we may begin to expect our dear Polly. It will be a circumstance of inexpressible comfort to me to have you both with me once more. The object most interesting to me for the residue of my life, will be to see you both developing daily those principles of virtue and goodness which will make you valuable to others and happy in yourselves, and acquiring those talents and that degree of science which will guard you at all times against ennui, the most dangerous poison of life. A mind always employed is always happy. This is the true secret, the grand recipe for felicity. The idle are the only wretched. In a world which furnishes so many emploiments which are useful, and so many which are amusing, it is our own fault if we ever know what ennui is, or if we are ever driven to the miserable resource of gaming, which corrupts our dispositions, and teaches us a habit of hostility against all mankind.—We are now entering the port of Toulouse, where I quit my bark; and of course must conclude my letter. Be good and be industrious, and you will be what I shall most love in this world. Adieu my dear child. Yours affectionately,

Th: Jefferson

61. TO WILLIAM SHORT

On the Canal of Languedoc,
Dear Sir   *approaching Toulouse. May 21. 1787.*
The only incalculable part of my journey now drawing to a close, I am able to give you a state of my future motions from which there will probably be no considerable variation, unless any considerable accident happen. I expect to arrive on the days following at the several places named.

May 23. Bourdeaux
31. Nantes
June 4. Lorient
7. Rennes
8. Nantes
11. Tours
13. Orleans
15. Paris

As there is a possibility that I may vary my route a little from Lorient, so as to avoid the repassage by Nantes, it will be adviseable to retain at Paris all letters which may arrive there after the 25th. of this month. I have passed through the Canal from it's entrance into the mediterranean at Cette to this place, and shall be immediately at Toulouse, in the whole 200 American miles, by water; having employed in examining all it's details nine days, one of which was spent in making a tour of 40 miles on horseback, among the Montagnes noires, to see the manner in which water has been collected to supply the canal; the other eight on the canal itself. I dismounted my carriage from it's wheels, placed it on the deck of a light bark, and was thus towed on the canal instead of the post road. That I might be perfectly master of all the delays necessary, I hired a bark to myself by the day, and have made from 20. to 35 miles a day, according to circumstances, always sleeping ashore. Of all the methods of travelling I have ever tried this is the pleasantest. I walk the greater part of the way along the banks of the canal, level, and lined with a double row of trees which furnish shade. When fatigued I take seat in my carriage where, as much at ease as if in my study, I read, write, or observe. My carriage being of glass all round, admits a full view of all the varying scenes thro' which I am shifted, olives, figs, mulberries, vines, corn and pasture, villages and farms. I have had some days of superb weather, enjoying two parts of the Indian's wish, cloudless skies and limpid waters: I have had another luxury which he could not wish, since we have driven him from the country of Mockingbirds, a double row of nightingales along the banks of the canal, in full song. This delicious bird gave me another rich treat at Vaucluse. Arriving there a little fatigued I sat down to repose myself at the fountain, which, in a retired hollow of the mountain, gushes out in a stream sufficient to turn 300 mills, the ruins of Petrarch's chateau perched on a rock 200 feet perpendicular over the fountain, and every tree and bush filled with nightingales in full chorus. I find Mazzei's observation just that their song is more varied, their tone fuller and stronger here than on the banks of the Seine. It explains to me another circumstance, why there never was a poet North of the Alps, and why there never will be one. A poet is as much the creature of climate as an orange or palm tree. What a bird the nightingale would be in the climates of America! We must colonize him thither. You should not think of returning to America without taking the tour which I have taken, extending it only further South. I intend to propose to Colo. T M Randolph the permitting his eldest son to take it the next spring, and suppose it would be an agreeable and oeconomical circumstance to you both to go together. You should not stop short of the country of Monsr. Pio, to whom be pleased to present me in the most friendly terms, as also to M. Mazzei, the M. de la fayette and Chastellux, maison de Chaville, two Abbés &c. Desire Frouillé to procure for me immediately le Recueil alphabetique des droits de traites uniformes 4. v. 8vo. printed in 1786, and, as is said, at Lyons. Petit should immediately make them plant the vacant space of the garden in Indian corn in rows 3. feet apart, the plants a foot apart in the row. I finish my page with assurances of the sincere esteem and attachment with which I am dear Sir your affectionate friend & servant,

Th: Jefferson

62. EXTRACTS FROM NOTES OF A TOUR INTO THE SOUTHERN PARTS OF FRANCE, &C.

Memorandums taken on a journey from Paris into the
Southern parts of France and Northern of Italy, in the year 1787.
CHAMPAGNE. March 3. SENS TO VERMANTON. The face of the country is in large hills, not too steep for the plough, somewhat resembling the Elk hill and Beverdam hills of Virginia. The soil is generally a rich mulatto loam, with a mixture of coarse sand and some loose stone. The plains of Yonne are of the same colour. The plains are in corn,[1] the hills in vineyard, but the wine not good. There are a few apple trees but none of any other kind, and no inclosures. No cattle, sheep, or swine. Fine mules.

Few chateaux. No farm houses, all the people being gathered in villages. Are they thus collected by that dogma of their religion which makes them believe that, to keep the Creator in good humor with his own works, they must mumble a mass every day? Certain it is that they are less happy and less virtuous in villages than they would be insulated with their families on the grounds they cultivate. The people are illy clothed. Perhaps they have put on their worst clothes at this moment as it is raining. But I observe women and children carrying heavy burthens, and labouring with the hough. This is an unequivocal indication of extreme poverty. Men, in a civilised country, never expose their wives and children to labour above their force or sex, as long as their own labour can protect them from it. I see few beggars. Probably this is the effect of a police.

BURGUNDY. Mar. 4. Lucy le bois. Cussy les forges. Rouvray. Maisonneuve. Vitteaux. La Chaleure. Pont de Panis. Dijon. The hills are higher and more abrupt. The soil a good red loam and sand, mixed with more or less grit, small stone, and sometimes rock. All in corn. Some forest wood here and there, broom, whins and holly, and a few inclosures of quick hedge. Now and then a flock of sheep.

The people are well clothed, but it is Sunday. They have the appearance of being well fed. The Chateau de Sevigny, near Cussy les forges is in a charming situation. Between Maison neuve and Vitteaux the road leads through an avenue of trees 8. American miles long in a right line. It is impossible to paint the ennui of this avenue. On the summits of the hills which border the valley in which Vitteaux is, there is a parapet of rock, 20. 30. or 40. feet perpendicular, which crowns the hills. The tops are nearly level and appear to be covered with earth. Very singular. Great masses of rock in the hills between la Chaleure and Pont de Panis, and a conical hill in the approach to the last place.

DIJON. The tavern price of a bottle of the best wine (e.g. of Vaune) is 4.^{tt} The best round potatoes here I ever saw. They have begun a canal 30. feet wide, which is to lead into the Saone at   . It is fed by springs. They are not allowed to take any water out of the riviere d'Ouche, which runs through this place on account of the mills on that river. They talk of making a canal to the Seine, the nearest navigable part of which at present is 15. leagues from hence. They have very light waggons here for the transportation of their wine. They are long and narrow, the fore wheels as high as the hind. Two peices of wine are drawn by one horse in one of these waggons. The road, in this part of the country, is divided into portions of 40. or 50. feet by stones, numbered, which mark the task of the labourers.

March 7. 8. From LA BARAQUE to CHAGNY. On the left are plains which extend to the Saone, on the right the ridge of mountains called the Cote. The plains are of a reddish-brown, rich loam, mixed with much small stone. The Cote has for it's basis a solid rock on which is about a foot of soil, and small stone in equal quantities, the soil red and of midling quality. The plains are in corn, the Cote in vines. The former has no inclosures, the latter is in small ones of dry stone wall. There is a good deal of forest. Some small herds of small cattle and sheep. Fine mules which come from Provence and cost 20. Louis. They break them at 2. years old, and they last to 30.

The corn lands here rent for about 15^{tt} the arpent. They are now planting, pruning, and sticking their vines. When a new vineyard is made they plant the vines in gutters about 4. feet apart. As the vines advance they lay them down. They put out new shoots, and fill all the intermediate space till all trace of order is lost. They have ultimately about 1. foot square to each vine. They begin to yeild good profit at 5. or 6. years old and last 100. or 150. years. A vigneron at Voulenay carried me into his vineyard, which was of about 10. arpents. He told me that some years it produced him 60. peices of wine, and some not more than 3. peices. The latter is the most advantageous produce, because the wine is better in quality and higher in price in proportion as less is made: and the expences at the same time diminish in the same proportion. Whereas when much is made, the expences are increased, while the quality and price become less. In very plentiful years they often give one half the wine for casks to contain the other half. The cask for 250. bottles costs 6^{tt} in scarce years and 10^{tt} in plentiful. The FEUILLETTE is of 125. bottles, the PIECE of 250., and the QUEUE, or BOTTE of 500. An arpent rents for from 20.^{tt} to 60.^{tt} A farmer of 10. arpents has about three labourers engaged by the year. He pais 4. Louis to a man, and half as much to a woman, and feeds them. He kills one hog, and salts it, which is all the meat used in the family during the year. Their ordinary food is bread and vegetables. At Pommard and Voulenay I observed them eating good wheat bread; at Meursault, rye. I asked the reason of the difference. They told me that the white wines fail in quality much oftener than the red, and remain on hand. The farmer therefore cannot afford to feed his labourers so well. At Meursault, only white wines are made, because there is too much stone for the red. On such slight circumstances depends the condition of man!—The wines which have given such celebrity to Burgundy grow only on the Cote, an extent of about 5 leagues long, and half a league wide. They begin at Chambertin, and go on through Vougeau, Romanie, Veaune, Nuys, Beaune, Pommard, Voulenay, Meursault, and end at Monrachet. The two last are white; the others red. Chambertin, Voujeau, and Veaune are strongest, and will bear transportation and keeping. They sell therefore on the spot for 1200.^{tt} the Queue, which is 48. sous the bottle. Voulenaye is the best of the other reds, equal in flavor to Chambertin &c. but being lighter, will not keep, and therefore sells for not more than 300^{tt} the Queue, which is 12. sous the bottle. It ripens sooner than they do and consequently is better for those who wish to broach at a year old. In like manner of the White wines, and for the same reason, Monrachet sells at 1200^{tt} the Queue (48s. the bottle) and Meursault of the best quality, viz. the Goutte d'or, at only 150^{tt} (6s. the bottle). It is remarkeable that the best of each kind, that is, of the Red and White, is made at the extremities of the line, to wit, at Chambertin and Monrachet. It is pretended that the adjoining vineyards produce the same qualities, but that, belonging to obscure individuals, they have not obtained a name, and therefore sell as other wines. The aspect of the Cote is a little South of the East. The Western side is also covered with vines, is apparently of the same soil; yet the wines are only of the coarsest kinds. Such too are those which are produced in the Plains: but there the soil is richer and less stony. Vougeau is the property of the monks of Citeaux, and produces about 200 pieces. Monrachet contains about 50 arpents, and produces one year with another about 120 peices. It belongs to two proprietors only, Monsr. de Clermont, who leases to some wine merchants, and the Marquis de Sarsnet of Dijon, whose part is farmed to a Monsr. de la Tour whose family, for many generations, have had the farm. The best

wines are carried to Paris by land. The transportation costs 36^{tt} the peice. The more indifferent go by water. Bottles cost 4½ sous each.
March 9. CHALONS. SENNECY. TOURNUS. ST. ALBIN. MACON. On the left are the fine plains of the Saone; on the right, high lands, rather waving than hilly, sometimes sloping gently to the plains, sometimes dropping down in precipices, and occasionally broken into beautiful vallies by the streams which run into the Saone. The Plains are a dark rich loam, in pasture and corn; the heights more or less red or reddish, always gritty, of midling quality only; their sides in vines, and their summits in corn. The vineyards are inclosed with dry stone walls, and there are some quickhedges in the corn grounds. The cattle are few and indifferent. There are some good oxen however. They draw by the head. Few sheep, and small. A good deal of wood lands.

I passed three times the canal called le Charollois, which they are opening from Chalons on the Saone to Digoïn on the Loire. It passes near Chagny, and will be 23. leagues long. They have worked on it 3. years, and will finish it in 4. more. It will reanimate the languishing commerce of Champagne and Burgundy, by furnishing a water transportation for their wines to Nantes, which also will receive new consequence by becoming the emporium of that commerce. At some distance on the right are high mountains, which probably form the separation between the waters of the Saone and Loire.—Met a malefactor in the hands of one of the Marechaussée; perhaps a dove in the talons of the hawk. The people begin now to be in separate establishments, and not in villages. Houses are mostly covered with tile.
BEAUJOLOIS. Maison blanche. St. George. Chateau de Laye Epinaye. The face of the country is like that from Chalons to Macon. The Plains are a dark rich loam, the hills a red loam, of midling quality, mixed generally with more or less coarse sand and grit, and a great deal of small stone. Very little forest. The vineyards are mostly inclosed with dry stone wall. A few small cattle and sheep. Here, as in Burgundy, the cattle are all white.

This is the richest country I ever beheld. It is about 10. or 12. leagues in length, and 3. 4. or 5. in breadth; at least that part of it which is under the eye of the traveller. It extends from the top of a ridge of mountains running parallel with the Saone, and sloping down to the plains of that river scarcely any where too steep for the plough. The whole is thick sown with farm houses, chateaux, and the Bastides of the inhabitants of Lyons. The people live separately, and not in villages. The hillsides are in wine and corn: the plains in corn and pasture. The lands are farmed either for money, or on half-stocks. The rents of the corn lands farmed for money are about 10. or 12.^{lt} the arpent. A farmer takes perhaps about 150. arpents for 3. 6. or 9. years. The 1st. year they are in corn, the 2d. in other small grain, with which he sows red clover; the 3d. is for the clover. The spontaneous pasturage is of greenswerd, which they call fromenteau. When lands are rented on half stocks, the cattle, sheep &c. are furnished by the landlord. They are valued and must be left of equal value. The increase of these, as well as the produce of the farm, are divided equally. These leases are only from year to year. They have a method of mixing beautifully the culture of vines, trees and corn. Rows of fruit trees are planted about 20. feet apart. Between the trees, in the row, they plant vines 4. feet apart and espalier them. The intervals are sowed alternately in corn, so as to be one year in corn the next in pasture, the 3d. in corn, the 4th in pasture &c. 100. toises of vines in length yeild generally about 4. peices of wine. In Dauphiné, I am told, they plant vines only at the roots of the trees and let them cover the whole trees. But this spoils both the wine and the fruit. Their wine, when distilled, yeilds but one third it's quantity in brandy. The wages of a labouring man here are 5. Louis, of a woman one half. The women do not work with the hough: they only weed the vines, the corn, &c. and spin. They speak a Patois very difficult to understand. I passed some time at the chateau de Laye epinaye. Monsieur de Laye has a seignory of about 15,000 arpens, in pasture, corn, vines, and wood. He has over this, as is usual, a certain jurisdiction both criminal and civil. But this extends only to the first crude examination, which is before his judges. The subject is referred for final examination and decision to the regular judicatures of the country. The Seigneur is keeper of the peace on his domains. He is therefore subject to the expences of maintaining it. A criminal prosecuted to sentence and execution, costs M. de Laye about 5000.^{lt} This is so burthensome to the Seigneurs, that they are slack in criminal prosecutions. A good effect from a bad cause. Thro' all Champagne, Burgundy and the Beaujolois, the husbandry seems good, except that they manure too little. This proceeds from the shortness of their leases. The people of Burgundy and Beaujolois are well clothed, and have the appearance of being well fed. But they experience all the oppressions which result from the nature of the general government, and from that of their particular tenures, and of the Seignorial government to which they are subject. What a cruel reflection that a rich country cannot long be a free one.—M. de Laye has a Diana and Endymion, a very superior morsel of sculpture by Michael Angelo Slodtz, done in 1740. The wild gooseberry is in leaf, the wild pear and sweet briar in bud.

LYONS. There are some feeble remains here of an amphitheatre of 200. feet diameter and of an aqueduct in brick. The Pont d'Ainay has 9. arches of 40. feet from center to center. The piers are of 6. feet.—The Almond is in bloom.

DAUPHINE. From St. Fond to Mornas. March 15. 16. 17. 18. The Rhone makes extensive plains, which lie chiefly on the Eastern side, and are often in two stages. Those of Montelimart are 3. or 4. miles wide, and rather good. Sometimes, as in the neighborhood of Vienne, the hills come in precipices to the river, resembling then very much our Susquehanna and it's hills, except that the Susquehanna is ten times as wide as the Rhone. The high lands are often very level.—The soil, both of hill and plain, where there is soil, is generally tinged, more or less, with red. The hills are sometimes mere masses of rock, sometimes a mixture of loose stone and earth. The plains are always stony and, as often as otherwise, covered perfectly with a coat of round stones of the size of the fist so as to resemble the remains of inundations from which all the soil has been carried away. Sometimes they are midling good, sometimes barren. In the neighborhood of Lyons there is more corn than wine, towards Tains more wine than corn. From thence the Plains, where best, are in corn, clover, almonds, mulberries, walnuts. Where there is still some earth they are in corn, almonds, and oaks; the hills are in vines.—There is a good deal of forest wood near Lyons, but not much afterwards. Scarcely any inclosures. There are a few small sheep before we reach Tains; there the number increases.

Nature never formed a country of more savage aspect than that on both sides the Rhone. A huge torrent, rushing like an arrow between high precipices often of massive rock, at other times of loose stone with but little earth. Yet has the hand of man subdued this savage scene, by planting corn where there is a little fertility, trees where there is still less, and vines where there is none. On the whole, it assumes a romantic, picturesque and pleasing air. The hills on the opposite side of the river, being high, steep, and laid up in terrasses, are of a singular appearance. Where the hills are quite in waste, they are covered with broom, whins, box, and some clusters of small pines. The high mountains of Dauphiné and Languedoc are now covered with snow. The Almond is in general bloom, and the willow putting out it's leaf. There were formerly OLIVES at Tains: but a great cold some years ago killed them, and they have not been replanted. I am told at Montelimart that an Almond tree yeilds about 3. livres profit a year. Supposing them 3. toises apart there will be 100 to the Arpent, which give 300.ᵗ a year, besides the corn growing in the same ground.—A league below Vienne, on the opposite side of the river is COTE ROTIE. It is a string of broken hills, extending a league on the river from the village of Ampuys to the town of Condrieux. The soil is white, tinged a little, sometimes with yellow, sometimes with red, stony, poor and laid up in terrasses. Those parts of the hills only which look to the sun at Midday or the earlier hours of the afternoon produce wines of the first quality. 700 vines 3 feet apart, yeild a feuillette, which is about 2½ peices to the arpent. The best red wine is produced at the upper end in the neighborhood of Ampuys; the best white next to Condrieux. They sell of the first quality and last vintage at 150ᵗ the Piece, equal to 12.s the bottle. Transportation to Paris is 60.ᵗ and the bottle 4.s so it may be delivered at Paris in bottles at 20s. When old it costs 10. or 11. Louis the Piece. There is a quality which keeps well, bears transportation, and cannot be drunk under 4. years. Another must be drunk at a year old. They are equal in flavor and price. The best vintages of red wine are of Monsieur de la Condamine seigneur d'Ampuys, dans son fief de Monlis, le Marquis de Leusse dans son grand tupin, M. de Montjoli, M. du Vivier, and M. du Prunel. The best of white are at Chateau grillé by Madame la veuve Peyrouse.

The wine called HERMITAGE is made on the hills impending over the village of Tains; on one of which is the hermitage which gives name to the hills for about two miles, and to the wine made on them. There are but three of those hills which produce wine of the 1st. quality, and of these the middle regions only. They are about 300 feet perpendicular height, ¼ of a mile in length and have a Southern aspect. The soil is scarcely tinged red, consists of small rotten stone, and, in it's most precious parts, without any perceptible mixture of earth. It is in sloping terrasses. They use a little dung. An Homme de vignes, which consist of 700 plants 3. feet apart, yeilds generally about ¾ of a peice, which is nearly 4 peices to the arpent. When new the Peice is sold at about 225,^{tt} old at 300.^{tt} It cannot be drunk under 4. years, and improves fastest in a hot situation. There is so little White made in proportion to the red, that it is difficult to buy it separate. They make the White sell the Red. If bought separately it is from 15. to 18. Louis the peice, new, and 3^{tt} the bottle old. To give quality to the Red, they mix ⅛ of white grapes. Portage to Paris is 72^{tt} the peice, weighing 600 lb. There are but about 1000. peices of both red and white of the 1st. quality made annually. They are made by M. Meus, seigneur of the place, M. de Loche avocat, M. Berger avocat, M. Chanoine Monron, M. Gaillet, M. de Beausace, M. Deure, M. Chalamelle, M. Monnet and two or three others. Vineyards are never rented here, nor are labourers in the vineyard hired by the year. They leave buds proportioned to the strength of the vine: sometimes as much as 15. inches. The last Hermit died in 1751.

In the neighborhood of Montelimart and below that they plant vines in rows 6. 8. or 10. feet apart, and 2. feet asunder in the row, filling the intervals with corn. Sometimes the vines are in double rows 2. feet apart. I saw single asses in ploughs proportioned to their strength. The plough formed of three peices, thus a. is the beam, to which the

share is fixed, b. a crooked bough of a tree sometimes single, sometimes forked, c. a crooked bough also to which the swingletree was fastened. Asses or mules, working in pairs, are coupled by square yokes in

ℿ this form the side peices only sliding out to disengage the animal. There are few chateaux in this province. The people too are mostly gathered into villages. There are however some scattering farm houses. These are made either of mud or of round stone and mud. They make inclosures also in both those ways. Day laborers receive 16.s or 18.s the day, and feed themselves. Those by the year receive, men 3. Louis and women half that, and are fed. They rarely eat meat; a single hog salted being the year's stock for a family. But they have plenty of cheese, eggs, potatoes and other vegetables, and walnut oil with their sallad. It is a trade here to gather dung along the road for their vines. This proves they have few cattle. I have seen neither hares nor partridges since I left Paris, nor wild fowl on any of the rivers. The roads from Lyons to St. Rambert are neither paved nor gravelled. After that they are coated with broken flint. The ferry boats on the Rhone, and the Isere, are moved by the stream, and very rapidly. On each side of the river is a moveable stage, one end of which is on an axle and two wheels, which, according to the tide, can be advanced or withdrawn so as to apply to the gunwale of the boat. The Pretorian palace at Vienne is 44. feet wide, of the Corinthian order, 4. columns in front, and 4. in flank. It was begun in the year 400. and finished by Charlemagne. The Sepulchral pyramid, a little way out of the town, has an order for it's basement, the pedestal of which from point to point of it's cap is 24f. 1.I. At each angle is a column, engaged one fourth in the wall. The circumference of the three fourths disengaged is 4.f. 4.I. Consequently the diameter is 23.I. The base of the column indicates it to be Ionic, but the capitals are not formed. The Cornice too is a bastard Ionic without modillions or dentils. Between the columns on each side is an arch of 8.f. 4.I. opening, with a pilaster on each side of it. On the top of the basement is a zocle, in the plane of the frieze below. On that is the pyramid, it's base in the plane of the collanno of the pilaster below. The pyramid is a little truncated on it's top. This monument is inedited.[2]

Mar. 18. Principality of ORANGE. The plains on the Rhone here are 2. or 3. leagues wide, reddish, good, in corn, clover, almonds, olives. No forest. Here begins the country of olives, there being very few till we enter this principality. They are the only tree which I see planted among vines. Thyme growing wild here on the hills. Asses very small, sell here for 2. or 3. Louis. The high hills in Dauphiné are covered with snow. The remains of the Roman aqueduct are of brick. A fine peice of Mosaic, still on it's bed, forming the floor of a cellar. 20 feet of it still visible. They are taking down the circular wall of the Amphitheatre to pave a road.

March 19. to 23. LANGUEDOC. Pont St. Esprit. Bagnols. Connault. Valignieres. Remoulins. St. Gervasy. Nismes. Pont d'Arles. To Remoulins there is a mixture of hill and dale. Thence to Nismes, hills on the right, on the left plains extending to the Rhone and the sea. The hills are rocky. Where there is soil it is reddish and poor. The plains generally reddish and good, but stony. When you approach the Rhone, going to Arles, the soil becomes a dark grey loam, with some sand, and very good. The culture is corn, clover, St. foin, olives, vines, mulberries, willow, and some almonds. There is no forest. The hills are inclosed in dry stone wall. Many sheep.

From the summit of the first hill after leaving Pont St. Esprit, there is a beautiful view of the bridge at about 2. miles distance, and a fine landscape of the country both ways. From thence an excellent road, judiciously conducted, thro very romantic scenes. In one part, descending the face of a hill, it is laid out in Serpentine, and not zig-zag, to ease the descent. In others it passes thro' a winding meadow, from 50. to 100. yards wide, walled as it were on both sides by hills of rock; and at length issues into plane country. The waste hills are covered with thyme, box, and chenevert.[3] Where the body of the mountains has a surface of soil, the summit has sometimes a crown of rock, as observed in Champagne. At Nismes the earth is full of limestone. They use square yokes as in Dauphiné. The horses are shorn. They are now pruning the olive. A very good tree produces 60. ℔. of olives, which yield 15 ℔. of oil: the best quality selling at 12.s the ℔. retail, and 10.s wholesale. The high hills of Languedoc still covered with snow. The horse chestnut and mulberry are leafing; appletrees and peas blossoming. The first butterfly I have seen. After the vernal equinox they are often 6. or 8. months without any rain. Many separate farmhouses, numbers of people in rags, and abundance of beggars. The Mine of wheat, weighing 30. ℔. costs 4^{tt} 10.s, wheat bread 3.s the pound. Vin ordinaire, good and of a strong body 2.s or 3.s the bottle. Oranges 1.s apeice. They are nearly finishing at Nismes a grist mill worked by a steam engine, which pumps water from a lower into an upper cistern, from whence two overshot wheels are supplied, each of which turns two pair of stones. The upper cistern being once filled with water, it passes thro the wheels into the lower one from whence it is returned into the upper by the pumps. A stream of water of ¼ or ½ inch diameter supplies the waste of evaporation, absorption, &c. This is furnished from a well by a horse. The arches of the pont St. Esprit are of 88. feet. Wild figs, very flourishing, grow out of the joints of the Pont du Gard. The fountain of Nismes is so deep, that a stone was 13″ descending from the surface to the bottom.

March 24. From NISMES to ARLES. The plains extending from Nismes to the Rhone in the direction of Arles is broken in one place by a skirt of low hills. They are red and stony at first, but as you approach the Rhone they are of a dark grey mould, with a little sand, and very good. They are in corn and clover, vines, olives, almonds, mulberries, and willow. There are some sheep, no wood, no inclosures.

The high hills of Languedoc are covered with snow. At an antient church in the suburbs of Arles are perhaps some hundreds of antient stone coffins along the road side. The ground is thence called les champs elysées. In a vault in the church are some preciously wrought, and in a back yard are many antient statues, inscriptions &c. Within the town are a part of two Corinthian columns, and of the pediment with which they were crowned, very rich, having belonged to the antient Capitol of the place. But the principal monument here is an Amphitheatre, the external portico of which is tolerably compleat. How many of these porticoes there were, cannot be seen: but at one of the principal gates there are still 5. measuring from out to in 78f. 10I., the vault diminishing inwards. There are 64. arches, each of which is from center to center 20.f. 6.I. Of course the diameter is of 438. feet, or of 450. feet if we suppose the 4. principal arches a little larger than the rest. The ground floor is supported on innumerable vaults. The first story, externally, has a tall pedestal, like a pilaster, between every two arches: the upper story a column, the base of which would indicate it Corinthian. Every column is truncated as low as the impost of the arch, but the arches are all entire. The whole of the upper entablature is gone, and of the Attic, if there was one. Not a single seat of the internal is visible. The whole of the inside, and nearly the whole of the outside is masked by buildings. It is supposed there are 1000. inhabitants within the Amphitheatre. The walls are more entire and firm than those of the Amphitheatre at Nismes. I suspect it's plan and distribution to have been very different from that.

TERRASSON. The plains of the Rhone from Arles to this place are a league or two wide: the mould is of a dark grey, good, in corn and lucerne. Neither wood, nor inclosures. Many sheep.

ST. REMIS. From Terrasson to St. Remis is a plain of a league or two wide, bordered by broken hills of massive rock. It is grey and stony, mostly in olives. Some almonds, mulberries, willows, vines, corn and lucerne. Many sheep. No forest, nor inclosures.

A labouring man's wages here are 150^{tt}, a woman's the half, and fed. 280. ℔. of wheat sells for 42.^{tt} They make no butter here. It costs, when brought, 15.s the ℔. Oil is 10.s the ℔. Tolerable good olive trees yeild one with another, about 20. ℔. of oil. An olive tree must be 20 years old before it has paid it's own expences. It lasts for ever. In 1765. it was so cold that the Rhone was frozen over at Arles for 2. months. In 1767. there was a cold spell of a week which killed all the olive trees. From being fine weather in one hour there was ice hard enough to bear a horse. It killed people on the road. The old roots of the olive trees put out again. Olive grounds sell at 24^{tt} a tree, and lease at 24 sous the tree. The trees are 15. pieds apart. But Lucerne is a more profitable culture. An arpent yeilds 100. quintals of hay a year, worth 3^{tt} a quintal. It is cut 4. or 5. times a year. It is sowed in the broad cast and lasts 5. or 6. years. An arpent of ground for corn rents at 30.^{tt} to 36.^{tt} Their leases are for 6. or 9. years. They plant willow for fire wood, and for hoops to their casks. It seldom rains here in summer. There are some chateaux, many separate farm houses, good and ornamented in the small way, so as to shew that the tenant's whole time is not occupied in procuring physical necessaries.

March 25. ORGON. PONTROYAL. ST. CANNAT. From Orgon to Pontroyal, after quitting the plains of the Rhone, the country seems still to be a plain cut into compartments, by chains of mountains of massive rock running thro it in various directions. From Pontroyal to St. Cannat the land lies rather in basons. The soil is very various. Grey and clay, grey and stony, red and stony; sometimes good, sometimes midling, often barren. We find some golden willows. Towards Pontroyal the hills begin to be in vines, and afterwards is some pasture of green swerd and clover. About Orgon are some inclosures of quickset, others of conical yews planted close. Towards St. Cannat they begin to be of stone.

The high mountains are covered with snow. Some separate farm houses of mud. Near Pontroyal is a canal for watering the country. One branch goes to Terrasson, the other to Arles. At St. Cannat a hill covered with pines. There is no forest; many sheep.

March. 25. 26. 27. 28. AIX. The country is waving, in vines, pasture of green swerd and clover, much inclosed with stone, and abounding with sheep.

On approaching Aix the valley which opens from thence towards the mouth of the Rhone and the sea is rich and beautiful: a perfect grove of olive trees, mixt among which is corn, lucerne and vines. The waste grounds throw out thyme and lavender. Wheat-bread is 3s. the ℔., cow's milk 16s. the quart, sheep's milk 6s., butter of sheep's milk 20s. the ℔., oil of the best quality 12s. the ℔., and 16s. if it be virgin oil. This is what runs from the olive when put into the press, spontaneously: afterwards they are forced by the press and by hot water. Dung costs 10s. the 100 ℔. Their fire wood is chene-vert and willow. The latter is lopped every three years. An ass sells for from 1. to 3. Louis; the best mules for 30. Louis. The best asses will carry 200. ℔., the best horses 300 ℔., the best mules 600 ℔. The temperature of the mineral waters of Aix is 90.° of Farenheit's thermometer at the spout. A mule eats half as much as a horse. The allowance to an ass for the day is a handful of bran mixed with straw. The price of mutton and beef about 6½s the ℔. The beef comes from Auvergne, is poor and bad. The mutton is small but of excellent flavor. The wages of a labouring man are 150ᵗᵗ the year, a woman's 60ᵗᵗ to 66ᵗᵗ and fed. Their bread is half wheat, half rye, made once in 3. or 4. weeks to prevent too great a consumption. In the morning they eat bread with an anchovy, or an onion. Their dinner in the middle of the day is bread, soupe, and vegetables.

Their supper the same. With their vegetables they have always oil and vinegar. The oil costs about 8s. the ℔. They drink what is called Piquette. This is made after the grapes are pressed, by pouring hot water on the pumice. On Sunday they have meat and wine. Their wood for building comes mostly from the Alps down the Durance and Rhone. A stick of pine 50. feet long, girting 6.f. 3.I. at one end, and 2.f. 3.I. at the other costs delivered here 54.^{tt} to 60.^{tt} 60 lb. of wheat cost 7.^{tt} One of their little asses will travel with his burthen about 5. or 6. leagues a day, and day by day: a mule from 6. to 8. leagues. (Note it is 20. American miles from Aix to Marseilles, and they call it 5. leagues. Their league then is of 4. American miles.)

MARSEILLES. The country is hilly, intersected by chains of hills and mountains of massive rock. The soil is reddish, stony and indifferent where best. Whenever there is any soil it is covered with olives. Among these are vines, corn, some lucerne, mulberry, some almonds and willow. Neither inclosures, nor forest. A very few sheep.

On the road I saw one of those little whirlwinds which we have in Virginia. Also some gullied hill-sides. The people are in separate establishments. 10 morning observations of the thermometer, from the 20th. to the 31st. of March inclusive, made at Nismes, St. Remy, Aix and Marseilles give me an average of 52½° and 46° and 61° for the greatest and least morning heats. 9. afternoon observations yeild an average of 62⅔° and 57.° and 66.° the greatest and least. The longest day here from sunrise to sunset is 15H. 14.′ The shortest is 8H.-46.′ The latitude being   . There are no tides in the Mediterranean. It is observed to me that the olive tree grows no where more than 30 leagues distant from that sea. I suppose however that both Spain and Portugal furnish proofs to the contrary, and doubt it's truth as to Asia, Africa and America. There are 6. or 8. months at a time here without rain. The most delicate figs known in Europe are those growing about this place, called figues Marcelloises, or les veritables Marcelloises, to distinguish them from others of inferior quality growing here. These keep any length of time. All others exude a sugar in the spring of the year and become sour. The only process for preserving them is drying them in the sun, without putting any thing to them whatever. They sell at 15s. the lb. while there are others as cheap as   the ℔. I meet here a small dried grape from Smyrna without a seed. There are a few of the plants growing in this neighborhood. The best grape for drying known here is called des Panses. They are very large, with a thick skin and much juice. They are best against a wall of Southern aspect, as their abundance of juice requires a great deal of sun to dry it. Pretty good fig trees are about the size of the Apricot tree and yeild about 20. ℔. of figs when dry, each. But the largest will yeild the value of a Louis. They are sometimes 15.I. diameter. It is said that the Marseilles fig degenerates when transplanted into another part of the country. The leaves of a Mulberry tree will sell for about 3,^{tt} the purchaser gathering them. The CAPER is a creeping plant. It is killed to the roots every winter. In the spring it puts out branches which creep to the distance of 3.f. from the center. The fruit forms on the stem as that extends itself, and must be gathered every day as it forms. This is the work of women. The pistache grows in this neighborhood also, but not very good. They eat them in their milky state. Monsieur de BERGASSE has a wine-cellar 240. pieds long, in which are 120. tons of from 50. to 100 peices each. These tons are 12. pieds diameter; the staves 4.I. thick, the heading 2½ pouces thick. The temperature of his cellar is of 9½° of Reaumur. The best method of packing wine, when bottled, is to lay the bottles on their side, and cover them with sand. The 2d. of April the young figs are formed: the 4th. we have Windsor beans. They have had Asparagus ever since the middle of March. The 5th. I see strawberries and the Guelder rose in blossom. To preserve the raisin, it is first dipped into lye and then dried in the sun. The Aloe grows in the open ground. I measure a mule, not the largest, 5f. 2.I. high. Marseilles is in an amphitheatre, at the mouth of the Vaune, surrounded by high mountains of naked rock, distant 2. or 3. leagues. The country within that amphitheatre is a mixture of small hills, vallies and plains. The latter are naturally rich. The hills and vallies are forced into production. Looking from the chateau de Notre dame de la garde, it would seem as if there was a Bastide for every arpent. The plain lands sell for 100. Louis the Carterelle which is less than an acre. The ground of the arsenal in Marseilles sold for from 15. to 40. Louis the square verge, being nearly the square yard English. In the feilds open to the sea they are obliged to plant rows of canes every here and there to break the force of the wind. Saw at the Chateau Borelli pumps worked by the wind; the axis of the vanes vertical, the house open thus the radius 12.f. 5.I, external circumference 103. feet. 16 windows. The sails 4. feet wide and 12 feet high.

. . . ROZZANO. PARMESAN CHEESE. It is supposed this was formerly made at Parma, and took it's name thence, but none is made there now. It is made thro all the country extending from Milan 150. miles. The most is made about Lodi. The making of butter being connected with the making cheese, both must be described together. There are, in the stables I saw, 85. cows, fed on hay and grass, not on grain. They are milked twice in the 24. hours, 10 cows yeilding at the two milkings a brenta of milk, which is 24. of our gallons. The night's milk is scummed in the morning at day break, when the cows are milked again and the new milk mixed with the old. In 3. hours the whole mass is scummed a second time, the milk remaining in a kettle for cheese, and the cream being put into a cylindrical churn, shaped like a grindstone, 18.I. radius and 14.I. thick. In this churn there are three staves pointing inwardly endwise to break the current of the milk. Thro it's center passes an iron axis with a handle at each end. It is turned about an hour and an half by two men till the butter is produced. Then they pour off the buttermilk and put in some water which they agitate backwards and forwards about a minute, and pour it off. They take out the butter, press it with their hands into loaves, and stamp it. It has no other washing. 16 American gallons of milk yield 15 ℔. of butter, which sells at 24 sous the ℔.

The milk which after being scummed as before had been put into a copper kettle receives it's due quantity of rennet and is gently warmed if the season requires it. In about 4. hours it becomes a slip. Then the whey begins to separate. A little of it is taken out. The curd is then thoroughly broken by a machine like a chocolate mill. A quarter of an ounce of saffron is put to 7. brenta of milk to give colour to the cheese. The kettle is then moved over the hearth, and heated by a quick fire till the curd is hard enough, being broken into small lumps by continual stirring. It is moved off the fire, most of the whey taken out, the curd compressed into a globe by the hand, a linen cloth slipped under it, and it is drawn out in that. A loose hoop is then laid on a bench and the curd, as wrapped in the linen is put into the hoop. It is a little pressed by the hand, the hoop drawn tight, and made fast. A board 2.I. thick is laid on it, and a stone on that of about 20 lb. weight. In an hour the whey is run off and the cheese finished. They sprinkle a little salt on it every other day in summer and every day in winter for 6. weeks. 7. brentas of milk make a cheese of 50. ℔., which requires 6. months to ripen, and is then dried to 45 ℔. It sells on the spot for 88ᵗ the 100. ℔. There are now 150. cheeses in this dairy. They are 19.I. diameter and 6.I. thick. They make a cheese a day in summer, and 2. in 3. days, or 1. in 2. days in winter.

The whey is put back into the kettle, the butter milk poured into it, and of this they make a poor cheese for the country people. The whey of this is given to the hogs. 8. men suffice to keep the cows and do all the business of this dairy. Mascarponi, a kind of curd, is made by pouring some butter milk into cream, which is thereby curdled, and is then pressed in a linen cloth.[4]

May 24. 25. 26. 27. 28. BORDEAUX. The cantons in which the most celebrated wines of Bordeaux are made are MEDOC down the river, GRAVE adjoining the city and the parishes next above; all on the same side of the river. In the first is made red wine principally, in the two last, white. In Medoc they plant the vines in cross rows of 3½ pieds. They keep them so low that poles extended along the rows one way, horizontally, about 15. or 18.I. above the ground, serve to tye the vines to, and leave the cross row open to the plough. In Grave they set the plants in quincunx, i.e. in equilateral triangles of 3½ pieds every side; and they stick a pole of 6. or 8. feet high to every vine separately. The vine stock is sometimes 3. or 4.f. high. They find these two methods equal in culture, duration, quantity and quality. The former however admits the alternative of tending by hand or with the plough. The grafting of the vine, tho a critical operation, is practised with success. When the graft has taken, they bend it into the earth and let it take root above the scar. They begin to yeild an indifferent wine at 3. years old, but not a good one till 25. years, nor after 80, when they begin to yield less, and worse, and must be renewed. They give three or four workings in the year, each worth 70.ᵗ or 75.ᵗ, the journal, which is of

840. square toises, and contains about 3000 plants. They dung a little in Medoc and Grave, because of the poverty of the soil; but very little; as more would affect the wine. The journal yeilds, communibus annis, about 3. pieces of 240. or 250 bottles each. The vineyards of first quality are all worked by their proprietors. Those of the 2d. rent for 300.ᵗ the journal: those of the 3d. at 200.ᵗ They employ a kind of overseer at four or five hundred livres the year, finding him lodging and drink; but he feeds himself. He superintends and directs, but is expected to work but little. If the proprietor has a garden the overseer tends that. They never hire labourers by the year. The day wages for a man are 30. sous, a woman's 15. sous, feeding themselves. The women make the bundles of sarment,⁵ weed, pull off the snails, tie the vines, gather the grapes. During the vintage they are paid high and fed well.

Of RED WINES, there are 4. vineyards of first quality, viz. 1. Chateau Margau, belonging to the Marquis d'Agicourt, who makes about 150. tonneaux of 1000 bottles each. He has engaged to Jernon a merchant. 2. La Tour de Segur, en Saint Lambert, belonging to Monsieur Mirosmenil, who makes 125. tonneaux. 3. Hautbrion, belonging ⅔ to M. le comte de Femelle, who has engaged to Barton a merchant, the other third to the Comte de Toulouse at Toulouse. The whole is 75. tonneaux. 4. Chateau de la Fite, belonging to the President Pichard at Bordeaux, who makes 175 tonneaux. The wines of the three first are not in perfection till 4 years old. Those [of] de la Fite, being somewhat lighter, are good at 3 years, that is, the crop of 1786 is good in the spring of 1789. These growths, of the year 1783 sell now at 2000.ᵗ the tonneau, those of 1784, on account of the superior quality of that vintage, sell at 2400,ᵗ those of 1785 at 1800,ᵗ those of 1786 at 1800,ᵗ tho they sold at first for only 1500.ᵗ RED WINES of the 2d. quality are ROZAN belonging to Madame de Rozan, Dabbadie, ou Lionville, la Rose, Quirouen, Durfort; in all 800 tonneaux, which sell at 1000.ᵗ new. The 3d. class are Calons, Mouton, Gassie, Arboete, Pontette, de Terme, Candale; in all, 2000 tonneaux at 8 or 900.ᵗ After these they are reckoned common wines and sell from 500.ᵗ down to 120.ᵗ the ton. All red wines decline after a certain age, losing colour, flavour, and body. Those of Bordeaux begin to decline at about 7. years old.

Of WHITE WINES, those made in the canton of Grave are most esteemed at Bordeaux. The best crops are 1. PONTAC, which formerly belonged to M. de Pontac, but now to M. de Lamont. He makes 40. tonneaux which sell at 400.ᵗ new. 2. ST. BRISE, belonging to M. de Pontac, 30 tonneaux at 350.ᵗ 3. DE CARBONIUS, belonging to the Benedictine monks, who make 50 tonneaux, and never selling till 3. or 4. years old, get 800.ᵗ the tonneau. Those made in the three parishes next above Grave, and more esteemed at Paris are 1. SAUTERNE. The best crop belongs to M. Diquem at Bordeaux, or to M. de Salus his son in law. 150. tonneaux at 300.ᵗ new and 600.ᵗ old. The next best crop is M. de Fillotte's 100. tonneaux sold at the same price. 2. PRIGNAC. The best is the President du Roy's at Bordeaux. He makes 175 tonneaux, which sell at 300.ᵗ new, and 600.ᵗ old. Those of 1784, for their extraordinary quality sell at 800.ᵗ 3. Barsac. The best belongs to the President Pichard, who makes 150. tonneaux at 280.ᵗ new and 600.ᵗ old. Sauterne is the pleasantest; next Prignac, and lastly Barsac; but Barsac is the strongest; next Prignac, and lastly Sauterne; and all stronger than Grave. There are other good crops made on the same paroisses of Sauterne, Prignac, and Barsac; but none as good as these. There is a Virgin wine, which tho' made of a red grape, is of a light rose colour, because, being made without pressure the colouring matter of the skin does not mix with the juice. There are other white wines from the preceding prices down to 75.ᵗ In general the white wines keep longest. They will be in perfection till 15. or 20. years of age. The best vintage now to be bought is of 1784, both of red and white. There has been no other good year since 1779.

The celebrated vineyards beforementioned are plains, as is generally the canton of Medoc, and that of Grave. The soil of Hautbrion particularly, which I examined, is a sand, in which is near as much round gravel or small stone, and a very little loam: and this is the general soil of Medoc. That of Pontac, which I examined also, is a little different. It is clayey, with a fourth or fifth of fine rotten stone; and of 2. feet depth it becomes all a rotten stone. M. de Lamont tells me he has a kind of grape without seeds, which I did not formerly suppose to exist, but I saw at Marseilles dried raisins from Smyrna, without seeds. I see in his farm at Pontac some plants of white clover and a good deal of yellow; also some small peach trees in the open ground. The principal English wine merchants at Bordeaux are Jernon, Barton, Johnston, Foster, Skinner, Copinger and McCartey. The chief French wine merchants are Feger, Nerac, Brunneau, Jauge, and du Verget. Desgrands, a wine broker, tells me they never mix the wines of first quality: but that they mix the inferior ones to improve them. The smallest wines make the best brandy. They yield about a fifth or sixth.

. . . TOURS is at the 119th. mile stone. Being desirous of enquiring here into a fact stated by Voltaire in his Questions encyclopediques. art. Coquilles, relative to the growth of shells unconnected with animal bodies at the chateau of Monsr. de la Sauvagiere near Tours, I called on M. Gentil premier Secretaire de l'Intendance, to whom the Intendant had written on my behalf at the request of the Marquis de Chastellux. I stated to him the fact as advanced by Voltaire and found he was, of all men, the best to whom I could have addressed myself. He told me he had been in correspondence with Voltaire on that very subject, and was perfectly acquainted with M. de la Sauvagiere, and the Faluniere where the fact is said to have taken place. It is at the Chateau de Grille mont, 6. leagues from Tours on the road to Bordeaux, belonging now to M. d'Orçai. He sais that de la Sauvagiere was a man of truth, and might be relied on for whatever facts he stated as of his own observation: but that he was overcharged with imagination, which, in matters of opinion and theory, often led him beyond his facts: that this feature in his character had appeared principally in what he wrote on the antiquities of Touraine: but that as to the fact in question he believed him. That he himself indeed had not watched the same identical shells, as Sauvagiere had done, growing from small to great: but that he had often seen such masses of those shells of all sizes, from a point to full size, as to carry conviction to his mind that they were in the act of growing: that he had once made a collection of shells for the Emperor's cabinet, reserving duplicates of them for himself; and that these afforded proofs of the same fact: that he afterwards gave those duplicates to a M. du Verget, a physician of Tours of great science and candour, who was collecting on a larger scale, and who was perfectly in sentiment with M. de la Sauvagiere: that not only the Faluniere, but many other places about Tours, would convince any unbiassed observer that shells are a fruit of the earth, spontaneously produced: and he gave me a copy of de la Sauvagiere's Recueil de dissertations, presented him by the author, wherein is one Sur la vegetation spontanée des coquilles du chateau des Places. So far I repeat from him. What are we to conclude? That we have not materials enough yet to form any conclusion. The fact stated by Sauvagiere is not against any law of nature, and is therefore possible: but it is so little analogous to her habitual processes that, if true, it would be extraordinary: that, to command our belief therefore, there should be such a suite of observations as that their untruth would be more extraordinary than the existence of the fact they affirm. The bark of trees, the skin of fruits and animals, the feathers of birds receive their growth and nutriment from the internal circulation of a juice thro' the vessels of the individual they cover. We conclude from analogy then that the shells of the testaceous tribe receive also their growth from a like internal circulation. If it be urged that this does not exclude the possibility of a like shell being produced by the passage of a fluid thro the pores of the circumjacent body, whether of earth, stone, or water; I answer that it is not within the usual oeconomy of nature to use two processes for one species of production. While I withold my assent however from this hypothesis, I must deny it to every other I have ever seen by which their authors pretend to account for the origin of shells in high places. Some of these are against the laws of nature and therefore impossible: and others are built on positions more difficult to assent to than that of de la Sauvagiere. They all suppose these shells to have covered submarine animals, and have then to answer the question How came they 15,000 feet above the level of the sea? and they answer it by demanding what cannot be conceded. One therefore who had rather have no opinion, than a false one, will suppose this question one of those beyond the investigation of human sagacity; or wait till further and fuller observations enable him to decide it....

63. TO MADAME DE CORNY[1]

Paris June 30. 1787.

On my return to Paris, it was among my first attentions to go to the rue Chaussée d'Antin No. 17. and enquire after my friends whom I had left there. I was told they were in England. And how do you like England, madam? I know your taste for the works of art gives you a little disposition to Anglomany. Their mechanics certainly excel all others in some lines. But be just to your own nation. They have not patience, it is true, to sit rubbing a peice of steel from morning to night as a lethargic Englishman will do, full charged with porter. But does not their benevolence, their chearfulness, their amability, when compared with the growling temper and manners of the people among whom you are, compensate their want of patience? I am in hopes that when the splendor of their shops, which is all that is worth seeing in London, shall have lost the charm of novelty, you will turn a wishful eye to the good people of Paris, and find that you cannot be so happy with any others. The Bois de Boulogne invites you earnestly to come and survey it's beautiful verdure, to retire to it's umbrage from the heats of the season. I was through it to-day, as I am every day. Every tree charged me with this invitation to you. Passing by la Muette, it wished for you as a mistress. You want a country house. This is for sale, and in the Bois de Boulogne, wh[ich] I have always insisted to be most worthy of your preference. Come then and buy it.   If I had had confidence in your speedy return, I should have embarrassed you in earnest with my little daughter. But an impatience to have her with me after her separation from her friends, added to a respect for your ease, have induced me to send a servant for her.

I tell you no news, because you have correspondents infinitely more au fait of the details of Paris than I am. And I offer you no services, because I hope you will come as soon as the letter could which should command them. Be assured however that no body is more disposed to render them, nor entertains for you a more sincere and respectful attachment than him who, after charging you with his compliments to Monsieur de Corny, has the honour of offering you the homage of those sentiments of distinguished esteem & regard with which he is, dear Madam, your most obedient & most humble servant.

Th: Jefferson

64. TO JOHN ADAMS

Dear Sir   *Paris July 1. 1787.*
I returned about three weeks ago from a very useless voiage. Useless, I mean, as to the object which first suggested it, that of trying the effect of the mineral waters of Aix en Provence on my hand. I tried these because recommended among six or eight others as equally beneficial, and because they would place me at the beginning of a tour to the seaports of Marseilles, Bourdeaux, Nantes and Lorient which I had long meditated, in hopes that a knowlege of the places and persons concerned in our commerce and the information to be got from them might enable me sometimes to be useful. I had expected to satisfy myself at Marseilles of the causes of the difference of quality between the rice of Carolina and that of Piedmont which is brought in quantities to Marseilles. Not being able to do it, I made an excursion of three weeks into the rice country beyond the Alps, going through it from Vercelli to Pavia about 60 miles. I found the difference to be, not in the management as had been supposed both here and in Carolina, but in the species of rice, and I hope to enable them in Carolina to begin the Cultivation of the Piedmont rice and carry it on hand in hand with their own that they may supply both qualities, which is absolutely necessary at this market. I had before endeavored to lead the depot of rice from Cowes to Honfleur and hope to get it received there on such terms as may draw that branch of commerce from England to this country. It is an object of 250,000 guineas a year. While passing thro' the towns of Turin, Milan and Genoa, I satisfied myself of the practicability of introducing our whale oil for their consumption and I suppose it would be equally so in the other great cities of that country. I was sorry that I was not authorized to set the matter on foot. The merchants with whom I chose to ask conferences, met me freely, and communicated fully, knowing I was in a public character. I

could however only prepare a disposition to meet our oil merchants. On the article of tobacco I was more in possession of my ground, and put matters into a train for inducing their government to draw their tobaccos directly from the U.S. and not as heretofore from G.B. I am now occupied with the new ministry here to put the concluding hand to the new regulations for our commerce with this country, announced in the letter of M. de Calonnes which I sent you last fall. I am in hopes in addition to those, to obtain a suppression of the duties on Tar, pitch, and turpentine, and an extension of the privileges of American *whale* oil, to their *fish* oils in general. I find that the quantity of Codfish oil brought to Lorient is considerable. This being got off hand (which will be in a few days) the chicaneries and vexations of the farmers[1] on the article of tobacco, and their elusions of the order of Bernis, call for the next attention. I have reason to hope good dispositions in the new ministry towards our commerce with this country. Besides endeavoring on all occasions to multiply the points of contact and connection with this country, which I consider as our surest mainstay under every event, I have had it much at heart to remove from between us every subject of misunderstanding or irritation. Our debts to the king, to the officers, and the farmers are of this description. The having complied with no part of our engagements in these draws on us a great deal of censure, and occasioned a language in the Assemblées des notables very likely to produce dissatisfaction between us. Dumas being on the spot in Holland, I had asked of him some time ago, in confidence, his opinion on the practicability of transferring these debts from France to Holland, and communicated his answer to Congress, pressing them to get you to go over to Holland and try to effect this business. Your knowledge of the ground and former successes occasioned me to take this liberty without consulting you, because I was sure you would not weigh your personal trouble against public good. I have had no answer from Congress, but hearing of your journey to Holland have hoped that some money operation had led you there. If it related to the debts of this country I would ask a communication of what you think yourself at liberty to communicate, as it might change the form of my answers to the eternal applications I receive. The debt to the officers of France carries an interest of about

2000 guineas, so we may suppose it's principal is between 30. and 40,000. This makes more noise against [us] than all our other debts put together.

I send you the arrets which begin the reformation here, and some other publications respecting America: together with copies of letters received from Obryon and Lambe. It is believed that a naval armament has been ordered at Brest in correspondence with that of England. We know certainly that orders are given to form a camp in the neighborhood of Brabant, and that Count Rochambeau has the command of it. It's amount I cannot assert. Report says 15,000 men. This will derange the plans of oeconomy. I take the liberty of putting under your cover a letter for Mrs. Kinloch of South Carolina, with a packet, and will trouble you to enquire for her and have them delivered. The packet is of great consequence, and therefore referred to her care, as she will know the safe opportunities of conveying it. Should you not be able to find her, and can forward the packet to it's address by any very safe conveiance I will beg you to do it. I have the honour to be with sentiments of the most perfect friendship & esteem Dear Sir your most obedient & most humble servant,

Th: Jefferson

65. TO MARIA COSWAY

Paris July 1. 1787.

You conclude, Madam, from my long silence that I am gone to the other world. Nothing else would have prevented my writing to you so long. I have not thought of you the less. But I took a peep only into Elysium. I entered it at one door, and came out at another, having seen, as I past, only Turin, Milan, and Genoa. I calculated the hours it would have taken to carry me on to Rome. But they were exactly so many more than I had to spare. Was not this provoking? In thirty hours from Milan I could have been at the espousals of the Doge and Adriatic. But I am born to lose every thing I love. Why were you not with me? So many enchanting scenes which only wanted your pencil to consecrate them to fame. Whenever you go to Italy you must pass at the Col de Tende. You may go in your chariot in full trot from Nice to Turin, as if there were no mountain. But have your pallet and pencil ready: for you will be sure to stop in the passage, at the chateau de Saorgio. Imagine to yourself, madam, a castle and village hanging to a cloud in front. On one hand a mountain cloven through to let pass a gurgling stream; on the other a river, over which is thrown a magnificent bridge; the whole formed into a bason, it's sides shagged with rocks, olive trees, vines, herds, &c. I insist on your painting it.

How do you do? How have you done? and when are you coming here? If not at all, what did you ever come for? Only to make people miserable at losing you. Consider that you are but 4. days from Paris. If you come by the way of St. Omers, which is but two posts further, you will see a new and beautiful country. Come then, my dear Madam, and we will breakfast every day á l'Angloise, hie away to the Desert,[1] dine under the bowers of Marly, and forget that we are ever to part again.   I received, in the moment of my departure your favor of Feb. 15. and long to receive another: but lengthy, warm, and flowing from the heart, as do the sentiments of friendship & esteem with which I have the honor to be, dear Madam, your affectionate friend & servant,

Th: Jefferson

66. TO THOMAS MANN RANDOLPH, JR.

Sir   *Paris July 6. 1787.*
Your favor of April 14. came here during my absence on a journey through the Southern parts of France and Northern of Italy, from which I am but lately returned: this cause alone has prevented your receiving a more early answer to it. I am glad to find that among the various branches of science presenting themselves to your mind you have fixed on that of Politics as your principal pursuit. Your country will derive from this a more immediate and sensible benefit. She has much for you to do. For tho' we may say with confidence that the worst of the American constitutions is better than the best which ever existed before in any other country, and that they are wonderfully

perfect for a first essay, yet every human essay must have defects. It will remain therefore to those now coming on the stage of public affairs to perfect what has been so well begun by those going off it. Mathematics, Natural philosophy, Natural history, Anatomy, Chemistry, Botany, will become amusements for your hours of relaxation, and auxiliaries to your principal studies. Precious and delightful ones they will be. As soon as such a foundation is laid in them as you may build on as you please hereafter, I suppose you will proceed to your main objects, Politics, Law, Rhetoric and History. As to these, the place where you study them is absolutely indifferent. I should except Rhetoric, a very essential member of them, and which I suppose must be taught to advantage where you are: you would do well therefore to attend the public exercises in this branch also, and to do it with very particular diligence. This being done, the question arises, where you shall fix yourself for studying Politics, Law, and History? I should not hesitate to decide in favor of France, because you will at the same time be learning to speak the language of that country, become absolutely essential under our present circumstances. The best method of doing this would be to fix yourself in some family where there are women and children, in Passy, Auteuil or some other of the little towns in reach of Paris. The principal hours of the day you will attend to your studies, and in those of relaxation associate with the family. You will learn to speak better from women and children in three months, than from men in a year. Such a situation too will render more easy a due attention to oeconomy of time and money. Having pursued your main studies here about two years, and acquired a facility in speaking French, take a tour of 4. or 5. months through this country and Italy, return then to Virginia and pass a year in Williamsburg under the care of Mr. Wythe, and you will be ready to enter on the public stage, with superior advantages. I have proposed to you to carry on the study of the law, with that of Politics and History. Every political measure will for ever have an intimate connection with the laws of the land; and he who knows nothing of these will always be perplexed and often foiled by adversaries having the advantage of that knolege over him. Besides it is a source of infinite comfort to reflect that under every change of fortune we have a resource in ourselves from which we may be able to derive an honourable subsistence. I would therefore propose not only the study, but the practice of the law for some time, to possess yourself of the habit of public speaking.   With respect to modern languages, French, as I have before observed, is indispensible. Next to this the Spanish is most important to an American. Our connection with Spain is already important and will become daily more so. Besides this the antient part of American history is written chiefly in Spanish. To a person who would make a point of reading and speaking French and Spanish, I should doubt the utility of learning Italian. These three languages, being all degeneracies from the Latin, resemble one another so much that I doubt the possibility of keeping in the head a distinct knowledge of them all. I suppose that he who learns them all will speak a compound of the three, and neither perfectly.— The journey which I propose to you need not be expensive, and would be very useful. With your talents and industry, with science, and that stedfast honesty which eternally pursues right, regardless of consequences, you may promise yourself every thing—but health, without which there is no happiness. An attention to health then should take place of every other object. The time necessary to secure this by active exercises, should be devoted to it in preference to every other pursuit. I know the difficulty with which a studious man tears himself from his studies at any given moment of the day. But his happiness and that of his family depends on it. The most uninformed mind with a healthy body, is happier than the wisest valetudinarian.—I need not tell you that if I can be useful to you in any part of this or any other plan you shall adopt, you will make me happy by commanding my services.

Will you be so good, Sir, as to return my most respectful thanks for the diploma with which I am honored by the society instituted with you for the encouragement of the study of Natural history. I am afraid it will never be in my power to contribute any thing to the object of the institution. Circumstances have thrown me into a very different line of life; and not choice, [as] I am happy to find is your case.—In the year 1781. while confined to my room by a fall from my horse, I wrote some Notes in answer to the enquiries of M. de Marbois as to the Natural and Political state of Virginia. They were hasty and indigested: yet as some of these touch slightly on some objects of it's natural history, I will take the liberty of asking the society to accept a copy of them. For the same reason, and because too they touch on the political condition of our country, I will beg leave to present you with a copy, and ask the favor of you to find a conveyance for them from London to Edinburgh. They are printing by Stockdale, bookseller Piccadilly, and will be ready in 3. or 4. weeks from this time. I will direct him to deliver two copies to your order.   Repeating constantly the proffer of my services, I shall only add assurances of the esteem and attachment with which I am Dear Sir Your friend & servt.,

Th: Jefferson

67. TO NICHOLAS LEWIS

Dear Sir   *Paris July 29. 1787.*
In my letter of Dec. 19. 1786. I informed you that, as you had supposed in your's of March 14. that the balance of bonds and profits of the estate to that time would pay all the debts then known to you except my sister Nancy's,[1] I was desirous of laying our shoulder seriously to the paiment of Farrell & Jones's, and McCaul's debts; that I should make propositions to them on that subject. I did so. These propositions were 1. To pay to Jones 400£ sterl. a year and to McCaul 200£ sterl., or to the former if he preferred it two thirds of the profits of my estate and to the latter one third. 2. That the crop of 1787. should commence these paiments. 3. That no interest should be allowed on their debts from Apr. 19. 1775 to Apr. 19. 1783 (being 8. years). 4. That their accounts should remain perfectly open to settlement and rectification, notwithstanding the paiments which should be made. McCaul has acceded very contentedly to these proposals. I added some other conditions to Jones, not worth mentioning as he does not accede as yet. I think however he will accede. I consider myself as so much bound in honor to the sacred execution of this agreement that what the profits fall short of enabling us to pay at any time I would chuse to have made up by a sale of something or another. I mentioned to you in my letter also that I could always get 36/ Virginia money for my tobacco deliv-

ered at Havre and proposed your having it sent there. Further reflection and information of the Virginia prices convince me it would be best to send them either to Havre or to Bordeaux, at either of which places I could have them attended to. I find that my old friend A. Donald is settled at Richmond, is concerned in the tobacco trade, and particularly sends to Havre. I am confident he would take on himself the having my tobaccoes shipped to me. The earlier they would come in the season, the better alwais. So far I had settled in my own mind the plan for extinguishing as fast as we could these two great debts, when I received from Mr. Eppes a letter of May 2. 1787. wherein he tells me he had been with you in Sep. 1786. that you had computed together all the former debts (except my sister Nancy's) due from the estate, and all due to it; and that there was still a balance of 1200£ against it, to pay which there would be nothing but the crop of 1786. two thirds of which would be consumed by negroes clothing and taxes. This account threatens a total derangement of my plan for payment of my great debts. I had observed that by a statement in your letter of March 14. of the probable proceeds of the crop of 1785 (about 50 hogsheads of tobacco) that the profits of the few house servants and tradesmen hired out were as much as those of the whole estate, and therefore suggested to you the hiring out the whole estate. The torment of mind I endure till the moment shall arrive when I shall not owe a shilling on earth is such really as to render life of little value. I cannot decide to sell my lands. I have sold too much of them already, and they are the only sure provision for my children. Nor would I willingly sell the slaves as long as there remains any prospect of paying my debts with their labour. In this I am governed solely by views to their happiness which will render it worth their while to use extraordinary cautions for some time to enable me to put them ultimately on an easier footing, which I will do the moment they have paid the debts due from the estate, two thirds of which have been contracted by purchasing them. I am therefore strengthened in the idea of renting out my whole estate; not to any one person, but in different parts to different persons, as experience proves that it is only small concerns that are gainful, and it would be my interest that the tenants should make a reasonable gain. The lease I made to Garth and Moseley would be a good model.

I do not recollect whether in that there was reserved a right of distraining on the lands for the whole rent. If not, such a clause would be essential, especially in the present relaxed state of the laws. I know there was in that no provision against paper money. This is still more essential. The best way of stating the rent would be in ounces of silver. The rent in that lease, tho expressed in current money, was meant to be 11.£ sterling a titheable.[2] When we consider the rise in the price of tobacco, it should balance any difference for the worse which may have taken place in the lands in Albemarle, so as to entitle us there to equal terms. In Cumberland, Goochland, Bedford, where the lands are better, perhaps better terms might be expected. Calculating this on the number of working slaves, it holds up to us a clear revenue capable of working off the debts in a reasonable time. Think of it, my dear Sir, and if you do not find it disadvantageous be so good as to try to execute it, by leases of 3, 4, or 5 years: not more, because no dependance can be reposed in our laws continuing the same for any length of time. Indeed 3. years might be the most eligible term. The mill should be separated from the lease, finished, and rented by itself. All the lands reserved to my own use in Garth and Mousley's lease should still be reserved, and the privileges of that lease in general. House negroes still to be hired separately. The old and infirm, who could not be hired, or whom it would be a pity to hire, could perhaps be employed in raising cotton, or some other easy culture on lands to be reserved; George still to be reserved to take care of my orchards, grasses &c. The lands in Albemarle should be relieved by drawing off a good number of the labourers to Bedford, where a better hire might be expected and more lands be opened there. I feel all the weight of the objection that we cannot guard the negroes perfectly against ill usage. But in a question between hiring and selling them (one of which is necessary) the hiring will be temporary only, and will end in their happiness; whereas if we sell them, they will be subject to equal ill usage, without a prospect of change. It is for their good therefore ultimately, and it appears to promise a relief to me within such a term as I would be willing to wait for. I do not mention the rate of hire with a view to tie you up to that, but merely to shew that hiring presents a hopeful prospect. I should rely entirely on your judgment for that, for the choice of kind and hopeful tenants, and for every other circumstance. The bacon hams you were so kind as to send to Mr. Buchanan for me, I never heard of. The difficulty of getting them here renders it not worth attempting again. I will put into this letter some more seeds of the Spanish Sainfoin lest those formerly sent should have miscarried. The present situation of Europe threatens a war, which if it breaks out will probably be a very general one. France and England are so little in a condition for war that we may still expect they will do much to avoid it. Should it take place, I fear the scale against this country would be too heavy.

I must pray of you to make all the arrangements possible for enabling me to comply with the first years paiment of my debts, that is to say the paiment for this present year, which is to be made in the city of London the next spring. Apologies for all the trouble I give you would only shew you how sensible I am of your goodness. I have proposed the extraordinary trouble of the leases with less reluctance, because it will be taken once for all, and will be a relief in the end. Be so good as to assure Mrs. Lewis of my attachment and my wishes for her health and happiness as well as that of your whole family. I am with sentiments of the most sincere esteem and respect Dear Sir Your friend & servant,

Th: Jefferson

68. TO PETER CARR, WITH ENCLOSURE

Dear Peter   *Paris Aug. 10. 1787.*
I have received your two letters of Decemb. 30. and April 18. and am very happy to find by them, as well as by letters from Mr. Wythe, that you have been so fortunate as to attract his notice and good will: I am sure you will find this to have been one of the most fortunate events of your life, as I have ever been sensible it was of mine. I inclose you a sketch of the sciences to which I would wish you to apply in such order as Mr. Wythe shall advise: I mention also the books in them worth your reading, which submit to his correction. Many of these are among your father's books, which you should have brought to you. As

I do not recollect those of them not in his library, you must write to me for them, making out a catalogue of such as you think you shall have occasion for in 18 months from the date of your letter, and consulting Mr. Wythe on the subject. To this sketch I will add a few particular observations.

1. Italian. I fear the learning this language will confound your French and Spanish. Being all of them degenerated dialects of the Latin, they are apt to mix in conversation. I have never seen a person speaking the three languages who did not mix them. It is a delightful language, but late events having rendered the Spanish more useful, lay it aside to prosecute that.

2. Spanish. Bestow great attention on this, and endeavor to acquire an accurate knowledge of it. Our future connections with Spain and Spanish America will render that language a valuable acquisition. The antient history of a great part of America too is written in that language. I send you a dictionary.

3. Moral philosophy. I think it lost time to attend lectures in this branch. He who made us would have been a pitiful bungler if he had made the rules of our moral conduct a matter of science. For one man of science, there are thousands who are not. What would have become of them? Man was destined for society. His morality therefore was to be formed to this object. He was endowed with a sense of right and wrong merely relative to this. This sense is as much a part of his nature as the sense of hearing, seeing, feeling; it is the true foundation of morality, and not the το χαλον[1] truth, &c., as fanciful writers have imagined. The moral sense, or conscience, is as much a part of man as his leg or arm. It is given to all human beings in a stronger or weaker degree, as force of members is given them in a greater or less degree. It may be strengthened by exercise, as may any particular limb of the body. This sense is submitted indeed in some degree to the guidance of reason; but it is a small stock which is required for this: even a less one than what we call Common sense. State a moral case to a ploughman and a professor. The former will decide it as well, and often better than the latter, because he has not been led astray by artificial rules. In this branch therefore read good books because they will encourage as well as direct your feelings. The writings of Sterne particularly

form the best course of morality that ever was written. Besides these read the books mentioned in the inclosed paper; and above all things lose no occasion of exercising your dispositions to be grateful, to be generous, to be charitable, to be humane, to be true, just, firm, orderly, couragious &c. Consider every act of this kind as an exercise which will strengthen your moral faculties, and increase your worth.

4. Religion. Your reason is now mature enough to receive this object. In the first place divest yourself of all bias in favour of novelty and singularity of opinion. Indulge them in any other subject rather than that of religion. It is too important, and the consequences of error may be too serious. On the other hand shake off all the fears and servile prejudices under which weak minds are servilely crouched. Fix reason firmly in her seat, and call to her tribunal every fact, every opinion. Question with boldness even the existence of a god; because, if there be one, he must more approve the homage of reason, than that of blindfolded fear. You will naturally examine first the religion of your own country. Read the bible then, as you would read Livy or Tacitus. The facts which are within the ordinary course of nature you will believe on the authority of the writer, as you do those of the same kind in Livy and Tacitus. The testimony of the writer weighs in their favor in one scale, and their not being against the laws of nature does not weigh against them. But those facts in the bible which contradict the laws of nature, must be examined with more care, and under a variety of faces. Here you must recur to the pretensions of the writer to inspiration from god. Examine upon what evidence his pretensions are founded, and whether that evidence is so strong as that it's falshood would be more improbable than a change of the laws of nature in the case he relates. For example in the book of Joshua we are told the sun stood still several hours. Were we to read that fact in Livy or Tacitus we should class it with their showers of blood, speaking of statues, beasts &c., but it is said that the writer of that book was inspired. Examine therefore candidly what evidence there is of his having been inspired. The pretension is entitled to your enquiry, because millions believe it. On the other hand you are Astronomer enough to know how contrary it is to the law of nature that a body revolving on it's axis, as the earth does, should have stopped, should not by that

sudden stoppage have prostrated animals, trees, buildings, and should after a certain time have resumed it's revolution, and that without a second general prostration. Is this arrest of the earth's motion, or the evidence which affirms it, most within the law of probabilities? You will next read the new testament. It is the history of a personage called Jesus. Keep in your eye the opposite pretensions. 1. Of those who say he was begotten by god, born of a virgin, suspended and reversed the laws of nature at will, and ascended bodily into heaven: and 2. of those who say he was a man, of illegitimate birth, of a benevolent heart, enthusiastic mind, who set out without pretensions to divinity, ended in believing them, and was punished capitally for sedition by being gibbeted according to the Roman law which punished the first commission of that offence by whipping, and the second by exile or death *in furcâ.*[2] See this law in the Digest Lib. 48. tit. 19 § 28.3. and Lipsius Lib. 2. de cruce. cap. 2. These questions are examined in the books I have mentioned under the head of religion, and several others. They will assist you in your enquiries, but keep your reason firmly on the watch in reading them all. Do not be frightened from this enquiry by any fear of it's consequences. If it ends in a belief that there is no god, you will find incitements to virtue in the comfort and pleasantness you feel in it's exercise, and the love of others which it will procure you. If you find reason to believe there is a god, a consciousness that you are acting under his eye, and that he approves you, will be a vast additional incitement. If that there be a future state, the hope of a happy existence in that increases the appetite to deserve it; if that Jesus was also a god, you will be comforted by a belief of his aid and love. In fine, I repeat that you must lay aside all prejudice on both sides, and neither believe nor reject any thing because any other person, or description of persons have rejected or believed it. Your own reason is the only oracle given you by heaven, and you are answerable not for the rightness but uprightness of the decision.—I forgot to observe when speaking of the New testament that you should read all the histories of Christ, as well of those whom a council of ecclesiastics have decided for us to be Pseudo-evangelists, as those they named Evangelists, because these Pseudo-evangelists pretended to inspiration as much as the others, and you are to judge their pretensions by your own reason, and not by the reason of those ecclesiastics. Most of these are lost. There are some however still extant, collected by Fabricius which I will endeavor to get and send you.

5. Travelling. This makes men wiser, but less happy. When men of sober age travel, they gather knowlege which they may apply usefully for their country, but they are subject ever after to recollections mixed with regret, their affections are weakened by being extended over more objects, and they learn new habits which cannot be gratified when they return home. Young men who travel are exposed to all these inconveniences in a higher degree, to others still more serious, and do not acquire that wisdom for which a previous foundation is requisite by repeated and just observations at home. The glare of pomp and pleasure is analogous to the motion of their blood, it absorbs all their affection and attention, they are torn from it as from the only good in this world, and return to their home as to a place of exile and condemnation. Their eyes are for ever turned back to the object they have lost, and it's recollection poisons the residue of their lives. Their first and most delicate passions are hackneyed on unworthy objects here, and they carry home only the dregs, insufficient to make themselves or any body else happy. Add to this that a habit of idleness, an inability to apply themselves to business is acquired and renders them useless to themselves and their country. These observations are founded in experience. There is no place where your pursuit of knowlege will be so little obstructed by foreign objects as in your own country, nor any wherein the virtues of the heart will be less exposed to be weakened. Be good, be learned, and be industrious, and you will not want the aid of travelling to render you precious to your country, dear to your friends, happy within yourself. I repeat my advice to take a great deal of exercise, and on foot. Health is the first requisite after morality. Write to me often and be assured of the interest I take in your success, as well as of the warmth of those sentiments of attachment with which I am, dear Peter, your affectionate friend,

Th: Jefferson

P.S. Let me know your age in your next letter. Your cousins here are well and desire to be remembered to you.

ENCLOSURE

Antient history. Herodot. Thucyd. Xenoph. hellen. Xenoph. Anab. Q. Curt. Just.

Livy. Polybius. Sallust. Caesar. Suetonius. Tacitus. Aurel. Victor. Herodian.

Gibbons' decline of the Roman empire. Milot histoire ancienne.

Mod. hist. English. Tacit. Germ. & Agricole. Hume to the end of H.VI. then Habington's E.IV.—Sr. Thomas Moor's E.5. & R.3.—Ld. Bacon's H.7.—Ld. Herbert of Cherbury's H.8.—K. Edward's journal (in Burnet) Bp. of Hereford's E.6. & Mary.—Cambden's Eliz. Wilson's Jac.I. Ludlow (omit Clarendon as too seducing for a young republican. By and by read him) Burnet's Charles 2. Jac.2. Wm. & Mary & Anne.—Ld. Orrery down to George 1. & 2.—Burke's G.3. Robertson's hist. of Scotland.

American. Robertson's America.—Douglass's N. America.—Hutcheson's Massachusets, Smith's N. York.—Smith's N. Jersey.—Franklin's review of Pennsylvania. Smith's, Stith's, Keith's, & Beverley's hist. of Virginia.

Foreign. Mallet's Northn. Antiquities by Percy.—Puffendorf's histy. of Europe & Martiniere's of Asia, Africa & America.—Milot histoire Moderne. Voltaire histoire universelle.—Milot hist. de France. —Mariana's hist. of Spain in Spa[nish.]—Robertson's Charles V.— Watson's Phil. II. & III.—Grotii Belgica.

Mosheim's Ecclesiastical history.

Poetry. Homer—Milton—Ossian—Sophocles—Aeschylus—Eurip.— Metastasio—Shakesp.—Theocritus—Anacreon [. . .]

Mathematics. Bezout & whatever else Mr. Madison recommends.

Astronomy. Delalande &c. as Mr. Madison shall recommend.

Natural Philosophy. Musschenbroeck.

Botany. Linnaei Philosophia Botanica—Genera Plantarum—Species plantarum—Gronovii flora [Virginica.]

Chemistry. Fourcroy.

Agriculture. Home's principles of Agriculture—Tull &c.

Anatomy. Cheselden.

Morality. The Socratic dialogues—Cicero's Philosophies—Kaim's principles of Natl. religion—Helvetius de l'esprit et de l'homme. Locke's Essay.—Lucretius—Traité de Morale & du Bon[heur]

Religion. Locke's Conduct of the mind.—Middleton's works—Boling-
broke's philosoph. works—Hume's essays—Voltaire's works—Beattie.
Politics & Law. Whatever Mr. Wythe pleases, who will be so good as to
correct also all the preceding articles which are only intended as a
ground work to be finished by his pencil.

69. TO GEORGE GILMER[1]

Dear Doctor   *Paris Aug. 12. 1787.*
Your letter of Jan. 9. 1787. came safely to hand in the month of June
last. Unluckily you forgot to sign it, and your hand writing is so Pro-
tean that one cannot be sure it is yours. To increase the causes of in-
certitude it was dated *Pen-park,* a name which I only knew as the seat
of John Harmer. The hand writing too being somewhat in his style
made me ascribe it hastily to him, indorse it with his name, and let it
lie in my bundle to be answered at leisure. That moment of leisure arriving, I set down to answer it to John Harmer, and now for the first
time discover marks of it's being yours, and particularly those expressions of friendship to myself and family which you have ever been so
good as to entertain, and which are to me among the most precious
possessions. I wish my sense of this, and my desires of seeing you rich
and happy may not prevent my seeing any difficulty in the case you
state of George Harmer's wills: which as you state them are thus.
    1. A will dated Dec. 26. 1779. written in his own hand and devising
to his brother the estates he had received from him.
    2. Another will dated June 25. 1782. written also in his own hand,
devising his estate to trustees to be conveyed to such of his relations
J.H. J.L. or H.L. as should become capable of acquiring property, or, on
failure of that, to be sold and the money remitted them.
    3. A third will dated Sep. 12. 1786. devising all his estate at Mar-
rowbone and his tracts at Horsepasture and Poison feild to you, which
will is admitted to record and of course has been duly executed. You
say the learned are divided on these wills. Yet I see no cause of division, as it requires little learning to decide that 'the first deed, and last

will must always prevail.' I am afraid therefore the difficulty may arise on the want of words of inheritance in the devise to you: for you state it as a devise to 'George Gilmer' (without adding 'and to his heirs') of 'all the *estate* called Marrowbone' 'the *tract* called Horsepasture' and 'the *tract* called Poisoned feild.' If the question is on this point, and you have copied the words of the will exactly, I suppose you take an estate in fee simple in Marrowbone, and for life only in Horsepasture and Poisoned feild, the want of words of inheritance in the two last cases being supplied as to the first by the word 'estate' which has been re-peatedly decided to be descriptive of the quantum of interest devised, as well as of it's locality. I am in hopes however you have not copied the words exactly, that there are words of inheritance to all the de-vises, as the testator certainly knew their necessity, and that the con-flict will be only between the different wills, in which case I see nothing which can be opposed to the last. I shall be very happy to eat at Pen-park some of the good mutton and beef of Marrowbone, Horsepasture and Poisoned feild, with yourself and Mrs. Gilmer and my good old neighbors. I am as happy no where else and in no other society, and all my wishes end, where I hope my days will end, at Monticello. Too many scenes of happiness mingle themselves with all the recollections of my native woods and feilds, to suffer them to be supplanted in my affection by any other. I consider myself here as a traveller only, and not a resident. My commission expires the next spring, and if not renewed, I shall of course return then. If renewed, I shall remain here some time longer. How much I cannot say; yet my wishes shorten the period. Among the strongest inducements will be that of your society and Mrs. Gilmer's, which I am glad to find brought more within reach by your return to Pen-park. My daughters are importunate to return also. Patsy enjoys good health, and is grow-ing to my stature. Polly arrived here about a month ago, after a favor-able voiage, and in perfect health. My own health has been as good as ever, after the first year's probation. The accident of a dislocated wrist, badly set, has I fear deprived me for ever of almost every use of my right hand. Nor is the extent of the evil as yet known, the hand with-ering, the fingers remaining swelled and crooked, and losing rather than gaining in point of suppleness. It is now eleven months since the accident. I am able however to write, tho for a long time I was not so. This inability was succeeded by a journey into the Southern parts of France and Northern of Italy, which added to the length of the chasm in my correspondence with my friends. If you knew how agreeable to me are the details of the small news of my neighborhood, your charity would induce you to write frequently. Your letters lodged in the post office at Richmond (to be forwarded to N. York) come with certainty. We are doubtful yet whether there will be war or not. Present me with warm affection to Mrs. Gilmer and be assured yourself of the unvarying sentiments of esteem and attachment with which I am Dear Doctor your sincere friend & servant,

Th: Jefferson

70. TO DAVID HUMPHREYS

Dear Sir   *Paris Aug. 14. 1787.*
I remember when you left us, it was with a promise to supply all the defects of correspondence in our friends, of which we complained, and which you had felt in common with us. Yet I have received but one letter from you which was dated June 5. 1786. and I answered it Aug. 14. 1786. Dropping that however and beginning a new account, I will observe to you that wonderful improvements are making here in various lines. In architecture the wall of circumvallation round Paris and the palaces by which we are to be let in and out are nearly compleated, 4 hospitals are to be built instead of the old hotel-dieu, one of the old bridges has all it's houses demolished and a second nearly so, a new bridge is begun at the Place Louis XV. the Palais royal is gutted, a considerable part in the center of the garden being dug out, and a subterranean circus begun wherein will be equestrian exhibitions &c. In society the habit habillé is almost banished, and they begin to go even to great suppers in frock[1]: the court and diplomatic corps however must always be excepted. They are too high to be reached by any improvement. They are the last refuge from which etiquette, formality and folly will be driven. Take away these and they would be on a level with other people. The assemblée des Notables have done a great deal

of good here. Various abolitions of abusive laws, have taken place and will take place. The government is allotted into subordinate administrations, called Provincial assemblies, to be chosen by the people; great reductions of expence in the trappings of the king, queen, and princes, in the department of war &c. Notwithstanding this, the discovery of the abuses of public money, some expences of the court not in unison with the projects of reform, and the new taxes, have raised within a few weeks a spirit of discontent so loud and so general as I did not think them susceptible of. They speak in all companies, in coffeehouses, in the streets, as if there was no Bastile: and indeed to confine all offenders in this way, the whole kingdom should be converted into a Bastile. The parliament of Paris puts itself at the head of this opposition. The king has been obliged to hold a bed of justice to enforce the registering the new taxes. The parliament proposes to forbid their execution, and this may possibly be followed by their exile. The mild and patriotic spirit of the new ministry, and the impossibility of finding subjects to make a new parliament, may perhaps avoid this extremity. It is not impossible but that all the domestic disturbances may be calmed by foreign difficulties. War has within a few days past become more probable. Tho the kings of England and Prussia had openly espoused the views of the Stadholder, yet negotiations were going on which gave hopes of accomodation. But the stoppage of the Princess of Orange, on her way to excite commotions at the Hague, kindled the kingly pride of her brother, and without consulting any body, he ordered 20,000 men to march instantly to revenge this insult. The stoppage of the sister of a king then is sufficient cause to sacrifice the lives of hundreds of thousands of better people and to lay the most fertile parts of Europe in ashes. Since this hasty movement, which is pertinaciously pursued, the English squadron has sailed Westwardly, and will be followed by a squadron from Brest, while a land army moves on to the confines of Holland. Still however the negociations are continued, and it is thought that the fiscal distresses of the principal powers may yet prevent war. So much for the blessings of having kings, and magistrates who would be kings. From these events our young republics may learn many useful lessons, never to call on foreign powers to settle their differences, to guard against hereditary magistrates, to prevent their citizens from becoming so established in wealth and power as to be thought worthy of alliance by marriage with the neices, sisters &c. of kings, and in short to besiege the throne of heaven with eternal prayers to extirpate from creation this class of human lions, tygers and mammouts called kings; from whom, let him perish, who does not say 'good lord deliver us,' and that so we may say, one and all, or perish is the fervent prayer of him who has the honor to mix with it sincere wishes for your health and happiness, and to be with real attachment and respect dear Sir your affectionate friend & humble servant,

Th: Jefferson

P.S. Aug. 15. The Parliament is exiled to Troyes this morning.

71. TO THE EDITOR OF THE *JOURNAL DE PARIS*[1]

Sir   *Paris Aug. 29. 1787.*
I am a citizen of the United states of America, and have passed in those states almost the whole of my life. When young, I was passionately fond of reading books of history, and travels. Since the commencement of the late revolution which separated us from Great Britain, our country too has been thought worthy to employ the pens of historians and travellers. I cannot paint to you, Sir, the agonies which these have cost me, in obliging me to renounce these favorite branches of reading and in discovering to me at length that my whole life has been employed in nourishing my mind with fables and falshoods. For thus I reason. If the histories of d'Auberteuil and of Longchamps, and the travels of the Abbé Robin can be published in the face of the world, and can be read and believed by those who are cotemporary with the events they pretend to relate, how may we expect that future ages shall be better informed? Will those rise from their graves to bear witness to the truth, who would not, while living, lift their voices against falshood? If cotemporary histories are thus false, what will future compilations be. And what are all those of preceding times? In your Journal of this day, you announce and criticize a book under the title of 'les ligues Acheenne, Suisse, and Hollan-

doise, et revolution des etats unis de l'Amerique par M. de Mayer.' I was no part of the Achaeen Swiss or Dutch confederacies and have therefore nothing to say against the facts related of them. And you cite only one fact from his account of the American revolution. It is in these words, 'Monsieur Mayer assure qu'une seule voix, un seul homme, prononça l'independance des Etats unis. "Ce fut, dit il, John Dickinson, un des Deputés de la Pensilvanie au Congrés. Le veille, il avoit voté pour la soumission. L'egalité des suffrages avoit suspendu la resolution; s'il eut persisté, le Congrés ne deliberoit point. Il fut foible: il cede aux instances de ceux qui avoient plus d'energie, plus d'elo-quence, et plus de lumieres; il donna sa voix: l'Amerique lui doit une reconnoissance eternelle; c'est Dickinson qui l'a affranchie." '[2] The modesty and candour of Mr. Dickinson himself, Sir, would disavow every word of this paragraph, except these 'il avoit voté pour la soumission.' These are true, every other tittle false. I was on the spot, and can relate to you this transaction with precision. On the 7th. of June 1776. the delegates from Virginia moved, in obedience to in-structions from their constituents, that Congress should declare the 13. united colonies to be independant of Great Britain, that a Confed-eration should be formed to bind them together, and measures be taken for procuring the assistance of foreign powers. The house or-dered a punctual attendance of all their members the next day at ten o'clock, and then resolved themselves into a Committee of the whole and entered on the discussion. It appeared in the course of the debates that 7. states, viz. N. Hampshire, Massachusets, Rhodeisland, Con-necticut, Virginia, North Carolina and Georgia were decided for a separation, but that 6. others still hesitated, to wit, New York, New Jersey, Pennsylvania, Delaware, Maryland and South Carolina. Con-gress, desirous of unanimity, and seeing that the public mind was ad-vancing rapidly to it, referred the further discussion to the 1st. of July, appointing in the mean time a Committee to prepare a declaration of independance, a second to form Articles for the confederation of the states, and a third to propose measures for obtaining foreign aid. On the 28th. of June the Declaration of Independance was reported to the house, and was laid on the table for the consideration of the members. On the 1st. day of July they resolved themselves into a committee of the whole, and resumed the consideration of the motion of June 7. It was debated through the day, and at length was decided in the affirmative by the votes of 9. states, viz. New Hampshire, Massachusets, Rhode island, Connecticut, *N. Jersey, Maryland,* Virginia, North Carolina and Georgia. Pennsylvania and South Carolina voted against it. Delaware, having but two members present, was divided. The delegates from New York declared they were for it, and their constituents also: but that the instructions against it, which had been given them a twelvemonth before, were still unrepealed; that their convention was to meet in a few days, and they asked leave to suspend their vote till they could obtain a repeal of their instructions. Observe that all this was in committee of the whole Congress, and that according to the mode of their proceedings the Resolution of that Committee to declare themselves independant was to be put to the same persons reassuming their form as a Congress. It was now evening, the members exhausted by a debate of 9 hours, during which all the powers of the soul had been distended with the magnitude of the object without refreshment, without a pause; and the delegates of S. Carolina desired that the final decision might be put off to the next morning that they might still weigh in their own minds their ultimate vote. It was put off, and in the morning of the 2d. of July they joined the other nine states in voting for it. The members of the Pennsylvania delegation too, who had been absent the day before, came in and decided the vote of their state in favor of Independance, and a 3d member of the state of Delaware, who, hearing of the division of the sentiments of his two colleagues, had travelled post to arrive in time, now came in and decided the vote of that state also for the resolution. Thus twelve states voted for it at the time of it's passage, and the delegates of New York, the 13th. state received instructions within a few days to add theirs to the general vote: so that, instead of the 'egalité des suffrages' spoken of by Mr. Mayer, there was not a dissenting voice. Congress proceeded immediately to consider the Declaration of Independence which had been reported by their committee on the 28th. of June. The several paragraphs of that were debated for three days. viz. the 2d. 3d. and 4th. of July. In the evening of the 4th. they were finally closed, and the instrument approved by an unanimous vote, and signed by every member, *except Mr. Dickinson.* Look into the Journals of congress of that day, Sir, and you will see the instrument, and the names of the signers, and that Mr. Dickinson's name is not among them. Then read again those words of your paper. 'Il (Mr. Mayer) assure qu'une seule voix, un seul homme, prononça l'independance des etats unis. "Ce fut John Dickinson. L'Amerique lui doit une reconnoissance eternal; c'est Dickinson qui l'a affranchie." ' With my regrets, and my Adieus to History, to Travels, to Mayer, and to you, Sir, permit me to mingle assurances of the great respect with which I have the honor to be, Sir, your most obedient & most humble servant,

An American

72. TO JOHN ADAMS

Dear Sir   *Paris Aug. 30. 1787.*
Since your favor of July 10. mine have been of July 17. 23 and 28. The last inclosed a bill of exchange from Mr. Grand on Tessier for £46-17-10 sterl. to answer Genl. Sullivan's bill for that sum. I hope it got safe to hand, tho' I have been anxious about it as it went by post and my letters thro' that channel sometimes miscarry.

From the separation of the Notables to the present moment has been perhaps the most interesting interval ever known in this country. The propositions of the Government, approved by the Notables, were precious to the nation and have been in an honest course of execution, some of them being carried into effect, and others preparing. Above all the establishment of the Provincial assemblies, some of which have begun their sessions, bid fair to be the instrument for circumscribing the power of the crown and raising the people into consideration. The election given to them is what will do this. Tho' the minister who proposed these improvements seems to have meant them as the price of the new supplies, the game has been so played as to secure the improvements to the nation without securing the price. The Notables spoke softly on the subject of the additional supplies, but the parliament took them up roundly, refused to register the edicts for the new taxes, till compelled in a bed of justice and prefered themselves to be transferred to Troyes rather than withdraw their opposition. It is urged principally against the king, that his revenue is 130. millions more than that of his predecessor was, and yet he demands 120. millions further. You will see this well explained in the 'Conference entre un ministre d'etat et un Conseiller au parlement' which I send you with some other small pamphlets. In the mean time all tongues in Paris (and in France as it is said) have been let loose, and never was a license of speaking against the government exercised in London more freely or more universally. Caracatures, placards, bon mots, have been indulged in by all ranks of people, and I know of no well attested instance of a single punishment. For some time mobs of 10; 20; 30,000 people collected daily, surrounded the parliament house, huzzaed the members, even entered the doors and examined into their conduct, took the horses out of the carriages of those who did well, and drew them home. The government thought it prudent to prevent these, drew some regiments into the neighborhood, multiplied the guards, had the streets constantly patrolled by strong parties, suspended privileged places, forbad all clubs, &c. The mobs have ceased: perhaps this may be partly owing to the absence of parliament. The Count d'Artois, sent to hold a bed of justice in the Cour des Aides, was hissed and hooted without reserve by the populace; the carriage of Madame de (I forget the name) in the queen's livery was stopped by the populace under a belief that it was Madame de Polignac's whom they would have insulted, the queen going to the theater at Versailles with Madame de Polignac was received with a general hiss. The king, long in the habit of drowning his cares in wine, plunges deeper and deeper; the queen cries but sins on. The Count d'Artois is detested, and Monsieur[1] the general favorite. The Archbishop of Thoulouse is made Ministre principale, a virtuous, patriotic and able character. The Marechal de Castries retired yesterday notwithstanding strong sollicitations to remain in office. The Marechal de Segur retired at the same time, prompted to it by the court. Their successors are not yet known. M. de St. Prist goes Ambassador to Holland in the room of Verac transferred to Switzerland, and the Count de Moustier goes to America in the room of the Chevalier de la Luzerne who has a promise of the first vacancy. These nominations are not yet made formally, but they are decided on and the parties are ordered to prepare for their destination. As it has been long since I have had a confidential conveiance to you, I have brought together the principal facts from the adjournment of the Notables to the present moment which, as you will perceive from their nature, required a confidential conveyance. I have done it the rather because, tho' you will have heard many of them and seen them in the public papers, yet floating in the mass of lies which constitute the atmospheres of London and Paris, you may not have been sure of their truth: and I have mentioned every truth of any consequence to enable you to stamp as false the facts pretermitted. I think that in the course of three months the royal authority has lost, and the rights of the nation gained, as much ground, by a revolution of public opinion only, as England gained in all her civil wars under the Stuarts. I rather believe too they will retain the ground gained, because it is defended by the young and the middle aged, in opposition to the old only. The first party increases, and the latter diminishes daily from the course of nature. You may suppose that under this situation, war would be unwelcome to France. She will surely avoid it if not forced by the courts of London and Berlin. If forced, it is probable she will change the system of Europe totally by an alliance with the two empires, to whom nothing would be more desireable. In the event of such a coalition, not only Prussia but the whole European world must receive from them their laws. But France will probably endeavor to preserve the present system if it can be done by sacrifising to a certain degree the pretensions of the patriotic party in Holland. But of all these matters you can judge, in your position, where less secrecy is observed, better than I can. I have news from America as late as July 19. Nothing had then transpired from the Federal convention. I am sorry they began their deliberations by so abominable a precedent as that of tying up the tongues of their members. Nothing can justify this example but the innocence of their intentions, and ignorance of the value of public discussions. I have no doubt that all their other measures will be good and wise. It is really an assembly of demigods. Genl. Washington was of opinion they should not separate till October. I have the honour to be with every sentiment of friendship and respect Dear Sir Your most obedient & most humble servant,

Th: Jefferson

73. TO NICHOLAS LEWIS

Dear Sir   *Paris Sep. 17. 1787.*
... I cultivate in my own garden here Indian corn for the use of my own table, to eat green in our manner. But the species I am able to get here for seed, is hard, with a thick skin, and dry. I had at Monticello a species of small white rare ripe corn which we called Homony-corn, and of which we used to make about 20. barrels a year for table use, green, in homony, and in bread. Great George will know well what kind I mean. I wish it were possible for me to receive an ear of this in time for the next year. I think too it might be done if you would be so good as to find an opportunity of sending one to Mr. Madison at New York, and another to Mr. A. Donald at Richmond. More at your leisure I would ask you to send me also an ear of two of the drying corn from the Cherokee country, some best watermelon seeds, some fine Cantaloupe melon seeds, seeds of the common sweet potato (I mean the real seeds and not the root which cannot be brought here without rotting) an hundred or two acorns of the willow oak and about a peck of acorns of the ground oak or dwarf oak, of the kind that George gathered for me one year upon the barrens of buck island creek. As these will be of some bulk, I will ask the favor of you to send them to Mr. Donald at Richmond who will find a conveiance for them to Havre. Perhaps I should do better to trouble Mrs. Lewis with this commission; I therefore take the liberty of recommending myself to her. The failure of the former attempt to send bacon hams to me discouraged me from proposing the attempt again. Yet I should think Mr. Donald could get them to me safely. A dozen or two would last me a year, would be better than any to be had on this side the Atlantic, which, inferior as they are, cost about a guinea apiece....

74. TO CHARLES THOMSON[1]

Dear Sir   *Paris Sep. 20. 1787.*
Your favor of April 28. did not come to my hands till the 1st. inst. Unfortunately the boxes of plants, which were a day too late to come by the April packet, missed the packet of June 10. also, and only came by that of July 25. They are not yet arrived at Paris, but I expect them daily. I am sensible of your kind attention to them, and that as you were leaving New York you took the course which bade fair to be the best. That they were forgotten in the hands in which you placed them, was probably owing to much business and more important. I have desired Mr. Madison to refund to you the money you were so kind as to advance for me. The delay of your letter will apologize for this delay of the repaiment. I thank you also for the extract of the letter you were so kind as to communicate to me on the antiquities found in the Western country.[2] I wish that the persons who go thither would make very exact descriptions of what they see of that kind, without forming any theories. The moment a person forms a theory, his imagination sees in every object only the tracts which favor that theory. But it is too early to form theories on those antiquities. We must wait with patience till more facts are collected. I wish our philosophical society would collect exact descriptions of the several monuments as yet known, and insert them naked in their transactions, and continue their attention to those hereafter to be discovered. Patience and observation may enable us in time to solve the problem whether those who formed the scattering monuments in our Western country, were colonies sent off from Mexico, or the founders of Mexico itself? Whether both were the descendants or the progenitors of the Asiatic red men. The Mexican tradition mentioned by Dr. Robertson is an evidence, but a feeble one, in favor of the one opinion. The number of languages radically different, is a strong evidence in favor of the contrary one. There is an American of the name of Ledyard, he who was with Capt. Cook on his last voiage and wrote an account of that voiage, who is gone to Petersburg, from thence he was to go to Kamschatka, to cross over thence to the Northwest coast of America, and to penetrate through the main continent to our side of it. He is a person of ingenuity and informa-

tion. Unfortunately he has too much imagination. However, if he escapes safely, he will give us new, various, and useful information. I had a letter from him dated last March, when he was about to leave St. Petersburgh on his way to Kamschatka.

With respect to the inclination of the strata of rocks, I had observed them between the Blue ridge and North Mountain in Virginia to be parallel with the pole of the earth. I observed the same thing in most instances in the Alps between Nice and Turin: but in returning along the precipices of the Appennines where they hang over the Mediterranean, their direction was totally different and various; and you mention that in our Western country they are horizontal. This variety proves they have not been formed by subsidence as some writers of theories of the earth have pretended, for then they should always have been in circular strata, and concentric. It proves too that they have not been formed by the rotation of the earth on it's axis, as might have been suspected had all these strata been parallel with that axis. They may indeed have been thrown up by explosions, as Whitehurst supposes, or have been the effect of convulsions. But there can be no proof of the explosion, nor is it probable that convulsions have deformed every spot of the earth. It is now generally agreed that rock grows, and it seems that it grows in layers in every direction, as the branches of trees grow in all directions. Why seek further the solution of this phaenomenon? Every thing in nature decays. If it were not reproduced then by growth, there would be a chasm.—I remember you asked me in a former letter whether the steam mill in London was turned by the steam immediately, or by the intermediate agency of water raised by the steam. When I was in London, Boulton made a secret of his mill. Therefore I was permitted to see it only superficially. I saw no waterwheels, and therefore supposed none. I answered you accordingly that there was none. But when I was at Nismes, I went to see the steam mill there, and they shewed it to me in all it's parts. I saw that their steam raised water, and that this water turned a wheel. I expressed my doubts of the necessity of the inter-agency of water, and that the London mill was without it. But they supposed me mistaken; perhaps I was so; I have had no opportunity since of clearing up the doubt.

We are here on the eve of great events. The contests in Holland seemed to render war probable. But it has actually begun in another quarter, between the Turks and Russians. The desertion of antient friends by the king of Prussia seems to render it necessary for them to seek new connections. New ones offer themselves, and I really suppose the offer will be accepted. A confederacy between France and the two empires may give law to the world. If it takes place the patriots of Holland will be saved, and the Turks expelled Europe. Constantinople, it is thought, will fall to the Empress of Russia, who, it is said, does not mean it as a dependance on her empire, but to make a separate kingdom of it for a younger son. Thus we may live to see the Greeks re-established as a people, and the language of Homer again a living language. Little will be wanting to amend the modern into antient Greek. It is whispered that the Mediterranean islands and Egypt would suit France well, the latter as the means of drawing the trade of the East Indies through the Red sea. Learning and civilisation will gain by the success of these projects, but it is first to be doubted whether they are seriously proposed, and then whether they may not be baffled by some event too small to be foreseen.

I had a letter from Mr. Churchman, but not developing his plan of knowing the longitude fully. I wrote him what was doubted about it so far as we could conjecture what it was.

I am with very great & sincere esteem Dear Sir Your friend & servant,

Th: Jefferson

75. TO BUFFON

Sir   *Paris Octob. 1. 1787.*
I had the honour of informing you some time ago that I had written to some of my friends in America, desiring they would send me such of the spoils of the Moose, Caribou, Elk and deer as might throw light on that class of animals; but more particularly to send me the complete skeleton, skin, and horns of the Moose, in such condition as that

the skin might be sowed up and stuffed on it's arrival here. I am happy to be able to present to you at this moment the bones and skin of a Moose, the horns of [another] individual of the same species, the horns of the Caribou, the el[k,] the deer, the spiked horned buck, and the Roebuck of America. They all come from New Hampshire and Massachusets. I give you their popular names, as it rests with yourself to decide their real names. The skin of the Moose was drest with the hair on, but a great deal of it has come off, and the rest is ready to drop off. The horns of the elk are remarkeably small. I have certainly seen of them which would have weighed five or six times as much. This is the animal which we call elk in the Southern parts of America, and of which I have given some description in the Notes on Virginia, of which I had the honour of presenting you a copy. I really doubt whether the flat-horned elk exists in America: and I think this may be properly classed with the elk, the principal difference being in the [horns.] I have seen the Daim, the Cerf, the Chevreuil of Europe. But the animal we call Elk, and which may be distinguished as the Round-horned elk, is very different from them. I have never seen the Brand-hirtz or Cerf d'Ardennes, nor the European elk. Could I get a sight of them I think I should be able to say to which of them the American elk resembles most, as I am tolerably well acquainted with that animal. I must observe also that the horns of the Deer, which accompany these spoils, are not of the fifth or sixth part of the weight of some that I have seen. This individual has been of three years of age, according to our method of judging. I have taken measures particularly to be furnished with large horns of our e[lk] and our deer, and therefore beg of you not to consider those now sent as furnishing a specimen of their ordinary size. I really suspect you will find that the Moose, the Round horned elk, and the American deer are species not existing in Europe. The Moose is perhaps of a new class. I wish these spoils, Sir, may have the merit of adding any thing new to the treasures of nature which [have] so fortunately come under your observation, and of which she seems [to] have given you the keys. They will in that case be some gratification to you, which it will always be pleasing to me to have procured, having the honor to be with sentiments of the most perfect esteem and respect, Sir, your most obedient & most humble servant,

Th: Jefferson

76. TO JAMES MADISON

Dear Sir   *Paris Oct. 8. 1787.*

The bearer hereof the count de Moustier,[1] successor to Monsr. de la Luzerne, would from his office need no letter of introduction to you or to any body. Yet I take the liberty of recommending him to you to shorten those formal approaches which the same office would otherwise expose him to in making your acquaintance. He is a great enemy to formality, etiquette, ostentation and luxury. He goes with the best dispositions to cultivate society without poisoning it by ill example. He is sensible, disposed to view things favorably, and being well acquainted with the constitution of England, it's manners and language, is the better prepared for his station with us. But I should have performed only the lesser, and least pleasing half of my task, were I not to add my recommendations of Madame de Brehan. She is goodness itself. You must be well acquainted with her. You will find her well disposed to meet your acquaintance and well worthy of it. The way to please her is to receive her as an acquaintance of a thousand years standing. She speaks little English. You must teach her more, and learn French from her. She hopes by accompanying M. de Moustier to improve her health which is very feeble, and still more to improve her son in his education and to remove him to a distance from the seductions of this country. You will wonder to be told that there are no schools in this country to be compared to ours, in the sciences. The husband of Madame de Brehan is an officer, and obliged by the times to remain with the army. Monsieur de Moustier brings your watch. I have worn her two months, and really find her a most incomparable one. She will not want the little re-dressing which new watches generally do, after going about a year. She costs 600 livres. To open her in all her parts, press the little pin on the edge, with the point of your nail. That opens the chrystal. Then open the dial plate in the usual way. Then press the stem, at the end within the loop, and it opens the back for winding up or regulating. *De Moutier is remarkably communicative. With adroitness he may be pumped of any thing. His openness is from character not from affection. An intimacy with him will on this account be politically valuable.* I am Dear Sir Your affectionate friend & servant,

Th: Jefferson

77. TO JOHN ADAMS

Dear Sir   *Paris Nov. 13. 1787.*
This will be delivered you by young Mr. Rutledge. Your knowledge of his father will introduce him to your notice. He merits it moreover on his own account.

I am now to acknolege your favors of Oct. 8 and 26. That of August 25. was duly received, nor can I recollect by what accident I was prevented from acknoleging it in mine of Sep. 28. It has been the source of my subsistence hitherto, and must continue to be so till I receive letters on the affairs of money from America. Van Staphorsts & Willinks have answered my draughts.—Your books for M. de la Fayette are received here. I will notify it to him, who is at present with his provincial assembly in Auvergne.

Little is said lately of the progress of the negociations between the courts of Petersburg, Vienna, and Versailles. The distance of the former and the cautious, unassuming character of it's minister here is one cause of delays: a greater one is the greediness and instable character of the emperor. Nor do I think that the Principal[1] here will be easily induced to lend himself to any connection which shall threaten a war within a considerable number of years. His own reign will be that of peace only, in all probability; and were any accident to tumble him down, this country would immediately gird on it's sword and buckler, and trust to occurrences for supplies of money. The wound their honour has sustained festers in their hearts, and it may be said with truth that the Archbishop and a few priests, determined to support his measures because proud to see their order come again into power, are the only advocates for the line of conduct which has been pursued. It is said and believed thro' Paris literally that the Count de Monmorin 'pleuroit comme un enfant'[2] when obliged to sign the counter declaration. Considering the phrase as figurative, I believe it expresses the distress of his heart. Indeed he has made no secret of his individual opinion. In the mean time the Principal goes on with a firm and patriotic spirit, in reforming the cruel abuses of the government and preparing a new constitution which will give to this people as much liberty as they are capable of managing. This I think will be the glory of his administration, because, tho' a good theorist in finance, he is thought to execute badly. They are about to open a loan of 100. millions to supply present wants, and it is said the preface of the Arret will contain a promise of the Convocation of the States general during the ensuing year. 12. or 15. provincial assemblies are already in action, and are going on well; and I think that tho' the nation suffers in reputation, it will gain infinitely in happiness under the present administration. I inclose to Mr. Jay a pamphlet which I will beg of you to forward. I leave it open for your perusal. When you shall have read it, be so good as to stick a wafer[3] in it. It is not yet published, nor will be for some days. This copy has been ceded to me as a favor.

How do you like our new constitution? I confess there are things in it which stagger all my dispositions to subscribe to what such an assembly has proposed. The house of federal representatives will not be adequate to the management of affairs either foreign or federal. Their President seems a bad edition of a Polish king. He may be reelected from 4. years to 4. years for life. Reason and experience prove to us that a chief magistrate, so continuable, is an officer for life. When one or two generations shall have proved that this is an office for life, it becomes on every succession worthy of intrigue, of bribery, of force, and even of foreign interference. It will be of great consequence to France and England to have America governed by a Galloman or Angloman. Once in office, and possessing the military force of the union, without either the aid or check of a council, he would not be easily dethroned, even if the people could be induced to withdraw their votes from him. I wish that at the end of the 4. years they had made him for ever ineligible a second time. Indeed I think all the good of this new constitution might have been couched in three or four new articles to be added to the good, old, and venerable fabrick, which should have been preserved even as a religious relique.—Present me and my daughters affectionately to Mrs. Adams. The younger one continues to speak of her warmly. Accept yourself assurances of the sincere esteem and respect with which I have the honour to be, Dear Sir, your friend & servant,

Th: Jefferson

78. TO WILLIAM STEPHENS SMITH

Dear Sir   *Paris Nov. 13. 1787.*
I am now to acknolege the receipt of your favors of October the 4th. 8th. and 26th. In the last you apologize for your letters of introduction to Americans coming here. It is so far from needing apology on your part, that it calls for thanks on mine. I endeavor to shew civilities to all the Americans who come here, and who will give me opportunities of doing it: and it is a matter of comfort to know from a good quarter what they are, and how far I may go in my attentions to them.—Can you send me Woodmason's bills for the two copying presses for the M. de la fayette, and the M. de Chastellux? The latter makes one article in a considerable account, of old standing, and which I cannot present for want of this article.—I do not know whether it is to yourself or Mr. Adams I am to give my thanks for the copy of the new constitution. I beg leave through you to place them where due. It will be yet three weeks before I shall receive them from America. There are very good articles in it: and very bad. I do not know which preponderate. What we have lately read in the history of Holland, in the chapter on the Stadtholder, would have sufficed to set me against a Chief magistrate eligible for a long duration, if I had ever been disposed towards one: and what we have always read of the elections of Polish kings should have forever excluded the idea of one continuable for life. Wonderful is the effect of impudent and persevering lying. The British ministry have so long hired their gazetteers to repeat and model into every form lies about our being in anarchy, that the world has at length believed them, the English nation has believed them, the ministers

themselves have come to believe them, and what is more wonderful, we have believed them ourselves. Yet where does this anarchy exist? Where did it ever exist, except in the single instance of Massachusets? And can history produce an instance of a rebellion so honourably conducted? I say nothing of it's motives. They were founded in ignorance, not wickedness. God forbid we should ever be 20. years without such a rebellion. The people can not be all, and always, well informed. The part which is wrong will be discontented in proportion to the importance of the facts they misconceive. If they remain quiet under such misconceptions it is a lethargy, the forerunner of death to the public liberty. We have had 13. states independant 11. years. There has been one rebellion. That comes to one rebellion in a century and a half for each state. What country before ever existed a century and half without a rebellion? And what country can preserve it's liberties if their rulers are not warned from time to time that their people preserve the spirit of resistance? Let them take arms. The remedy is to set them right as to facts, pardon and pacify them. What signify a few lives lost in a century or two? The tree of liberty must be refreshed from time to time with the blood of patriots and tyrants. It is it's natural manure. Our Convention has been too much impressed by the insurrection of Massachusets: and in the spur of the moment they are setting up a kite to keep the hen yard in order. I hope in god this article will be rectified before the new constitution is accepted.—You ask me if any thing transpires here on the subject of S. America? Not a word. I know that there are combustible materials there, and that they wait the torch only. But this country probably will join the extinguishers.— The want of facts worth communicating to you has occasioned me to give a little loose to dissertation. We must be contented to amuse, when we cannot inform. Present my respects to Mrs. Smith, and be assured of the sincere esteem of Dear Sir Your friend & servant,

Th: Jefferson

79. TO JAMES MADISON

Dear Sir   *Paris Dec. 20. 1787.*

My last to you was of Oct. 8 by the Count de Moustier. Yours of July 18. Sep. 6. and Oct. 24. have been successively received, yesterday, the day before and three or four days before that. I have only had time to read the letters, the printed papers communicated with them, however interesting, being obliged to lie over till I finish my dispatches for the packet, which dispatches must go from hence the day after tomorrow. I have much to thank you for. First and most for the cyphered paragraph respecting myself.[1] These little informations are very material towards forming my own decisions. I would be glad even to know when any individual member thinks I have gone wrong in any instance. If I know myself it would not excite ill blood in me, while it would assist to guide my conduct, perhaps to justify it, and to keep me to my duty, alert. I must thank you too for the information in Thos. Burke's case, tho' you will have found by a subsequent letter that I have asked of you a further investigation of that matter. It is to gratify the lady who is at the head of the Convent wherein my daughters are, and who, by her attachment and attention to them, lays me under great obligations. I shall hope therefore still to receive from you the result of the further enquiries my second letter had asked.—The parcel of rice which you informed me had miscarried accompanied my letter to the Delegates of S. Carolina. Mr. Bourgoin was to be the bearer of both and both were delivered together into the hands of his relation here who introduced him to me, and who at a subsequent moment undertook to convey them to Mr. Bourgoin. This person was an engraver particularly recommended to Dr. Franklin and Mr. Hopkinson. Perhaps he may have mislaid the little parcel of rice among his baggage.—I am much pleased that the sale of Western lands is so successful. I hope they will absorb all the Certificates of our Domestic debt speedily in the first place, and that then offered for cash they will do the same by our foreign one.

The season admitting only of operations in the Cabinet, and these being in a great measure secret, I have little to fill a letter. I will therefore make up the deficiency by adding a few words on the Constitution proposed by our Convention. I like much the general idea of framing a government which should go on of itself peaceably, without needing continual recurrence to the state legislatures. I like the organization of the government into Legislative, Judiciary and Executive. I like the power given the Legislature to levy taxes; and for that reason solely approve of the greater house being chosen by the people directly. For tho' I think a house chosen by them will be very illy qualified to legislate for the Union, for foreign nations &c. yet this evil does not weigh against the good of preserving inviolate the fundamental principle that the people are not to be taxed but by representatives chosen immediately by themselves. I am captivated by the compromise of the opposite claims of the great and little states, of the latter to equal, and the former to proportional influence. I am much pleased too with the substitution of the method of voting by persons, instead of that of voting by states: and I like the negative given to the Executive with a third of either house, though I should have liked it better had the Judiciary been associated for that purpose, or invested with a similar and separate power. There are other good things of less moment. I will now add what I do not like. First the omission of a bill of rights providing clearly and without the aid of sophisms for freedom of religion, freedom of the press, protection against standing armies, restriction against monopolies, the eternal and unremitting force of the habeas corpus laws, and trials by jury in all matters of fact triable by the laws of the land and not by the law of Nations. To say, as Mr. Wilson does that a bill of rights was not necessary because all is reserved in the case of the general government which is not given, while in the particular ones all is given which is not reserved might do for the Audience to whom it was addressed, but is surely gratis dictum, opposed by strong inferences from the body of the instrument, as well as from the omission of the clause of our present confederation which had declared that in express terms. It was a hard conclusion to say because there has been no uniformity among the states as to the cases triable by jury, because some have been so incautious as to abandon this mode of trial, therefore the more prudent states shall be reduced to the same level of calamity. It would have been much more just and wise to have concluded the other way that as most of the states had judiciously preserved this palladium,[2] those who had wandered should be brought back to it, and to have established general right instead of general wrong. Let me add that a bill of rights is what the people are entitled to against every government on earth, general or particular, and what no just government should refuse, or rest on inference. The second feature I dislike, and greatly dislike, is the abandonment in every instance of the necessity of rotation in office, and most particularly in the case of the President. Experience concurs with reason in concluding that the first magistrate will always be re-elected if the constitution permits it. He is then an officer for life. This once observed it becomes of so much consequence to certain nations to have a friend or a foe at the head of our affairs that they will interfere with money and with arms. A Galloman or an Angloman will be supported by the nation he befriends. If once elected, and at a second or third election outvoted by one or two votes, he will pretend false votes, foul play, hold possession of the reins of government, be supported by the states voting for him, especially if they are the central ones lying in a compact body themselves and separating their opponents: and they will be aided by one nation of Europe, while the majority are aided by another. The election of a President of America some years hence will be much more interesting to certain nations of Europe than ever the election of a king of Poland was. Reflect on all the instances in history antient and modern, of elective monarchies, and say if they do not give foundation for my fears, the Roman emperors, the popes, while they were of any importance, the German emperors till they became hereditary in practice, the kings of Poland, the Deys of the Ottoman dependancies. It may be said that if elections are to be attended with these disorders, the seldomer they are renewed the better. But experience shews that the only way to prevent disorder is to render them uninteresting by frequent changes. An incapacity to be elected a second time would have been the only effectual preventative. The power of removing him every fourth year by the vote of the people is a power which will not be exercised. The king of Poland is removeable every day by the Diet, yet he is never removed.—Smaller objections are the Appeal in fact as well as law, and the binding all persons Legislative, Executive and Judiciary by oath to maintain that constitution. I do not pretend to decide what would be the best method of procuring the establishment of the manifold good things in this constitution, and of getting rid of the bad. Whether by adopting it in hopes of future amendment, or, after it has been duly weighed and canvassed by the people, after seeing the parts they generally dislike, and those they generally approve, to say to them 'We see now what you wish. Send together your deputies again, let them frame a constitution for you omitting what you have condemned, and establishing the powers you approve. Even these will be a great addition to the energy of your government.'—At all events I hope you will not be discouraged from other trials, if the present one should fail of it's full effect.—I have thus told you freely what I like and dislike: merely as a matter of curiosity for I know your own judgment has been formed on all these points after having heard every thing which could be urged on them. I own I am not a friend to a very energetic government. It is always oppressive. The late rebellion in Massachusets has given more alarm than I think it should have done. Calculate that one rebellion in 13 states in the course of 11 years, is but one for each state in a century and a half. No country should be so long without one. Nor will any degree of power in the hands of government prevent insurrections. France with all it's despotism, and two or three hundred thousand men always in arms has had three insurrections in the three years I have been here in every one of which greater numbers were engaged than in Massachusets and a great deal more blood was spilt. In Turkey, which Montesquieu supposes more despotic, insurrections are the events of every day. In England, where the hand of power is lighter than here, but heavier than with us they happen every half dozen years. Compare again the ferocious depredations of their insurgents with the order, the moderation and the almost self extinguishment of ours.—After all, it is my principle that the will of the Majority should always prevail. If they approve the proposed Convention in all it's parts, I shall concur in it chearfully, in hopes that they will amend it whenever they shall find it work wrong. I think our governments will remain virtuous for many centuries; as long as they are chiefly agricultural; and this will be as long as there shall be vacant lands in any part of America. When they get piled upon one another in large cities, as in Europe, they will become corrupt as in Europe. Above all things I hope the education of the common people will be attended to; convinced that on their good sense we may rely with the most security for the preservation of a due degree of liberty. I have tired you by this time with my disquisitions and will therefore only add assurances of the sincerity of those sentiments of esteem and attachment with which I am Dear Sir your affectionate friend & servant,

Th: Jefferson

P.S. The instability of our laws is really an immense evil. I think it would be well to provide in our constitutions that there shall always be a twelvemonth between the ingrossing a bill and passing it: that it should then be offered to it's passage without changing a word: and that if circumstances should be thought to require a speedier passage, it should take two thirds of both houses instead of a bare majority.

80. TO MARIA COSWAY

Paris Jan. [31, 1788]

I went to breakfast with you according to promise, and you had gone off at 5. oclock in the morning. This spared me indeed the pain of parting, but it deprives me of the comfort of recollecting that pain. Your departure was the signal of distress to your friends. You know the accident which so long confined the Princess to her room. Madame de Corny too was immediately thrown into great alarm for the life of her husband. After being long at death's door he is reviving. Mrs. Church seemed to come to participate of the distress of her friend instead of the pleasures of Paris. I never saw her before: but I find in her all the good the world has given her credit for. I do not wonder at your fondness for each other. I have seen too little of her, as I did of you. But in your case it was not my fault, unless it be a fault to love my friends so dearly as to wish to enjoy their company in the only way it yeilds enjoiment, that is, en petite comité.[1] You make every body love you. You are sought and surrounded therefore by all. Your mere domestic cortege was so numerous, et si imposante, that one could not approach you quite at their ease. Nor could you so unpremeditately mount into the Phaeton and hie away to the bois de Boulogne, St. Cloud, Marly, St. Germains &c. Add to this the distance at which you were placed from me. When you come again, you must be nearer, and move more extempore. You complain, my dear Madam, of my not writing to you, and you have the appearance of cause for complaint. But I have been above a month looking out for a private conveiance, without being able to find one, and you know the infidelity of the post office. Sometimes they mislay letters to pocket the frankmoney: and always they open those of people in office. As if your friendship and mine could be interesting to government! As if, instead of the effusions of a sincere esteem, we would fill our letters with the miserable trash called state secrets!—I am flattered by your attention to me in the affair of the tea vase. I like perfectly the form of the one Mrs. Church brought. But Mr. Trumbull and myself have seen one made for the count de Moustier, wherein the spout is suppressed, and the water made to issue at a pretty little ornament. When he returns he will explain this to you, and try to get me a vase of the size and form of Mrs. Church's, but with this improvement. In this business I shall beg leave to associate your taste with his. Present my compliments to Mr. Cosway. I am obliged to trust this letter through the post office, as I see no immediate chance of a private conveiance. Adieu, my dear Madam: think of me often and warmly, as I do of you.

81. TO ALEXANDER DONALD[1]

Dear Sir   *Paris Feb. 7. 1788.*
I received duly your friendly letter of Nov. 12. By this time you will have seen published by Congress the new regulation obtained from this court in favor of our commerce. I should have made them known to you at the same time but that there is a sort of decency which requires that first communications should be made to government. You will observe that the arrangement relative to tobacco is a continuation of the order of Berni for five years, only leaving the price to be settled between the buyer and seller. You will see too that all contracts for tobacco are forbidden till it arrives in France. Of course your proposi-

tion for a contract is precluded. I fear the prices here will be low, especially if the market be crowded. You should be particularly attentive to the article which requires that the tobacco should come in French or American bottoms, as this article will in no instance be departed from.

I wish with all my soul that the nine first Conventions may accept the new Constitution, because this will secure to us the good it contains, which I think great and important. But I equally wish that the four latest conventions, whichever they be, may refuse to accede to it till a declaration of rights be annexed. This would probably command the offer of such a declaration, and thus give to the whole fabric, perhaps as much perfection as any one of that kind ever had. By a declaration of rights I mean one which shall stipulate freedom of religion, freedom of the press, freedom of commerce against monopolies, trial by juries in all cases, no suspensions of the habeas corpus, no standing armies. These are fetters against doing evil which no honest government should decline. There is another strong feature in the new constitution which I as strongly dislike. That is the perpetual re-eligibility of the President. Of this I expect no amendment at present because I do not see that any body has objected to it on your side the water. But it will be productive of cruel distress to our country even in your day and mine. The importance to France and England to have our government in the hands of a Friend or a foe, will occasion their interference by money, and even by arms. Our President will be of much more consequence to them than a king of Poland. We must take care however that neither this nor any other objection to the new form produce a schism in our union. That would be an incurable evil, because near friends falling out never reunite cordially; whereas, all of us going together, we shall be sure to cure the evils of our new constitution, before they do great harm.—The box of books I had taken the liberty to address to you is but just gone from Havre for New York. I do not see at present any symptoms strongly indicating war. It is true that the distrust existing between the two courts of Versailles and London is so great that they can scarcely do business together. However the difficulty and doubt of obtaining money makes both afraid to enter into war. The little preparations for war, which we see, are the effect of distrust rather than of a design to commence hostilities. However, in such a state of mind, you know small things may produce a rupture. So that tho peace is rather probable, war is very possible.

Your letter has kindled all the fond recollections of antient times, recollections much dearer to me than any thing I have known since. There are minds which can be pleased by honors and preferments, but I see nothing in them but envy and enmity. It is only necessary to possess them to know how little they contribute to happiness, or rather how hostile they are to it. No attachments soothe the mind so much as those contracted in early life: nor do I recollect any societies which have given me more pleasure than those of which you have partaken with me. I had rather be shut up in a very modest cottage, with my books, my family and a few old friends, dining on simple bacon, and letting the world roll on as it liked, than to occupy the most splendid post which any human power can give. I shall be glad to hear from you often. Give me the small news as well as the great. Tell Dr. Currie that I believe I am indebted to him a letter, but that, like the mass of my countrymen I am not at this moment able to pay all my debts: the post being to depart in an hour, and the last stroke of a pen I am able to send by it being that which assures you of the sentiments of esteem and attachment with which I am dear Sir your affectionate friend & servt.,

Th: Jefferson

82. TO ANGELICA SCHUYLER CHURCH

Paris Sunday. Feb. 17. 1788.

You speak, Madam, in your Note of Adieu, of civilities which I never rendered you. What you kindly call such were but the gratifications of my own heart: for indeed that was much gratified in seeing and serving you. The morning you left us, all was wrong. Even the sun shine was provoking, with which I never quarelled before. I took it into my head he shone only to throw light on our loss: to present a chearfulness not at all in unison with my mind. I mounted my horse earlier than common, and took by instinct the road you had taken. Some spirit whispered this to me: but he whispered by halves only: for, when I turned about at St. Denis, had he told me you were then broke down at Luzarches, I should certainly have spurred on to that place, and perhaps not have quitted you till I had seen the carriage perform it's office fully by depositing you at Boulogne. I went in the evening to Madame de Corny's, where we talked over our woes, and this morning I found some solace in going for Kitty and the girls. She is now here, just triste enough to shew her affection, and at the same time her discretion. I think I have discovered a method of preventing this dejection of mind on any future parting. It is this. When you come again, I will employ myself solely in finding or fancying that you have some faults, and I will draw a veil over all your good qualities, if I can find one large enough. I think I shall succeed in this. For, trying myself today, by way of exercise, I recollected immediately one fault in your composition. It is that you give all your attention to your friends, caring nothing about yourself. Now you must agree that I christian this very mildly when I call it a folly only. And I dare say I shall find many like it when I examine you with more sang froid.—I remember you told me, when we parted, you would come to see me at Monticello. Now tho' I believe this to be impossible, I have been planning what I would shew you: a flower here, a tree there; yonder a grove, near it a fountain; on this side a hill, on that a river. Indeed, madam, I know nothing so charming as our own country. The learned say it is a new creation; and I believe them; not for their reasons, but because it is made on an improved plan. Europe is a first idea, a crude production, before the maker knew his trade, or had made up his mind as to what he wanted. Let us go back to it together then. You intend it a visit; so do I. While you are indulging with your friends on the Hudson, I will go to see if Monticello remains in the same place. Or I will attend you to the falls of Niagara, if you will go on with me to the passage of the Patowmac, the Natural bridge &c. This done, we will come back together, you for a long, and I for a lesser time. Think of this plan, and when you come to pay your summer's visit to Kitty we will talk it over. In the mean time heavens bless you, Madam, fortify your health, and watch over your happiness. Your's affectionately,

Th: J.

83. NOTES OF A TOUR THROUGH
HOLLAND AND THE RHINE VALLEY

MEMORANDUMS ON A TOUR FROM PARIS TO AMSTERDAM,
STRASBURG AND BACK TO PARIS. 1788. MARCH. 3.

Post	Face of country	Soil	Produce	Animals	Inclosures	Wood
Bourget						
Louvres ⎤ Chapelle ⎦	broad low hills	reddish loam, some sand	corn	none	none	none
Senlis	do.	barren	nothing	none	none	scraggy trees

Amsterdam. Joists of houses placed, not with their sides horizontally and perpendicular[ly] but diamond-wise thus ◇ first for greater strength, 2. to arch between with brick thus ⬭. Windows opening so that they admit air, and not rain. The upper sash opens on [a hori]zontal axis, or pins in the center of the sides thus. The lower sash slides up.

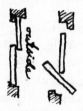

Manner of fixing a flag staff, or the mast of a vessel. a. is the bolt on which it turns. b. a bolt which is taken in and out to fasten it or to let it down. When taken out, the lower end of the staff is shoved out of it's case, and the upper end being heaviest brings itself down. A rope must have been previously fastened to the butt end, to pull it down again when you want to raise the flag end.

Dining tables letting down with single or double leaves so as to take the room of their thickness only with a single leaf when open,

thus ⬚ or thus ⬚ double leaves open ⬚

when shut, thus ⬚ or thus ⬚ shut, ⬚

Peat costs about 1. doit each, or 12½ stivers the 100. 100. makes 7. cubic feet, and to keep a tolerably comfortable fire for a study or chamber takes about 6. every hour and a half.

A machine for drawing light *empty* boats over a dam at Amsterdam. It is an Axis in peritrochio[1] fixed on the dam. From the dam each way is a sloping stage. The boat is presented to this, the rope of the axis made fast to it, and it is drawn up. The water [on one] side of the dam is about 4.f. higher than on the other.

The Camels used for lightering ships over the Pampus will raise the ship 8. fe[et.] There are beams passing through the ship's sides, projecting to the off side of the Came[l] and resting on it. Of course that alone would keep the Camel close to the ship. Besides this there are a great number of windlasses on the Camels, the ropes of which are made fast to the gunwale of the ship. The Camel is shaped to the ship on the near side, and straight on the off one. When placed alongside, water is let into it, so as nearly to sink it. In this state it receives the beams &c. of the ship: and then the water is pumped out.

Wind saw mills. See the plans detailed in the Moolen book which I bought.[2] A circular foundation of brick is raised about 3. or 4. feet high, and covered with a curb or [sill] of wood, and has little rollers under it's sill which make it turn easily on the cu[rb. A] hanging bridge projects at each end, about 15. or 20. feet beyond the circular area thus [*see Fig. 1*] horizontally, and thus [*see Fig. 2*] in the profile to increase the play of the timbers on the frame. The wings are at one side, as at a. There is a shelter over the hanging bridges, [b]ut of plank, with scarce any frame, very light.

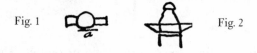

Fig. 1   Fig. 2

A bridge across a canal formed by two scows which open each to the opposite shore, and let boats pass.

A lanthern over the street door which gives light equally into the antichamber and the street. It is a hexagon, and occupies the place of the middle pane of [gla]ss in the circular top of the street door.

[A] bridge on a canal, turning on a swivel, by which means it is arranged along the [side] of the canal, so as not to be in the way of boats when not in use. When used it is turned across the canal. It is of course a little more than double the width of the canal.

Hedges of beach, which not losing the old leaf till the new bud pushes it off, has the effect of an evergreen, as to cover.

Mr. Ameshoff merchant at Amsterdam. The distribution of his aviary worthy notice. Each kind of the large birds has it's coop 8.f. wide and 4.f. deep. The middle of the front is occupied by a broad glass window, on one side of which is a door for the keeper to enter at, and on the other a little trap door for the birds to pass in and out. The floor strowed with clean hay. Before each coop is a court of 8. by 16.f. with wire in front, and netting above if the fowls be able to fly. For such as require it there are bushes of evergreen growing in their court for them to lay their eggs under. The coops are frequently divided into two stories, the upper for those birds which perch, such as pigeons &c. the lower for those which feed on the ground, as pheasants, partridges &c. The court is in common for both stories, because the birds do no injury to each other. For the waterfowl there is a pond of water passing thro' the courts, with a moveable separation. While they are breeding they must be separate. Afterwards they may come together. The small birds [are some] of them in a common aviary, and some in cages.

The Dutch wheel-barrow is in this form which is very convenient for loading and unloading.

Mr. Hermen Hend Damen, merchant-broker of Amsterdam tells me that the emigrants to America come from the Palatinate down the Rhine and take shipping from Amsterdam. Their passage is 10. guineas if paid here, and 11. if paid in America. He says they might be had in any number to go to America and settle lands as tenants on half stocks or metairies. Perhaps they would serve their employer one year as an indemnification for the passage, and then be bound to remain on his lands 7. years. They would come to Amsterdam at their own expence. He thinks they would employ more than 50. acres each. But qu? especially if they have 50. acres for their wife also?

Hodson the best house. Stadhouderian. His son in the government. Friendly, but old and very infirm.

Hope. The first house in Amsterdam. His first object England: but it is supposed he would like to have the American business also. Yet he would probably make our affairs subordinate to those of England.

Vollenhoven. An excellent old house, connected with no party.

Sapportus. A broker. Very honest and ingenuous. Well disposed. Acts for Hope; but will say with truth what he can do for us. The best person to consult with as to the best house to undertake a piece of business. He has brothers in London in business.

Jacob Van Staphorst tells me there are about 14. millions of florins, new money, placed in loans in Holland every year, being the savings of individuals out of their annual revenue &c. Besides this there are every year reimbursements of old loans from some quarter or other, to be replaced at interest in some new loan.

1788. March 16. Baron Steuben has been generally suspected of having suggested the first idea of the self-styled order of Cincinnati. But Mr. Adams tells me that in the year 1776. he had called at a tavern in the state of N. York to dine, just at the moment when the British army was landing at Frog's neck. Genls. Washington, Lee, Knox, and

Parsons came to the same tavern. He got into conversation with Knox. They talked of antient history, of Fabius who used to raise the Romans from the dust, of the present contest &c. and Genl. Knox, in the course of the conversation, said he should wish for some ribbon to wear in his hat, or in his button hole, to be transmitted to his descendants as a badge and a proof that he had fought in defence of their liberties. He spoke of it in such precise terms as shewed he had revolved it in his mind before. Mr. Adams says he and Knox were standing together in the door of the tavern, and does not recollect whether Genl. Washington and the others were near enough to hear the conversation, or were even in the room at that moment. Baron Steuben did not arrive in America till above a year after that. Mr. Adams is now 53. years old; i.e. 9. more than I am.

HOPE'S HOUSE NEAR HARLAEM.

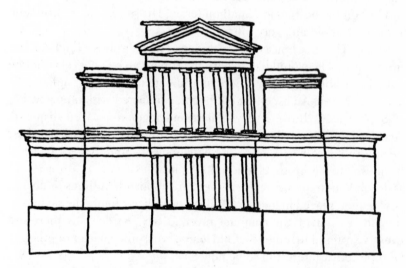

It is said this house will cost 4 tons of silver, [or] 40,000. £ sterl. The separation between the middle building and wings in the upper story has a capricious appearance, yet a pleasing one. The right wing of the house (which is the left in the plan) extends back to a great length so as to make the ground plan in the form of an L. The parapet has a pannel of wall, and a pannel of wall, and a pannel of ballusters alternately, which lighten it. There is no portico, the columns being backed against the wall of the front.

Mar. 30. 31. AMSTERDAM, UTRECHT, NIMEGUEN. The lower parts of the low countries seem partly to have been gained from the sea, and partly to be made up of the plains of the Yssel, the Rhine, the Maese and the Schelde united. To Utrecht nothing but plain is seen, a rich black mould, wet, lower than the level of the waters which intersect it; almost entirely in grass; few or no farm houses, as the business of grazing requires few labourers. The canal is lined with country houses which bespeak the wealth and cleanliness of the country; but generally in an uncouth state and exhibiting no regular architecture. After passing Utrecht the hills N.E. of the Rhine come into view, and gather in towards the river till, at Wyck Dursted they are within 3. or 4. miles and at Amelengen they join the river. The plains, after passing Utrecht become more sandy; the hills are very poor and sandy, generally waste in broom, sometimes a little corn. The plains are in corn, grass and willow. The plantations of the latter are immense, and give it the air of an uncultivated country. There are now few chateaux. Farm houses abound, built generally of brick, and covered with tile or thatch. There are some apple trees, but no forest. A few inclosures of willow wattling. In the gardens are hedges of beach 1. foot apart, which, not losing it's old leaves till they are pushed off in the spring by the young ones, gives the shelter of evergreens. The Rhine is here about 300. yards wide, and the road to Nimeguen passing it a little below Wattelingen leaves Hetern in sight on the left. On this side, the plains of the Rhine, the Ling, and the Waal unite. The Rhine and Waal are crossed on vibrating boats,[3] the rope supported by a line of 7. little barks. The platform by which you go on to the ferry boat is supported by boats. The view from the hill at Gress [Grebbe] is sublime. It commands the Waal, and extends far up the Rhine. That also up and down the Waal from the Bellevue of Nimeguen is very fine. The chateau here is pretended to have lodged Julius Caesar. This is giving it an antiquity of at least 18. centuries, which must be apocryphal. Some few sheep to-day, which were feeding in turnep-patches.

Apr. 1. CRANENBURG. CLEVES. SANTEN. REYNBERG. HOOGSTRAAT. The transition from ease and opulence to extreme poverty is remarkeable on crossing the line between the Dutch and Prussian territory. The soil and climate are the same. The governments alone differ. With the poverty, the fear also of slaves is visible in the faces of the Prussian subjects. There is an improvement however in the physiognomy, especially could it be a little brightened up. The road leads generally over the hills, but sometimes thro' skirts of the plains of the Rhine. These are always extensive and good. They want manure, being visibly worn down. The hills are almost always sandy, barren, uncultivated, and insusceptible of culture, covered with broom and moss. Here and there a little indifferent forest, which is sometimes of beach. The plains are principally in corn, some grass and willow. There are no chateaux, nor houses that bespeak the existence even of a middle class. Universal and equal poverty overspreads the whole. In the villages too, which seem to be falling down, the overproportion of women is evident. The cultivators seem to live on their farms. The farmhouses are of mud, the better sort of brick, all covered with thatch. Cleves is little more than a village. If there are shops or magazines of merchandize in it, they shew little. Here and there at a window some small articles are hung up within the glass. The gooseberry beginning to leaf.

Apr. 2. Passed the Rhine at ESSENBERG. It is there about ¼ of a mile wide, or 500 yds. It is crossed in a scow with sails. The wind being on the quarter we were 8. or 10′ only in the passage. Duysberg is but a village, in fact, walled in; the buildings mostly of brick. No new ones which indicate a thriving state. I had understood that near that were remains of the encampment of Varus, in which he and his legions fell by the arms of Arminius (in the time of Tiberius I think it was) but there was not a person to be found in Duysberg who could understand either English, French, Italian or Latin. So I could make no enquiry.

From DUYSBERG to DUSSELDORP the road leads sometimes over the hills, sometimes thro' the plains of the Rhine, the quality of which are as before described. On the hills however are considerable groves of oak, of spontaneous growth, which seems to be of more than a century: but the soil being barren, the trees, tho' high, are crooked and knotty. The undergrowth is broom and moss. In the plains is corn entirely, as they are become rather sandy for grass. There are no inclosures on the Rhine at all. The houses are poor and ruinous, mostly of brick and scantling mixed, a good deal of rape cultivated.

DUSSELDORP. The gallery of paintings is sublime, particularly the room of Vander Werff. The plains from Dusseldorp to Cologne are much more extensive, and go off in barren downs at some distance from the river. These downs extend far, according to appearance. They are manuring the plains with lime. A gate at the elector's chateau on this road in this form [*see Fig. 3*] [which would be better thus perhaps] [*see Fig 4*]. We cross at Cologne on a pendulum boat. I observe the hog

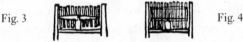

Fig. 3   Fig. 4

of this country (Westphalia) of which the celebrated ham is made, is tall, gaunt, and with heavy lop ears. Fatted at a year old, would weigh 100. or 120 ℔. at 2 years old 200 ℔. Their principal food is acorns. The pork fresh sells @ 2½d sterl. the ℔. The ham ready made @ 5½d sterl. the ℔. 106. ℔ of this country is equal to 100. ℔ of Holland. About 4. ℔ of fine Holland salt is put on 100. ℔ of pork. It is smoked in a room which has no chimney. Well informed people here tell me there is no other part of the world where the bacon is smoked. They do not know that we do it. Cologne is the principal market of exportation. They find that the small hog makes the sweetest meat.

COLOGNE is a sovereign city, having no territory out of it's walls. It contains about 60.000. inhabitants; appears to have much commerce, and to abound with poor. It's commerce is principally in the hands of protestants, of whom there are about 60. houses in the city. They are extremely restricted in their operations, and otherwise oppressed in every form by the government which is catholic, and excessively intolerant. Their Senate some time ago, by a majority of 22. to 18. allowed them to have a church: but it is believed this privilege will be revoked. There are about 250. catholic churches in the city. The Rhine is here about 400. yds. wide. This city is in 50.° Lat. wanting about 6.' Here the vines begin, and it is the most Northern spot on the earth on which wine is made. Their first grapes came from Orleans, since that from Alsace, Champagne &c. It is 32. years only since the first vines were sent from Cassel, near Mayence, to the Cape of good hope, of which the Cape wine is now made. Afterwards new supplies were sent from the same quarter. That I suppose is the most Southern spot on the globe where wine is made and it is singular that the same vine should have furnished two wines as much opposed to each other in quality, as in situation. Note I was addressed here by Mr. Damen of Amsterdam to Mr. Jean Jaques Peuchen of this place merchant.

Apr. 4. COLOGNE. BONNE. ANDERNACH. COBLENTZ. I see many walnut trees to-day in the open fields. It would seem as if this tree and wine required the same climate. The soil begins now to be reddish, both on the hills and in the plains. These from Cologne to Bonne extend about 3. miles from the river on each side: but, a little above Bonne, they become contracted, and continue from thence to be from 1. mile to nothing, comprehending both sides of the river. They are in corn, some clover, and rape, and many vines. These are planted in rows 3. feet apart both ways. The vine is left about 6. or 8.f. high, and stuck with poles 10. or 12.f. high. To these poles they are tied in two places, at the height of about 2. and 4.f. They are now performing this operation. The hills are generally excessively steep, a great proportion of them barren, the rest in vines principally, sometimes small patches of corn. In the plains, tho' rich, I observe they dung their vines plentifully; and it is observed here, as elsewhere, that the plains yield much wine, but bad. The good is furnished from the hills. The walnut, willow, and appletree beginning to leaf.

ANDERNACH is the port on the Rhine to which the famous millstones of Cologne are brought, the quarry, as some say, being at Mendich, 3. or 4. leagues from thence. I suppose they have been called Cologne millstones because the merchants of that place having the most extensive correspondence, have usually sent them to all parts of the world. I observed great collections of them at Cologne. This is one account.

Apr. 5. COBLENTZ, NASSAU. Another account is that these stones are cut at Triers, and brought down the Moselle. I could not learn the price of them at the quarry; but I was shewn a grindstone, of the same stone, 5.f. diam. which cost at Triers 6. florins. It was but of half the thickness of a millstone. I suppose therefore that two millstones would cost about as much as 3. of these grindstones, i.e. about a guinea and a half. This country abounds with slate.

The best Moselle wines are made about 15. leagues from hence, in an excessively mountainous country. The 1st. quality (without any comparison) is that made on the mountain of Brownberg, adjoining to the village of Dusmond, and the best crop is that of the Baron Breidbach Burrhesheim grand chambellan et grand Baillif de Coblentz. His Receveur, of the name of Mayer, lives at Dusmond. The last fine year was 1783. which sells now at 50. Louis the foudre, which contains 6 aumes of 170 bottles each = about 1100. bottles. This is about 22. sous Tournois the bottle. In general the Baron Burresheim's crop will sell as soon as made, say at the vintage, for 130. 140. 150. ecus the foudre (the ecu is 1½ florin of Holland) say 200*f.* 2. Vialen is the 2d. quality, and sells new at 120. ecus the futre. 3. Crach, Bisport are the 3d. and sell for about 105. ecus. I compared Crach of 1783. with Baron Burrhesheim's of the same year. The latter is quite clear of acid, stronger, and very sensibly the best. 4. Selting, which sells at 100. ecus. 5. Kous, Berncastle the 5th. quality sells at 80. or 90. After this there is a gradation of qualities down to 30. ecus.

These wines must be 5. or 6. years old before they are quite ripe for drinking. 1000. plants yield a foudre of wine a year in the most plentiful vineyards. In other vineyards it will take 2000. or 2500. plants to yield a foudre. The culture of 1000. plants costs about 1. Louis a year. A day's labour of a man is paid in Winter 20 kreitzers (i.e. ⅓ of a florin) in Summer 26. A woman's is half that. The red wines of this country are very indifferent and will not keep. The Moselle is here from 100. to 200. yds. wide, the Rhine 300. to 400. A jessamine in the Ct. de Moustier's garden in leaf.

In the Elector of Treves' palace at Coblentz, are large rooms very well warmed by warm air conveyed from an oven below through tubes which open into the rooms. An oil and vinegar cruet in this form. At

Coblentz we pass the river on a pendulum boat, and the road to Nassau is over tremendous hills, on which is here and there a little corn, more vines, but mostly barren. In some of these barrens are forests of beach and oak, tolerably large, but crooked and knotty, the undergrowth beach brush, broom and moss. The soil of the plains, and of the hills where they are cultivable, is reddish. Nassau is a village the whole rents of which should not amount to more than a hundred or two guineas, yet it gives the title of Prince to the house of Orange to which it belongs.

Apr. 6. NASSAU, SCHWELBACH, WISBADEN, HOCHHEIM, FRANKFORT. The road from Nassau to Schwelbach is over hills, or rather mountains, both high and steep; always poor, and above half of them barren in beach and oak. At Schwelbach there is some chesnut. The other parts are either in winter grain, or preparing for that of the Spring. Between Schwelbach and Wisbaden we come in sight of the plains of the Rhine, which are very extensive. From hence the lands, both high and low are very fine, in corn, vines, and fruit trees. The country has the appearance of wealth, especially in the approach to Frankfort.

Apr. 7. FRANCFORT. Among the poultry, I have seen no turkies in Germany till I arrive at this place. The Stork, or Crane, is very commonly tame here. It is a miserable, dirty, ill-looking bird. The Lutheran is the reigning religion here and is equally intolerant to the Catholic and Calvinist, excluding them from the free corps.

Apr. 8. FRANCFORT, HANAU. The road goes thro' the plains of the Maine, which are mulatto and very fine. They are well cultivated till you pass the line between the republic and the Landgraviate of Hesse, when you immediately see the effect of the difference of government, notwithstanding the tendency which the neighborhood of such a commercial town as Francfort has to counteract the effects of tyranny in it's vicinities, and to animate them in spite of oppression. In Francfort all is life, bustle and motion. In Hanau the silence and quiet of the mansions of the dead. Nobody is seen moving in the streets; every door is shut; no sound of the saw, the hammer, or other utensil of industry. The drum and fife is all that is heard. The streets are cleaner than a German floor, because nobody passes them. At Williamsbath, near Hanau, is a country seat of the Landgrave. There is a ruin which is clever. It presents the remains of an old castle. The ground plan is

in this form. The upper story in this, a circular room of 31½f. diameter within. The 4. little square towers, at the corners, finish at the floor of the upper story, so as to be only platforms to walk out on. Over the circular room is platform also, which is covered by the broken parapet which once crowned the top, but is now fallen off in some parts, whilst the other parts remain. I like better however the form of the ruin at Hagley in England which was thus. A centry box here covered over

with bark, so as to look exactly like the trunk of an old tree. This is a good idea, and may be of much avail in a garden. There is a hermitage in which is a good figure of a hermit in plaister, coloured to the life, with a table and book before him, in the attitude of reading and contemplation. In a little cell is his bed, in another his books, some tools &c., in another his little provision of fire wood &c. There is a monument erected to the son of the present landgrave in the form of a pyramid, the base of which is 18½f. The side declines from the perpendicular about 22½.° An arch is carried through it both ways so as to present a door in each side. In the middle of this, at the crossing of the two arches, is a marble monument with this inscription 'ante tempus.' He died at 12. years of age.   Between Hanau and Frankfort, in sight of the road, is the village of Bergen, where was fought the battle of Bergen in the war before last.—Things worth noting here are 1. a folding ladder, 2. manner of packing china cups and saucers, the former in a circle within the latter. 3. the marks of different manufactures of china, to wit. Dresden with two swords, Hecks with a wheel,

with a Ⱳ. Frankendaal with 𝒵ℬ (for Charles Theodore) and a

👑 over it. Berlin with   4. the top rail of the waggon sup-

ported by the washers on the ends of the axle-trees.

Apr. 10. FRANKFORT, HOCHEIM. MAYENCE. The little tyrants round about having disarmed their people, and made it very criminal to kill game, one knows when they quit the territory of Frankfort by the quantity of game which is seen. In the Republic, every body being allowed to be armed, and to hunt on their own lands, there is very little game left in it's territory. The hog hereabouts resembles extremely the little hog of Virginia, round like that, a small head, and short upright ears. This makes the ham of Mayence, so much esteemed at Paris.

We cross the Rhine at Mayence on a bridge 1840. feet long, supported by 47. boats. It is not in a direct line, but curved up against the stream, which may strengthen it, if the difference between the upper and lower curve be sensible, if the planks of the floor be thick, well jointed together, and forming sectors of circles, so as to act on the whole as the stones of an arch. But it has by no means this appearance. Near one end, one of the boats has an Axis in peritrochio, and a chain, by which it may be let drop down stream some distance, with the portion of the floor belonging to it, so as to let a vessel through. Then it is wound up again into place, and to consolidate it the more with the adjoining parts, the loose section is a little higher, and has at each end a folding stage, which folds back on it when it moves down, and when brought up again into place, these stages are folded over on the bridge. This whole operation takes but 4. or 5. minutes. In the winter the bridge is taken away entirely, on account of the ice, and then every thing passes on the ice, thro' the whole winter.

Apr. 11. MAYENCE. RUDESHEIM. JOHANSBERG. MARKEBRONN. The women do everything here. They dig the earth, plough, saw, cut, and split wood, row, tow the batteaux &c. In a small but dull kind of batteau, with two hands rowing with a kind of large paddle, and a square sail but scarcely a breath of wind we went down the river at the rate of

5. miles an hour, making it 3½ hours to Rudesheim. The floats of wood which go with the current only, go 1½ mile an hour. They go night and day. There are 5. boatmills abreast here. Their floats seem to be about 8.f. broad. The Rhine yields salmon, carp, pike, and perch, and the little rivers running into it yield speckled trout. The plains from Maintz to Rudesheim are good and in corn: the hills mostly in vines. The banks of the river are so low that, standing up in the batteau, I could generally see what was in the plains, yet they are seldom overflowed.

Though they begin to make wine, as has been said, at Cologne, and continue it up the river indefinitely, yet it is only from Rudesheim to Hocheim, that wines of the very first quality are made. The river happens there to run due East and West, so as to give to it's hills on that side a Southern aspect, and even in this canton, it is only Hocheim, Johansberg, and Rudesheim that are considered as of the very first quality. Johansberg is a little mountain (berg signifies mountain) wherein is a religious house, about 15. miles below Mayence, and near the village of Vingel. It has a Southern aspect, the soil a barren mulatto clay, mixed with a good deal of stone, and some slate. This wine used to be but on a par with Hocheim and Rudesheim; but the place having come to the Bp. of Fulda, he improved it's culture so as to render it stronger, and since the year 1775. it sells at double the price of the other two. It has none of the acid of the Hocheim and other Rhenish wines. There are about 60. tons made in a good year, which sell, as soon as of a drinkable age, at 1000.f. each. The ton here contains 7½ aumes of 170. bottles each. Rudesheim is a village about 18. or 20. miles below Mayence. It's fine wines are made on the hills about a mile below the village, which look to the South, and on the middle and lower parts of them. They are terrassed. The soil is grey, about one half of slate and rotten stone, the other half of barren clay, excessively steep. Just behind the village also is a little spot, called hinder house, belonging to the Counts of Sicken and Oschstein, wherein each makes about a ton of wine of the first quality. This spot extends from the bottom to the top of the hill. The vignerons of Rudesheim dung their vines about once in 5. or 6. years putting a one-horse tumbrel load of dung on every 12.f. square. 1000 plants yield about 4. aumes in a good year.

The best crops are
the Chanoines of Mayence, who makes 15. pieces of 7½ aumes
le Comte de Sicken	6.	" "
le Comte d'Oschstein	9.	
l'electeur de Mayence	6.	
le Comte de Meternisch	6.	
Monsr. de Boze	5.	
M. Ackerman, bailiff et Aubergiste des 3. couronnes	8.	
M. Ackerman le fils, aubergiste à la couronne	5.	
M. Lynn, aubergiste de l'Ange	5.	
Baron de Wetzel	7.	
Couvent de Mariahausen, des religieuses Benedictines	7.	
M. Johan Yung	8.	
M. de Rieden	5.	
	92.	

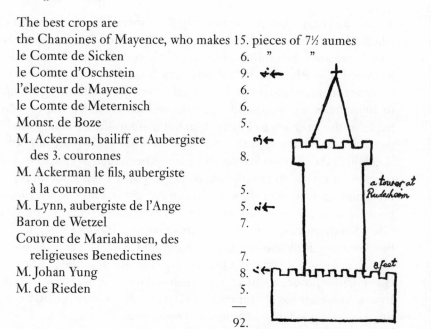

a tower at Rudesheim

8 feet

These wines begin to be drinkable at about 5. years old. The proprietors sell them old or young, according to the price offered, and according to their own want of money. There is always a little difference between different casks, and therefore when you chuse and buy a single cask, you pay 3, 4, 5, or 600. florins for it. They are not at all acid, and to my taste much preferable to Hocheim, tho' but of the same price. Hocheim is a village about 3. miles above Mayence, on the Maine where it empties into the Rhine. The spot whereon the good wine is made is the hill side from the church down to the plain, a gentle slope of about ¼ of a mile wide and extending half a mile towards Mayence. It is of South Western aspect, very poor, sometimes grey, sometimes mulatto, with a moderate mixture of small broken stone. The vines are planted 3.f. apart, and stuck with sticks about 6.f. high. The vine too is cut at that height. They are dunged once in 3. or 4. years. 1000 plants yield from 1. to 2. aumes a year. They begin to yield a little at 3. years old, and continue to 100. years, unless sooner killed by a cold winter. Dick, keeper of the Rothen-house tavern at Francfort, a great wine merchant, who has between 3. and 400. tons of wine in his cellars, tells me that Hocheim of the year 1783. sold, as soon as it was made, at 90. florins the aume, Rudesheim of the same year, as soon as made at 115. florins, and Markebronn 70. florins. But a peasant of Hocheim tells me that the best crops of Hocheim in the good years, when sold new, sell but for about 32. or 33. florins the aume: but that it is only the poorer proprietors who sell new. The fine crops are

Count Ingleheim	about 10. tons	⎫
Baron d'Alberg	8.	all of these keep till
Count Schimbon	14.	about 15. years old be-
the Chanoines of Mayence	18.	fore they sell, unless
Counsellor Schik de Vetsler	15.	they are offered a very
Convent of Jacobsberg	8.	good price sooner.
the Chanoine of Fechbach	10.	⎭
the Carmelites of Frankfort	8.	who only sell by the bottle in their own tavern in Francfort.
the Bailiff of Hocheim	11.	who sells at 3. or 4. years old
Zimmerman, a bourgeois	4.	⎫ these being poor sell new.
Feldman, a carpenter	2.	⎭

Markebronn (bronn signifies a spring, and is probably of affinity with the Scotch word, burn) is a little canton in the same range of hills, adjoining to the village of Hagenheim, about 3. miles above Johansberg, subject to the elector of Mayence. It is a sloping hill side of Southern aspect, mulatto, poor, and mixed with some stone. This yields wine of the 2d. quality.

Apr. 12. MAYENCE. OPPENHEIM. WORMS. MANHEIM. On the road between Mayence and Oppenheim are three cantons which are also esteemed as yielding wines of the 2d. quality. These are Laudenheim, Bodenheim, and Nierstein. Laudenheim is a village about 4. or 5. miles from Mayence. It's wines are made on a steep hill side, the soil of which is grey, poor and mixed with some stone. The river happens there to make a short turn to the S.W. so as to present it's hills to the S.E. Bodenheim is a village 9. miles, and Nierstein another about 10. or 11. miles from Mayence. Here too the river is N.E. and S.W. so as to give to the hills between these villages a S.E. aspect; and at Nierstein a valley making off, brings the face of the hill round to the South. The hills between these villages are almost perpendicular, of a vermillion red, very poor, and having as much rotten stone as earth. It is to be observed that these are the only cantons on the South side of the river which yield good wine, the hills on this side being generally exposed to the cold winds, and turned from the sun. The annexed bill of prices current will give an idea of the estimation of these wines respectively.

With respect to the grapes in this country, there are three kinds in use for making white wine (for I take no notice of the red wines as being absolutely worthless.) 1. The Klemperien, of which the inferior qualities of Rhenish wines are made, and is cultivated because of it's hardness. The wines of this grape descend as low as 100. florins the ton of 8. aumes. 2. The Rhysslin grape which grows only from Hocheim down to Rudesheim. This is small and delicate, and therefore succeeds only in this chosen spot. Even at Rudesheim, it yields a fine wine only in the little spot called Hinder-house before mentioned: the mass of good wines made at Rudesheim below the village being of the 3d. kind of grape, which is called the Orleans grape.

To Oppenheim the plains of the Rhine and Maine are united. From that place we see the commencement of the Berg-strasse, or mountains which separate at first the plains of the Rhine and Maine, then cross the Neckar at Heidelberg, and from thence forms the separation between the plains of the Neckar and Rhine, leaving those of the Rhine about 10. and 12. miles wide. These plains are sometimes black, sometimes mulatto, always rich. They are in corn, potatoes, and some willow. On the other side again, that is, on the West side, the hills keep at first close to the river. They are 150. or 200.f. high, sloping, red, good, and mostly in vines. Above Oppenheim, they begin to go off till they join the mountains of Lorraine and Alsace, which separate the waters of the Moselle and Rhine, leaving to the whole valley of the Rhine about 20. or 25. miles breadth. About Worms these plains are sandy, poor, and often covered only with small pine.

April 13. MANHEIM. There is a bridge over the Rhine here supported on 39. boats, and one over the Neckar on 11. boats. The bridge over the Rhine is 21½f. wide from rail to rail. The boats are 4.f. deep, 52.f. long, and 9f. 8I. broad. The space between boat and boat is 18f. 10I. From these data the length of the bridge should be 9f. − 8I + 18f − 10I × 40 = 1140. feet. In order to let vessels pass through, two boats well framed together, with their flooring are made to fall down stream together.—Here too they make good ham. It is fattened on round potatoes and Indian corn. The farmers smoke what is for their own use in their chimnies. When it is made for sale, and in greater quantities than the chimney will hold, they make the smoke of the chimney pass into an adjoining loft or apartment from which it has no issue; and here they hang their hams.

An economical curtain bedstead. The bedstead is 7.f. by 4.f.2I. From each leg there goes up an iron rod ⅜I. diam. Those from the legs at the foot of the bed meeting at top as in the margin, and those from the head meeting in like manner, so that the two at the foot form one point, and the two at the head another. On these points lays an oval iron rod, whose long diameter is 5.f. and short one 3f. 1.I. There is a hole through this rod at each end, by which it goes on firm on the point of the upright rods. Then a nut screws it down firmly. 10. breadths of stuff 2.f. 10I. wide and 8.f. 6.I. long form the curtains. There is no top nor vallons. The rings are fastened within 2½ or 3.I. of the top on the inside, which 2½I. or 3.I. stand up and are an ornament somewhat like a ruffle.

I have observed all along the Rhine that they make the oxen draw by the horns. A pair of very handsome chariot horses, large, bay, and 7. years old sell for 50. Louis. 1 ℔ of beef sells for 8 kreitzers (i.e. ⁸⁄₆₀ of a florin) 1 ℔ of mutton or veal 6. kreitzers, 1 ℔ of pork 7½ kr., of ham 12. kr., of fine wheat bread 2. kr., of butter 20. kr. 160 ℔ wheat 6 *f.* 160 ℔ maize 5.*f.* 160 ℔ potatoes 1 *f.* 100. ℔ hay 1 *f.* a cord of wood (which is 4.4 and 6.f.) 7 *f.* A labourer by the day receives 24. kr. and feeds himself. A journee or arpent of land (which is 8. by 200. steps) such as the middling plains of the Rhine will sell for 200. *f.* There are more souldiers here than other inhabitants, to wit, 6000. souldiers and 4000. males of full age of the citizens, the whole number of whom is reckoned at 20,000.

Apr. 14. MANHEIM. DOSSENHEIM. HEIDELBERG. SCHWETZINGEN. MANHEIM. The elector placed in 1768. 2. male and 5. females of the Angora goat at Dossenheim, which is at the foot of the Bergstrasse mountains. He sold 25. last year, and has now 70. They are removed into the mountains 4. leagues beyond Dossenheim. Heidelberg is on the Neckar just where it issues from the Bergstrasse mountains, occupying the first skirt of a plain which it forms. The Chateau is up the hill a considerable height. The gardens lie above the Chateau, climbing up the mountain in terrasses. This chateau is the most noble ruin I have ever seen, having been reduced to that state by the French in the time of Louis XIV. 1693. Nothing remains under cover but the chapel. The situation is romantic and pleasing beyond expression. It is on a great scale much like the situation of Petrarch's chateau at Vaucluse on a small one. The climate too is like that of Italy. The apple, the pear, cherry, peach, apricot and almond are all in bloom. There is a station in the garden to which the chateau re-echoes distinctly 4. syllables. The famous ton of Heidelberg was new built in 1751. and made to contain 30. foudres more than the antient one. It is said to contain 236. foudres of 1200. bottles each. I measured it, and found it's length external to be 28.f. 10.I. it's diameter at the end 20.f. 3.I. the thickness of the staves 7½I. thickness of the hoops 7½I. besides a great deal of external framing. There is no wine in it now. The gardens at Schwetzingen shew how much money may be laid out to make an ugly thing. What is called the English quarter however relieves the eye from the strait rows of trees, round and square basons which constitute the great mass of the garden. There are some tolerable morsels of Graecian architecture, and a good ruin. The Aviary too is clever. It consists of cells of about 8.f. wide, arranged round, and looking into, a circular area of about 40. or 50.f. diameter. The cells have doors both of wire and glass, and have small shrubs in them. The plains of the Rhine on this side are 12. miles wide, bounded by the Bergstrasse mountains. These appear to be 800. or 1000.f. high; the lower part in vines, from which is made what is called the vin de Nichar; the upper in chesnut.

There are some cultivated spots however quite to the top. The plains are generally mulatto, in corn principally; they are planting potatoes in some parts, and leaving others open for Maize and tobacco. Many peach and other fruit trees on the lower part of the mountain. The paths on some parts of these mountains are somewhat in the style represented in the margin.

MANHEIM. KAEFERTHAL. MANHEIM. Just beyond Kaeferthal is an extensive sandy waste planted in pine, in which the elector has about 200 sangliers[4] tamed. I saw about 50. The heaviest I am told would weigh about 300 ℔. They are fed on round potatoes and range in an extensive forest of small pines. At the village of Kaeferthal is a plantation of Rhubarb begun in 1769 by a private company. It contains 20 arpens or journees, and it's culture costs about 4. or 500ƒ a year. It sometimes employs 40 to 50 labourers at a time. The best age to sell the Rhubarb at is the 5th. or 6th. year; but the sale being dull they keep it sometimes to the 10th. year. They find it best to let it remain in the earth, because when taken out it is liable to the worm. At about 10. years old however it begins to rot in the ground. They sell about 200 quintals a year at 2 or 3ƒ a ℔. and could sell double that quantity from this ground if they could find a market. The apothecaries of Frankfort and of England are the principal buyers. It is in beds resembling lettuce beds, the plants 4. 5 or 6I. apart. When dug, a thread is passed thro' every peice of root and it is hung separate in a kind of rack. When dry it is rasped. What comes off is given to the cattle.

Apr. 15. MANHEIM. SPIRE. CARLSRUH. The valley preserves it's width, extending on each side of the river about 10. or 12. miles. But the soil loses much in it's quality, becoming sandy and lean, often barren and overgrown with pine thicket. At Spire is nothing remarkeable. Between that and Carlsruh we pass the Rhine in a common Skow with oars where it is between 3. and 400. yards wide. Carlsruh is the residence of the Margrave of Baden, a sovereign prince. His chateau is built in the midst of a natural forest of several leagues diameter, and of the best trees I have seen in these countries. They are mostly oak, and would be deemed but indifferent in America. A great deal of money has been spent to do more harm than good to the ground, cutting a number of straight allies through the forest. He has a pheasantry

of the gold and silver kind, the latter very tame, but the former excessively shy. A little inclosure of stone 2½f. high and 30.f. diameter in
which are two tamed beavers. There is a pond of 15.f. diameter in the
center and at each end a little cell for them to retire into, which is
stowed with boughs and twigs with leaves on them which are their
principal food. They eat bread also. Twice a week the water is changed.
They cannot get over this wall.—Some cerfs[5] of a peculiar kind, spot-
ted like fawns. The horns remarkeably long, small and sharp, with few
points. I am not sure there were more than two to each main beam,
and I saw distinctly there came out a separate and subordinate beam
from the root of each. 8 Ancora goats, beautiful animals, all white.
This town is only an appendage of the Chateau, and but a moderate
one. It is a league from Durlach, halfway between that and the
river.—I observe they twist the funnels of their stoves about in
any form, for ornament merely, without fearing their smoking,
as thus e.g.

Apr. 16. CARLSRUH. RASTADT. SCHOLHOVEN. BISCHOFHEIM. KEHL.
STRASBOURG. The valley of the Rhine still preserves it's width, but
varies in quality, sometimes a rich mulatto loam, sometimes a poor
sand, covered with small pine. The culture is generally corn. It is to be
noted that thro the whole of my route through the Netherlds. and the
valley of the Rhine there is a little red clover every here and there, and
a great deal of rape cultivated. The seed of this is sold to be made into
oil. The rape is now in blossom. No inclosures. The fruit trees are generally blossoming thro' the whole valley. The high mountains of the
Bergstrasse as also of Alsace are crowned with snow within this day or
two. The every day dress of the country women here is black. Rastadt
is a seat also of the Margrave of Baden. Scholhoven and Kehl are in his
territory but not Bischofheim. I see no beggars since I enter his government nor is the traveller obliged to ransom himself every moment
by a chaussée gold. The roads are excellent, and made so I presume
out of the coffers of the prince. From Cleves till I enter the Margra-
vate of Baden the roads have been strung with beggars, in Hesse the
most, and the road tax very heavy. We pay it chearfully however
through the territory of Frankfort and thence up the Rhine, because
fine gravelled roads are kept up. But through the Prussian and other

parts of the road below Frankfort the roads are only as made by the carriages, there not appearing to have been ever a day's work employed on them.—At Strasburg we pass the Rhine on a wooden bridge.

At Brussell and Antwerp the fuel is pit-coal, dug in Brabant. Thro' all Holland it is turf. From Cleves to Cologne it is pit coal brought from Engld. They burn it in open stoves. From thence it is wood burnt in close stoves, till you get to Strasbourg, where the open chimney comes again into use.

April 16. 17. 18. STRASBOURG. The Vin de paille is made in the neighborhood of Colmar in Alsace about   from this place. It takes it's name from the circumstance of spreading the grapes on straw where they are preserved till spring, and then made into wine. The little juice then remaining in them makes a rich sweet wine, but the dearest in the world without being the best by any means. They charge 9ᵗ the bottle for it in the taverns of Strasbourg. It is the caprice of wealth alone which continues so losing an operation. This wine is sought because dear, while the better wine of Frontignan is rarely seen at a good table because it is cheap.

STRASBOURG. SAVERNE. PHALSBOURG. As far as Saverne, the country is in waving hills and hollows, red, rich enough, mostly in small grain, but some vines. A little stone. From Saverne to Phalsbourg we cross a considerable mountain which takes an hour to rise it.

April 19. PHALSBOURG. FENESTRANGE. MOYENVIC. NANCY. Asparagus to-day at Moyenvic. The country is always either mountainous or hilly, red, tolerably good, and in small grain. On the hills about Fenestrange, Moyenvic and Nancy are some small vineyards where a bad wine is made. No inclosures. Some good sheep, indifferent cattle and small horses. The most forest I have seen in France, principally of beech, pretty large. The houses, as in Germany are of scantling, filled in with wicker and morter, and covered either with thatch or tiles. The people too here, as there, gathered in villages. Oxen plough here with collars and hames. The awkward figure of their mould board leads one to consider what should be it's form.[6] The offices of the mouldboard are to receive the sod after the share has cut under it, to raise it gradually and reverse it. The fore end of it then should be horizontal to enter under the sod, and the hind end perpendicular to throw it over, the intermediate surface changing gradually from the horizontal to the perpendicular. It should be as wide as the furrow, and of a length suited to the construction of the plough. The following would seem a good method of making it. Take a block whose length, breadth and thickness is that of your intended mouldboard, suppose 2½f. long and 8I. broad and thick. Draw the lines a. d. and c. d. Fig. 1. With a saw, the toothed edge of which is straight, enter at, a, and cut on, guiding the hind part of the saw on the line a. b. and the fore part on the line a. d. till the saw reaches the points b. and d. Then enter it at, c. and cut on, guiding it by the lines c. b. and c. d. till it reaches the points b. and d. The quarter a. b. c. d. will then be completely cut out, and the diagonal from d. to b. laid bare. The peice may now be represented as in fig. 2. Then saw in transversly, at every 2. inches, till the saw reaches

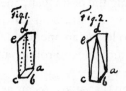

the line c. e. and the diagonal b. d. and cut out the peices with a chissel. The upper surface will thus be formed. With a gage opened to 8.I. and guided by the line c. e. scribe the upper edge of the board from d. to b. Cut that edge perpendicular to the face of the board and scribe it of the proper thickness. Then form the under side by the upper, by cutting transversely with the saw, and taking out the peices with a chissel. As the upper edge of the share fin rises a little, the fore end of the board b. c. will rise as much from a strict horizontal position, and will throw the hind end a. d. exactly as much beyond the perpendicular so as to ensure the reversing of the sod.—The women here, as in Germany do all sorts of work. While one considers them as useful and rational companions, one cannot forget that they are also objects of our pleasures. Nor can they ever forget it. While employed in dirt and drudgery some tag of a ribbon, some ring or bit of bracelet, earbob or necklace, or something of that kind will shew that the desire of pleasing is never suspended in them. How valuable is that state of society which allots to them internal emploiments only, and external to the men. They are formed by nature for attentions and not for hard labour. A woman never forgets one of the numerous train of little offices which belong to her; a man forgets often.

Apr. 20. NANCY. TOULE. VOID. LIGNY EN BARROIS. BAR LE DUC. ST. DIZIER. Nancy itself is a neat little town, and it's environs very agreeable. The valley of the little branch of the Moselle on which it is, is about a mile wide. The road then crossing the head waters of the Moselle, the Maes, and the Marne, the country is very hilly, and perhaps a third of it poor and in forests of beach. The other two thirds from poor up to midling, red, and stony, almost entirely in corn, now and then only some vines on the hills. The Moselle at Toul is 30 or 40 yds. wide, the Maese near Void about half that, the Marne at St. Dizier about 40. yds. They all make good plains of from a quarter of a mile to a mile wide. The hills of the Maese abound with chalk. The rocks coming down from the tops of the hills on all the road of this day at regular intervals like the ribs of an animal, have a very singular appearance. Considerable flocks of sheep and asses, and in the approach to St. Dizier great plantations of apple and cherry trees. Here and there a peach tree, all in general bloom. The roads thro' Lorraine are strung with beggars.

Apr. 21. ST. DIZIER. VITRY LE FRANÇAIS. CHALONS SUR MARNE. EPERNAY. The plains of the Marne and the Sault uniting, appear boundless to the eye till we approach their confluence at Vitry where the hills come in on the right. After that the plains are generally about a mile, mulatto, of middling quality sometimes stony. Sometimes the ground goes off from the river so sloping, that one does not know whether to call it high or low land. The hills are mulatto also but whitish, occasioned by the quantity of chalk which seems to constitute their universal base. They are poor and principally in vines. The streams of water are of the colour of milk, occasioned by the chalk also. No inclosures. Some flocks of sheep. Children gathering dung in the roads. Here and there a chateau, but none considerable.

Apr. 22. EPERNAY. The hills abound with chalk. Of this they make lime, not so strong as stone lime, and therefore to be used in greater proportion. They cut the blocks into regular forms also like stone and build houses of it. The common earth too, well impregnated with this, is made into mortar, moulded in the form of brick, dried in the sun, and houses built of them which last 100 or 200 years. The plains here are a mile wide, red, good, in corn, clover, Luzerne, St. foin. The hills are in vines, and this being precisely the canton where the most celebrated wines of Champagne are made details must be entered into. Remember however that they will relate always to the white wines unless where the red are expressly mentioned. The reason is that their red wines, tho much esteemed on the spot, are by no means esteemed elsewhere equally with their white, nor do they merit it.

A Topographical sketch of the position of the wine villages, the course of the hills, and consequently the aspect of the vine-yards.

Soil. Meagre mulatto clay mixt with small broken stones, and a little hue of chalk. Very dry.

Aspect. May be better seen by the annexed diagram, observing that the wine of Aij is made from a. to b. Dizy b. to c. Auvillij d. to e. Cumieres e. to f. Epernay g. to h. Perry l. to k. The hills from Aij to Cumieres are generally about 250f. high. The good wine is made only in the middle region. The lower region however is better than the upper because this last is exposed to cold winds and a colder atmosphere.

Culture. The vines are planted 2f. apart. Afterwards they are multi-plied (provignés) when a stock puts out two shoots they lay them down, spread them open and cover them with earth so as to have in the end about a plant for every square foot. This operation is per-formed with the aid of a hook formed thus ϒ and 9.I. long which being stuck in the ground holds down the main stock while the labourer separates and covers the new shoots. They leave two buds above the ground. When the vine has shot up high enough, they stick it with oak sticks of the size and length of our tobacco sticks and tie the vine to them with straw. These sticks cost 2^{tt} the hundred and will last 40. years. An arpent, one year with another in the fine vineyards gives 12. peices and in the inferior vineyards 25. pieces. Each piece is of 200. bottles. An arpent of the first quality sells for 3000^{tt} and there have been instances of 7200^{tt} (the arpent contains 100 verges of 22 pieds square). The arpent of inferior quality sells at 1000.^{tt} They plant the vines in a hole about a foot deep, and fill that hole with good mould to make the plant take. Otherwise it would perish. Afterwards if ever they put dung it is very little. During wheat harvest there is a month or 6. weeks that nothing is done in the vineyards. That is to say from the 1st. Aug. to the beginning of vintage. The vintage com-mences early in Sep. and lasts a month. A day's work of a labourer in the busiest season is 20s. and he feeds himself. In the least busy season it is 15s. Cornlands are rented from 4^{tt} to 24,^{tt} but vinelands never rented. The three façons of an arpent of vines cost 15.^{tt} The whole year's expence of an arpent is worth 100.^{tt}

Grapes. The bulk of their grapes are purple, which they prefer for making even white wine. They press them very lightly (without tread-ing them or permitting them to ferment at all) for about an hour, so that it is the beginning of the running only which makes the bright wine. What follows the beginning is of a straw colour and therefore not placed on a level with the first; the last part of the juice produced by strong pressure is red and ordinary. They chuse the bunches with as much care to make wine of the very 1st. quality as if to eat. Not above one eighth of the whole grapes will do for this purpose. The white grape, tho not so fine for wine as the red, when the red can be produced, and more liable to rot in a moist season, yet grows better if the soil be excessively poor, and therefore in such a soil it is preferred: because there indeed the red would not grow at all.

Wines. The white wines are either 1. mousseux (sparkling) or 2. non mousseux (still). The sparkling are little drank in France but are alone known and drank in foreign countries. This makes so great a demand and so certain a one that it is the dearest by about an eigth and therefore they endeavour to make all sparkling if they can. This is done by bottling in the spring from the beginning of March to June. If it succeeds they lose abundance of bottles from $\frac{1}{10}$ to $\frac{1}{3}$. This is another cause encreasing the price. To make the still wine they bottle in September. This is only done when they know from some circumstance that the wine will not be brisk. So if the spring bottling fails to make a brisk wine, they decant it into other bottles in the fall and it then makes the very best still wine. In this operation it loses from $\frac{1}{10}$ to $\frac{1}{20}$ by sediment. They let it stand in the bottles in this case 48. hours with only a napkin spread over their mouths, but no cork. The best sparkling wine decanted in this manner makes the best still wine and which will keep much longer than that originally made still by being bottled in September. The brisk wines lose their briskness the older they are, but they gain in quality with age to a certain length. These wines are in perfection from 2. to 10. years old, and will even be very good to 15. 1766 was the best year ever known. 1775. and 1776 next to that. 1783 is the last good year, and that not to be compared with those. These wines stand icing very well.

Aij. M. Dorsay makes 1100 peices which sell as soon as made at 300.^{tt} and in good years 400 in the cask. I paid in his cellar to M. Louis his homme d'affaires for the remains of the year 1783. 3^{tt}-10 the bottle. Brisk champaigne of the same merit would have cost 4.^{tt} (The piece and demiqueue are the same. The feuillette is 100. bouteilles.) M. le Duc 400 to 500 pieces. M. de Villermont 300. pieces. Mr. Janson 250. pieces. All of the 1st. quality, red and white in equal quantities.

Auvillij. Les moines Benedictins, 1000 peices red and white but three fourths red. Both of the first quality. The king's table is supplied by them. This enables them to sell at 550^{tt} the piece tho' their white is hardly as good as Dorsay's, and their red is the best. L'Abbatiale belonging to the bishop of the place 1000 to 1200 pieces red and white, three fourths red at 400.^{tt} to 550.^{tt} because neighbors to the monks.

Cumieres is all of a 2d quality. Both red and white 150^{tt} to 200^{tt} the piece.

Epernay. Mde. Jermont 200 pieces @ 300.^{tt}—M. Patelaine 150 pieces. M. Marc 200 peices. M. Chertems 60 pieces. M. Lauchay 50 peices. M. Cousin 100 pieces (Aubergiste de l'hotel de Rohan á Epernay.) M. Pierrot 100 pieces. Les Chanoines regulieres d'Epernay 200. pieces. Mesdames les Urselines religieuses 100. pieces. M. Gilette 200.p. All of the 1st quality red and white in equal quantities.

Pierrij. M. Casotte 500 pieces. M. de la Motte 300 pieces. M. de Failli 300 pieces. I tasted his wine of 1779 which was really very good, tho not equal to that of M. Dorsay of 1783. He sells it at 2–10 to merchants and 3.^{tt} to individuals. Les Semnaristes 150.p. M. Hoquart 200.p. all of 1st. quality, white and red in equal quantities. At Cramont also there are some wines of 1st. quality made. At Avize also, and Aucy, Le Meni, Mareuil, Verzy-Verzenni. This last place (Verzy Verzenni) belongs to the M. de Sillery, the wines are carried to Sillery and there stored, whence they are called Vins de Sillery, tho not made there.

All these wines of Epernay and Pierrij sell almost as dear as M. Dorsay's, their quality being nearly the same. There are many small proprietors who might make all wines of the 1st. quality if they would cull their grapes: but they are too poor for this. Therefore the proprietors beforenamed, whose names are established buy of the poorer ones the right to cull their vineyards, by which means they increase their quantity, as they find about ⅓ of the grapes fit to make wine of the 1st. quality.

The lowest priced wines of all are 30^{tt} the peice, red or white. They make brandy of the pumice. In very bad years when their wines become vinegar they are sold for 6^{tt} the peice and made into brandy. They yield ¹⁄₁₀ brandy.

White Champaigne is good in proportion as it is silky and still. Many circumstances derange the scale of wines. The proprietor of the best vineyard, in the best year, having bad weather come upon while he is gathering his grapes, makes a bad wine, while his neighbor holding a more indifferent vineyard, which happens to be ingathering while the weather is good, makes a better. The M. de Casotte at Pierrij formerly was the first house. His successors by some imperceptible change of culture have degraded the quality of their wines. Their cellars are admirably made, being about 6. 8. or 10f. wide vaulted and extending into the ground in a kind of labyrinth to a prodigious distance, with an air hole of 2.f. diameter every 50. feet. From the top of the vault to the surface of the earth is from 15. to 30f. I have no where seen cellars comparable to these. In packing their bottles they lay a row on their side, then across them at each end they lay laths, and on these another row of bottles, heads and points on the others. By this means they can take out a bottle from the bottom or where they will.

Apr. 23. Epernay. Chateau Thieray. St. Jean. Meaux. Vergalant. Paris. From Epernay to St. Jean the road leads over hills which in the beginning are indifferent, but get better towards the last. The plains wherever seen are inconsiderable. After passing St. Jean the hills become good and the plains increase. The country about Vert-galant is pretty. A skirt of a low ridge which runs in on the extensive plains of the Marne and Seine is very picturesque. The general bloom of fruit trees proves there are more of them than I had imagined from travelling in other seasons when they are less distinguishable at a distance from the Forest trees.

84. TO WILLIAM SHORT

Dear Sir   *Frankfort on the Maine April 9. 1788.*
I arrived here on the 6th. inst. having been overtaken at Cleves by the commencement of a storm of rain hail and snow which lasted to this place, with intermissions now and then. The roads however continued good to Bonne, where beginning to be clayey and to be penetrated with the wet they became worse than imagination can paint for about 100 miles which brought me to the neighborhood of this place where the chaussee[1] began. My old friend the Baron de Geismar met me

here, on a letter I had written him from Amsterdam, and has been my Cicerone. It happens to be the moment of the fair of Frankfort which is very great. Yesterday we made an excursion up the Maine to Hanau, passing the ground where the battle of Bergen was fought in the war before last. Tomorrow we shall go to the vineyards of Hocheim, and perhaps to Rudesheim and Johannesberg, where the most celebrated wines are made. Then I shall pass on to Mayence, Worms, Manheim, Heidelberg and Spires, and from this last place to Strasburg. Unless I find there any thing from you which may call me to Paris directly, I shall probably go a little circuitously, perhaps by the way of Reims in Champagne, so that I am unable to say exactly when I shall be at Paris. I guess about the 20th. I met at Hanau with many acquaintances, the officers who had been stationed in Albemarle while in captivity. I have seen much good country on the Rhine, and bad whenever I got a little off of it. But what I have met with the most wonderful in nature is a set of men absolutely incorruptible by money, by fair words or by foul: and that this should, of all others, be the class of postillions. This however is the real character of German postilions whom nothing on earth can induce to go out of a walk. This has retarded me not a little: so that I shall be glad to be delivered over to the great jack boots.

The neighborhood of this place is that which has been to us a second mother country. It is from the palatinate on this part of the Rhine that those swarms of Germans have gone, who, next to the descendants of the English, form the greatest body of our people. I have been continually amused by seeing here the origin of whatever is not English among us. I have fancied myself often in the upper parts of Maryland and Pennsylvania. I have taken some measures too for realizing a project which I have wished to execute for 20 years past without knowing how to go about it. I am not sure but that you will enter into similar views when I can have the pleasure of explaining them to you at Paris. Being too long for a letter, and having already given you a sufficiency of egoismes, for want of other subjects I shall conclude with assurances of the esteem & attachment with which I am Dear Sir your affectionate friend & servt.,

Th: Jefferson

85. TO MARIA COSWAY

Paris Apr. 24. 1788.

I arrived here, my dear friend, the last night, and in a bushel of letters presented me by way of reception, I saw that one was of your hand-writing. It is the only one I have yet opened, and I answer it before I open another. I do not think I was in arrears in our epistolary account when I left Paris. In affection I am sure you were greatly my debtor. I often determined during my journey to write to you: but sometimes the fatigue of exercise, and sometimes a fatigued attention hindered me. At Dusseldorp I wished for you much. I surely never saw so precious a collection of paintings. Above all things those of Van der Werff affected me the most. His picture of Sarah delivering Agar to Abraham is delicious. I would have agreed to have been Abraham though the consequence would have been that I should have been dead five or six thousand years. Carlo Dolce became also a violent favorite. I am so little of a connoisseur that I preferred the works of these two authors to the old faded red things of Rubens. I am but a son of nature, loving what I see and feel, without being able to give a reason, nor caring much whether there be one. At Heidelberg I wished for you too. In fact I led you by the hand thro' the whole garden. I was struck with the resemblance of this scene to that of Vaucluse as seen from what is called the chateau of Petrarch. Nature has formed both on the same sketch, but she has filled up that of Heidelberg with a bolder hand. The river is larger, the mountains more majestic and better clothed. Art too has seconded her views. The chateau of Petrarch is the ruin of a modest country house, that of Heidelbourg would stand well along side the pyramids of Egypt. It is certainly the most magnificent ruin after those left us by the antients. At Strasbourg I sat down to write to you. But for my soul I could think of nothing at Strasbourg but the promontory of noses, of Diego, of Slawkenburgius his historian, and the procession of the Strasburgers to meet the man with the nose.[1] Had I written to you from thence it would have been a continuation of Sterne upon noses, and I knew that nature had not formed me for a Continuator of Sterne: so I let it alone till I came here and received your angry letter. It is a proof of your esteem, but I love better to have soft testimonials of it. You must therefore now write me a letter teeming with affection; such as I feel for you. So much I have no right to ask.—Being but just arrived I am not au fait of the small news respecting your acquaintance here. I know only that the princess Lubomirski is still here, and that she has taken the house that was M. de Simoulin's. When you come again therefore you will be somewhat nearer to me, but not near enough: and still surrounded by a numerous cortege, so that I shall see you only by scraps as I did when you were here last. The time before we were half days, and whole days together, and I found this too little. Adieu! God bless you! Your's affectionately,

Th: Jefferson

86. TO JAMES MADISON

Dear Sir   *Paris May 3. 1788.*

... By Mr. Warville I send your pedometer. To the loop at bottom of it you must sew a tape, and, at the other end of the tape, a small hook (such as we use under the name of hooks and eyes.) Cut a little hole in the bottom of your left watch pocket. pass the hook and tape through it, and down between the breeches and drawers, and fix the hook on the edge of your knee band, an inch from the knee buckle. Then hook the instrument itself by it's swivel-hook on the upper edge of the watch-pocket. Your tape being well adjusted in length, your double steps will be exactly counted by the instrument, the shortest hand pointing out the thousands, the flat hand the hundreds, and the long hand the tens and units. Never turn the hands backward. Indeed it is best not to set them to any given place, but to note the number they stand at when you begin to walk. The adjusting the tape to it's exact length is a critical business, and will cost you many trials. But, once done, it is done for ever. The best way is to have a small buckle fixed on the middle of the tape, by which you can take it up and let it out at pleasure. When you chuse it should cease to count, unhook it from the top of the watch pocket and let it fall down to the bottom of the pocket....I am with sentiments of the most sincere esteem & attachment Dr. Sir your affectionate friend & servt,

Th: Jefferson

87. TO ANNE WILLING BINGHAM

Dear Madam   *Paris May 11. 1788.*
A gentleman going to Philadelphia furnishes me the occasion of sending you some numbers of the Cabinet des modes and some new theatrical peices. These last have had great success on the stage, where they have excited perpetual applause. We have now need of something to make us laugh, for the topics of the times are sad and eventful. The gay and thoughtless Paris is now become a furnace of Politics. All the world is run politically mad. Men, women, children talk nothing else; and you know that naturally they talk much, loud and warm. Society is spoilt by it, at least for those who, like myself, are but lookers on.—You too have had your political fever. But our good ladies, I trust, have been too wise to wrinkle their foreheads with politics. They are contented to soothe and calm the minds of their husbands returning ruffled from political debate. They have the good sense to value domestic happiness above all other, and the art to cultivate it beyond all others. There is no part of the earth where so much of this is enjoyed as in America. You agree with me in this: but you think that the pleasures of Paris more than supply it's want: in other words that a Parisian is happier than an American. You will change your opinion, my dear Madam, and come over to mine in the end. Recollect the women of this capital, some on foot, some on horses, and some in carriages hunting pleasure in the streets, in routs and assemblies, and forgetting that they have left it behind them in their nurseries; compare them with our own countrywomen occupied in the tender and tranquil amusements of domestic life, and confess that it is a comparison of Amazons and Angels.—You will have known from the public papers that Monsieur de Buffon, the father, is dead: and you have known long ago that the son and his wife are separated. They are pursuing pleasure in op-

posite directions. Madame de Rochambeau is well: so is Madame de la Fayette. I recollect no other Nouvelles de societé interesting to you, and as for political news of battles and sieges, Turks and Russians, I will not detail them to you, because you would be less handsome after reading them. I have only to add then, what I take a pleasure in repeating, tho' it be to the thousandth time that I have the honour to be with sentiments of very sincere respect & attachment, dear Madam, Your most obedient & most humble servant,

Th: Jefferson

88. JEFFERSON'S HINTS TO AMERICANS TRAVELING IN EUROPE

GENERAL OBSERVATIONS

Buy Dutens.[1] Buy beforehand the map of the country you are going into. On arriving at a town, the first thing is to buy the plan of the town, and the book noting it's curiosities. Walk round the ramparts when there are any. Go to the top of a steeple to have a view of the town and it's environs.

When you are doubting whether a thing is worth the trouble of going to see, recollect that you will never again be so near it, that you may repent the not having seen it, but can never repent having seen it. But there is an opposite extreme too. That is, the seeing too much. A judicious selection is to be aimed at, taking care that the indolence of the moment have no influence on the decision. Take care particularly not to let the porters of churches, cabinets &c. lead you thro' all the little details in their possession, which will load the memory with trifles, fatigue the attention and waste that and your time. It is difficult to confine these people to the few objects worth seeing and remembering. They wish for your money, and suppose you give it more willingly the more they detail to you.

When one calls in the taverns for the vin du pays they give you what is natural and unadulterated and cheap: when vin etrangere is called for, it only gives a pretext for charging an extravagant price for an unwholsome stuff, very often of their own brewing.

The people you will naturally see the most of will be tavern keepers, Valets de place, and postillions. These are the hackneyed rascals of every country. Of course they must never be considered when we calculate the national character.

Before entering Italy buy Addison's travels. He visited that country as a classical amateur, and it gives infinite pleasure to apply one's classical reading on the spot. Besides it aids our future recollection of the place.

Buy the Guide pour le voyage d'Italie en poste. The latest edition. It is the post book of Italy.

The theatres, public walks and public markets to be frequented. At these you see the inhabitants from high to low.

OBJECTS OF ATTENTION FOR AN AMERICAN

1. Agriculture. Every thing belonging to this art, and whatever has a near relation to it. Useful or agreeable animals which might be transported to America. New species of plants for the farm or garden, according to the climate of the different states.

2. Mechanical arts, so far as they respect things necessary in America, and inconvenient to be transported thither ready made. Such are forges, stonequarries, boats, bridges (very specially) &c. &c.

3. Lighter mechanical arts and manufactures. Some of these will be worth a superficial view. But circumstances rendering it impossible that America should become a manufacturing country during the time of any man now living, it would be a waste of attention to examine these minutely.

4. Gardens. Peculiarly worth the attention of an American, because it is the country of all others where the noblest gardens may be made without expence. We have only to cut out the superabundant plants.

5. Architecture worth great attention. As we double our numbers every 20 years we must double our houses. Besides we build of such perishable materials that one half of our houses must be rebuilt in

every space of 20 years. So that in that term, houses are to be built for three fourths of our inhabitants. It is then among the most important arts: and it is desireable to introduce taste into an art which shews so much.

6. Painting, statuary. Too expensive for the state of wealth among us. It would be useless therefore and preposterous for us to endeavor to make ourselves connoisseurs in those arts. They are worth seeing, but not studying.

7. Politics of each country. Well worth studying so far as respects internal affairs. Examine their influence on the happiness of the people: take every possible occasion of entering into the hovels of the labourers, and especially at the moments of their repast, see what they eat, how they are cloathed, whether they are obliged to labour too hard; whether the government or their landlord takes from them an unjust proportion of their labour; on what footing stands the property they call their own, their personal liberty &c.

8. Courts. To be seen as you would see the tower of London or Menagerie of Versailles with their Lions, tygers, hyaenas and other beasts of prey, standing in the same relation to their fellows. A slight acquaintance with them will suffice to shew you that, under the most imposing exterior, they are the weakest and worst part of mankind. Their manners, could you ape them, would not make you beloved in your own country, nor would they improve it could you introduce them there to the exclusion of that honest simplicity now prevailing in America, and worthy of being cherished....

89. TO ELIZABETH WAYLES EPPES

Dear Madam   *Paris July 12. 1788.*

Your kind favor of January 6. has come duly to hand. These marks of your remembrance are always dear to me, and recall to my mind the happiest portion of my life. It is among my greatest pleasures to receive news of your welfare and that of your family. You improve in your trade I see, and I heartily congratulate you on the double blessings of which heaven has just begun to open her stores to you. Polly is infinitely flattered to find a name sake in one of them. She promises in return to teach them both French. This she begins to speak easily enough and to read as well as English. She will begin Spanish in a few days, and has lately begun the harpsichord and drawing. She and her sister will be with me tomorrow and if she has any tolerable scrap of her pencil ready I will inclose it herein for your diversion. I will propose to her at the same time to write to you. I know she will undertake it at once as she has already done a dozen times. She gets all the apparatus, places herself very formally with pen in hand, and it is not till after all this and rummaging her head thoroughly that she calls out 'indeed Papa I do not know what to say, you must help me,' and as I obstinately refuse this her good resolutions have always proved abortive and her letters ended before they were begun. Her face kindles with love whenever she hears your name, and I assure you Patsy is not behind her in this. She remembers you with warm affection, recollects that she was bequeathed to you, and looks to you as her best future guide and guardian. She will have to learn from you things which she cannot learn here, and which after all are among the most valuable parts of education for an American. Nor is the moment so distant as you imagine. On this I will enter into explanations in my next letter. I will only engage, from her dispositions, that you will always find in her the most passive compliance. You say nothing to us of Betsy, whom we all remember too well not to remember her affectionately. Jack too has failed to write to me since his first letter. I should be much pleased if he would himself give me the details of his occupations and his progress. I would write to Mrs. Skipwith but I could only repeat to her what I say to you, that we love you both sincerely, and pass one day in every week, together, and talk of nothing but Eppington, Hors du monde and Monticello. And were we to pass the whole seven, the theme would still be the same. God bless you both, madam, your husbands, your children, and every thing near and dear to you: and be assured of the constant affection of your sincere friend and humble servant,

Th: Jefferson

90. TO WILLIAM GORDON[1]

Sir   *Paris July 16. 1788.*

In your favor of the 8th. instant you mention that you had written to me in February last. This letter never came to hand. That of Apr. 24. came here during my absence on a journey thro' Holland and Germany, and having been obliged to devote the first moments after my return to some very pressing matters, this must be my apology for not having been able to write to you till now. As soon as I knew that it would be agreeable to you to have such a disposal of your work for translation as I had made for Dr. Ramsay, I applied to the same bookseller with propositions on your behalf. He told me that he had lost so much by that work that he could hardly think of undertaking another, and at any rate not without first seeing and examining it. As he was the only bookseller I could induce to give any thing on the former occasion, I went to no other with my proposals, meaning to ask you to send me immediately as much of the work as is printed. This you can do by the Diligence which comes three times a week from London to Paris. Furnished with this, I will renew my propositions and do the best for you I can, tho' I fear that the ill success of the translation of Dr. Ramsay's work, and of another work on the subject of America, will permit less to be done for you than I had hoped. I think Dr. Ramsay's failed from the inelegance of the translation, and the translator's having departed entirely from the Doctor's instructions. I will be obliged to you to set me down as a subscriber for half a dozen copies, and to ask Mr. Trumbul (No. 2. North street, Rathbone place) to pay you the *whole* subscription price for me, which he will do on shewing him this letter. These copies can be sent by the Diligence. I have not yet received the pictures Mr. Trumbul was to send me, nor consequently that of the M. de la Fayette. I will take care of it when it arrives. His title is simply *le Marquis de la Fayette.*   You ask, in your letter of Apr. 24. details of my sufferings by Colo. Tarleton. I did not suffer by him. On the contrary he behaved very genteelly with me. On his approach to Charlottesville which is within 3. miles of my house at Monticello, he dispatched a troop of his horse under Capt. Mc.leod with the double object of taking me prisoner with the two Speakers of the Senate and

Delegates who then lodged with me and remaining there in vedette, my house commanding a view of 10. or 12 counties round about. He gave strict orders to Capt. Mc.leod to suffer nothing to be injured. The troop failed in one of their objects, as we had notice so that the two speakers had gone off about two hours before their arrival at Monticello, and myself with my family about five minutes. But Captn. Mc.leod preserved every thing with sacred care during about 18. hours that he remained there. Colo. Tarleton was just so long at Charlottesville being hurried from thence by news of the rising of the militia, and by a sudden fall of rain which threatened to swell the river and intercept his return. In general he did little injury to the inhabitants on that short and hasty excursion, which was of about 60. miles from their main army then in Spotsylvania, and ours in Orange. It was early in June 1781. Lord Cornwallis then proceeded to the point of fork, and encamped his army from thence all along the main James river to a seat of mine called Elkhill, opposite to Elk island and a little below the mouth of the Byrd creek. (You will see all these places exactly laid down in the map annexed to my Notes on Virginia printed by Stockdale.) He remained in this position ten days, his own head quarters being in my house at that place. I had had time to remove most of the effects out of the house. He destroyed all my growing crops of corn and tobacco, he burned all my barns containing the same articles of the last year, having first taken what corn he wanted, he used, as was to be expected, all my stocks of cattle, sheep, and hogs for the sustenance of his army, and carried off all the horses capable of service: of those too young for service he cut the throats, and he burnt all the fences on the plantation, so as to leave it an absolute waste. He carried off also about 30. slaves: had this been to give them freedom he would have done right, but it was to consign them to inevitable death from the small pox and putrid fever then raging in his camp. This I knew afterwards to have been the fate of 27. of them. I never had news of the remaining three, but presume they shared the same fate. When I say that Lord Cornwallis did all this, I do not mean that he carried about the torch in his own hands, but that it was all done under his eye, the situation of the house, in which he was, commanding a view of every part of the plantation, so that he must have seen every fire. I relate these things on my own knowlege in a great degree, as I was on the ground soon after he left it. He treated the rest of the neighborhood somewhat in the same stile, but not with that spirit of total extermination with which he seemed to rage over my possessions. Wherever he went, the dwelling houses were plundered of every thing which could be carried off. Lord Cornwallis's character in England would forbid the belief that he shared in the plunder. But that his table was served with the plate thus pillaged from private houses can be proved by many hundred eye witnesses. From an estimate I made at that time on the best information I could collect, I supposed the state of Virginia lost under Ld. Cornwallis's hands that year about 30,000 slaves, and that of these about 27,000 died of the small pox and camp fever, and the rest were partly sent to the West Indies and exchanged for rum, sugar, coffee and fruits, and partly sent to New York, from whence they went at the peace either to Nova Scotia, or England. From this last place I believe they have been lately sent to Africa. History will never relate the horrors committed by the British army in the *Southern* states of America. They raged in Virginia 6. months only, from the middle of April to the middle of October 1781. when they were all taken prisoners, and I give you a faithful specimen of their transactions for 10. days of that time and in one spot only. Expede Herculem.[2] I suppose their whole devastations during those 6. months amounted to about three millions sterling.—The copiousness of this subject has only left me space to assure you of the sentiments of esteem and respect with which I am Sir your most obedt. humble servt.,

Th: Jefferson

91. TO REV. JAMES MADISON

Dear Sir   *Paris July 19. 1788.*
My last letter to you was of the 13th. of August last. As you seem willing to accept of the crums of science on which we are subsisting here, it is with pleasure I continue to hand them on to you in proportion as they are dealt out.   Herschel's volcano in the moon you have doubtless heard of, and placed among the other vagaries of a head

which seems not organised for sound induction. The wildness of the theories hitherto proposed by him, on his own discoveries, seems to authorize us to consider his merit as that of a good Optician only. You know also that Doctor Ingenhousz had discovered, as he supposed, from experiment, that vegetation might be promoted by occasioning streams of the electrical fluid to pass through a plant, and that other Physicians had received and confirmed his theory. He now however retracts it, and finds, by more decisive experiments, that the electrical fluid can neither forward nor retard vegetation. Uncorrected still of the rage of drawing general conclusions from partial and equivocal observations, he hazards the opinion that *light* promotes vegetation. I have heretofore supposed from observation that light affects the *colour* of living bodies, whether vegetable or animal; but that either the one or the other receive *nutriment* from that fluid must be permitted to be doubted of till better confirmed by observation. It is always better to have no ideas than false ones; to believe nothing, than to believe what is wrong. In my mind, theories are more easily demolished than re-built. An Abbé here has shaken, if not destroyed, the theory of de Dominis, Descartes and Newton for explaining the phaenomenon of the rainbow. According to that theory, you know, a cone of rays issuing from the sun and falling on a cloud in the opposite part of the heavens, is reflected back in the form of a smaller cone, the apex of which is the eye of the observer: thus.

(a) the sun. (b) (c) the diameter of the rainbow (d) the eye of the observer. So that (d) the eye of the observer must be in the axis of both cones, and equally distant from every part of the bow. But he observes that he has repeatedly seen bows the one end of which has been very near to him, and the other at a great distance. I have often seen the same thing myself. I recollect well to have seen more than once the end of a rainbow between myself and a house, or between myself and a bank not twenty yards distant, and this repeatedly. But I never saw, what he sais he has seen, different rainbows at the same time intersecting each other. I never saw coexistent bows which were not concentric also.—Again, according to the theory, if the sun is in the horizon, the horizon intercepts the lower half of the bow, from (e) to (c). If above the horizon, that intercepts more than the half, in proportion. So that generally the bow is less than a semicircle and never more. He says he has seen it more than a semicircle. I have often seen a leg of the bow below my level. My situation at Monticello admitted this, because there is a mountain there in the opposite direction of the afternoon's sun, the valley between which and Monticello is 500 feet deep. I have seen a leg of a rainbow plunge down on the river running through that valley. But I do not recollect to have remarked at any time that the bow was of more than half a circle. It appears to me that these facts demolish the Newtonian hypothesis but they do not support that erected in it's stead by the Abbé. He supposes a cloud between the sun and observer, and that through some opening in that cloud the rays pass and form an Iris on the opposite part of the heavens, just as a ray passing through a hole in the shutter of a darkened room, and falling on a prism there, forms the prismatic colours on the opposite wall. According to this we might see bows of more than the half circle as often as of less. A thousand other objections occur to this hypothesis, which need not be suggested to you. The result is that we are wiser than we were, by having an error the less in our catalogue; but the blank occasioned by it must remain for some happier hypothesist to fill up.

The dispute about the conversion and reconversion of water and air is still stoutly kept up. The contradictory experiments of Chemists leave us at liberty to conclude what we please. My conclusion is that art has not yet invented sufficient aids to enable such subtle bodies to make a well defined impression on organs as blunt as ours: that it is laudable to encourage investigation, but to hold back conclusion. Speaking one day with Monsieur de Buffon on the present ardor of chemical enquiry, he affected to consider chemistry but as cookery, and to place the toils of the laboratory on a footing with those of the kitchen. I think it on the contrary among the most useful of sciences, and big with future discoveries for the utility and safety of the human race. It is yet indeed a mere embryon. It's principles are contested. Experiments seem contradictory: their subjects are so minute as to escape our senses; and their result too fallacious to satisfy the mind. It is probably an age too soon to propose the establishment of system. The attempt therefore of Lavoisier to reform the Chemical nomenclature is premature. One single experiment may destroy the whole filiation of his terms, and his string of Sulfates, Sulfites, and Sulfures may have served no other end than to have retarded the progress of the science by a jargon from the confusion of which time will be requisite to extricate us. Accordingly it is not likely to be admitted generally.

You are acquainted with the properties of the composition of nitre, salt of tartar and sulphur called Pulvis fulminens. Of this the explosion is produced by heat alone. Monsieur Bertholet by dissolving silver in the nitrous acid, precipitating it with lime water, and drying the precipitate on Ammoniac has discovered a powder which fulminates most powerfully on coming into contact with any substance whatever. Once made it cannot be touched. It cannot be put into a bottle, but must remain in the capsula where dried.—The property of the Spathic acid to corrode flinty substances, has been lately applied by a M. Puymaurin, of Toulouse, to engrave on glass, as artists engrave on copper with aquafortis.—M. de la Place has discovered that the secular acceleration and retardation of the moon's motion is occasioned by the action of the sun, in proportion as his eccentricity changes, or, in other words, as the orbit of the earth increases or diminishes. So that this irregularity is now perfectly calculable.—Having seen announced in a gazette that some person had found in a library of Sicily an Arabic translation of Livy, which was thought to be complete, I got the Chargé des affaires of Naples here to write to Naples to enquire into the fact. He obtained in answer that an Arabic translation was found, and that it would restore to us 17 of the books lost, to wit, from the 60th. to the 77th. inclusive: that it was in possession of an Abbe Vella at Palermo who, as soon as he shall have finished a work he has on hand, will give us an Italian and perhaps a Latin translation of this Livy. There are persons however, who doubt the truth of this discovery, founding their doubts on some personal circumstance relative to the person who sais he has this translation. I find nevertheless that the Chargé des affaires believes in the discovery, which makes me hope it may be true.

A country man of ours, a Mr. Lediard of Connecticut set out from hence some time ago for St. Petersburgh, to go thence to Kamschatka, thence to cross over to the Western coast of America, and penetrate through the continent to our side of it. He had got within a few days journey of Kamschatka, when he was arrested by order of the empress of Russia, sent back and turned adrift in Poland. He went to London, engaged under the auspices of a private society formed there for pushing discoveries into Africa, passed by this place, which he left a few days ago for Marseilles, where he will embark for Alexandria and Grand Cairo, thence explore the Nile to it's source, cross to the head of the Niger, and descend that to it's mouth. He promises me, if he escapes through this journey, he will go to Kentuckey and endeavour to penetrate Westwardly from thence to the South sea.

The death of M. de Buffon you have heard long ago. I do not know whether we shall have any thing posthumous of his.

As to political news, this country is making it's way to a good constitution. The only danger is they may press so fast as to produce an appeal to arms, which might have an unfavorable issue for them. As yet that appeal is not made. Perhaps the war which seems to be spreading from nation to nation may reach them. This would ensure the calling of the states general, and this, as is supposed, the establishment of a constitution.   I have the honor to be with sentiments of sincere esteem & respect, Dear Sir Your friend & servant,

Th: Jefferson

92. TO MARIA COSWAY

Paris July 27. 1788

Hail, dear friend of mine! for I am never so happy as when business, smoothing her magisterial brow, says 'I give you an hour to converse with your friends.' And with none do I converse more fondly than with my good Maria: not her under the poplar, with the dog and string at her girdle: but the Maria who makes the Hours her own, who teaches them to dance for us in so charming a round, and lets us think of nothing but her who renders them *si gracieuses.* Your Hours,[1] my dear friend, are no longer your own. Every body now demands them; and were it possible for me to want a memorandum of you, it is presented me in every street of Paris. Come then to see what triumph Time is giving you. Come and see every body stopping to admire the Hours, suspended against the walls of the Quai des Augustins, the Boulevards, the Palais royal &c. &c. with a 'Maria Cosway delint.' at the bottom. But you triumph every where; so, if you come here, it will be, not to see your triumphs but your friends, and to make them happy with your presence. Indeed we wish much for you. Society here is become more gloomy than usual. The civil dissensions, tho' they have yet cost no blood and will I hope cost none, still render conversation serious, and society contentious. How gladly would I take refuge every day in your coterie. Your benevolence, embracing all parties, disarms the party-dispositions of your friends, and makes of yours an asylum for tranquility. We are told you are becoming more recluse. This is a proof the more of your taste. A great deal of love given to a few, is better than a little to many. Besides, the world will derive greater benefit from your talents, as these will be less called off from their objects by numerous visits.   I remember that when under the hands of your Coëffeuse, you used to amuse yourself with your pencil. Take then, some of these days, when Fancy bites and the Coeffeuse is busy, a little visiting card, and crayon on it something for me. What shall it be? Cupid leading the lion by a thread? or Minerva clipping his wings? Or shall it be political? The father, for instance, giving the bunch of rods to his children to break, or Jupiter sending to the frogs a kite instead of the log for their king? Or shall it be something better than all this, a sketch of your own fancy? So that I have something from your hand, it will satisfy me; and it will be the better if of your own imagination. I will put a 'Maria Cosway delint.' at bottom, and stamp it on my visiting cards, that our names may be together if our persons cannot. Adieu, my dear friend, love me much, and love me always. Your's affectionately,

Th: Jefferson

93. TO MARIA COSWAY

My Dear Dear Friend   *Paris July 30. 1788.*
Cease to chide me. It is hard to have been chained to a writing table, drudging over business daily from morning to night ever since my return to Paris. It will be a cruel exaggeration, if I am to lose my friends into the bargain. The only letter of private friendship I wrote on my return, and before entering on business, was to you. The first I wrote after getting through my budget was to you. It had gone off on the morning of the last post, and in the evening of the same day, your's of the 15th. was brought here by I know not whom, while I was out. I am incapable of forgetting or neglecting you my dear friend; and I am sure if the comparison could be fairly made of how much I think of you, or you of me, the former scale would greatly preponderate. Of this I have no right to complain, nor do I complain. You esteem me as much as I deserve. If I love you more, it is because you deserve more. Of voluntary faults to you I can never be guilty, and you are too good not to pardon the involuntary. Chide me then no more; be to me what you have been; and give me without measure the comfort of your friendship. Adieu ma tres chere et excellente amie.

Th: J.

94. TO ANGELICA SCHUYLER CHURCH

Paris Aug. 17. 1788.
The urn is well worth acceptance, my dear Madam, on it's own account, for it is a perfect beauty: but it is more flattering to me to accept it on account of the giver. I shall preserve it as sacred as I would the urns of my forefathers, had I all of them from Adam to the present day, and with this difference of estimation that it recalls to my mind a living friend. The memorial of me which you have from Trumbul is of the most worthless part of me. Could he paint my friendship to you, it would be something out of the common line. I should have been happy indeed to have made a third at Down-place with yourself and Mrs. Cosway. Your society would have been amusement enough for

me. I never blame heaven so much as for having clogged the etherial spirit of friendship with a body which ties it to time and place. I am with you always in spirit: be you with me sometimes.   I have in contemplation to visit America in the Spring, as Madame de Corny has mentioned to you. I have not as yet asked a Congé, because, till the new government is in activity, I know not to whom to address my request. I presume it will not be denied me. The project of carrying with me colonies of animals and plants for my native country, will oblige me to embark at Havre, as being the nearest port. This is but twenty hours distant from London. Can you, my dear madam, sacrifice twenty hours of your life to make my daughters and myself happy? In this event we might make our trips in concert. I allow myself all the months of April, May, and June, to find a good ship. Embarking in either of these months we shall avoid being out during the equinoxes and be sure of fine weather. Think of it then, my friend, and let us begin a negociation on the subject. You shall find in me all the spirit of accomodation with which Yoric began his with the fair Piedmontese.[1] We have a thousand inducements to wish it on our part. On yours perhaps you may find one in the dispositions we shall carry with us to serve and amuse you on the dreary voiage. Madme. de Corny talks of your brother coming to Europe for you. How much easier for him to meet you in Williamsburgh! Besides, I am your brother. Should this proposition be absolutely inadmissible, I will flatter myself with the hope of seeing you at New York, or even at Albany if I am master enough of my time. To see the country will be one motive: but to see you a much stronger, and to become acquainted with your father who must be good, because you are so. The fruit is a specimen of the tree. I had the honour of serving with him in Congress in the year 1775. but probably he does not remember me.

I have just deposited Kitty in good health in the Chaussée d'Antin. I had a consultation with Madame de Corny last night, the result of which was to insist on her being translated from the drawing mistress to the drawing master of the Convent. Write to me sometimes, and permit me to answer your letters. God bless you, my dear madam, your affectionate friend

Th: Jefferson

95. TO MARIA COSWAY

Paris Sep. 26. 1788.

Your favor of Aug. the 19., my very dear friend, is put into my hands this 26th. day of September 1788. and I answer it in the same instant to shew you there is nothing nearer my heart than to meet all the testimonies of your esteem. It is a strong one that you will occupy yourself for me on such a trifle as a visiting card. But sketch it only with your pencil, my friend, and do not make of it a serious business. This would render me uneasy, because I did not mean such a trespass on your time. A few strokes of your pencil on a card will be enjoiment enough for me.

I am going to America, and you to Italy. The one or the other of us goes the wrong way, for the way will ever be wrong which leads us farther apart. Mine is a journey of duty and of affection. I must deposit my daughters in the bosom of their friends and country. This done, I shall return to my station. My absence may be as short as five months, and certainly not longer than nine. How long my subsequent stay here may be I cannot tell. It would certainly be the longer had I a single friend here like yourself.—In going to Italy, be sure to cross the Alps at the Col de Tende. It is the best pass, because you need never get out of your carriage. It is practicable in seasons when all the other passes are shut up by snow. The roads leading to and from it are as fine as can possibly be, and you will see the castle of Saorgio. Take a good day for that part of your journey, and when you shall have sketched it in your portefeuille, and copied it more at leisure for yourself, tear out the leaf and send it to me. But why go to Italy? You have seen it, all the world has seen it, and ransacked it thousands of times. Rather join our good friend Mrs. Church in her trip to America. There you will find original scenes, scenes worthy of your pencil, such as the Natural bridge or the Falls of Niagara. Or participate with Trumbull the historical events of that country. These will have the double merit of being new, and of coming from you. I should find excuses for being sometimes of your parties. Think of this, my dear friend, mature the project with Mrs. Church, and let us all embark together at Havre. Adieu ma tres chere et excellente amie. Your's affectionately,

Th: J.

96. TO THOMAS PAYNE

Sir   *Paris Octob. 2. 1788.*

Having occasion for a correspondent in your line in the city of London, I take the liberty of addressing myself to you on the recommendation of my friends Mr. Trumbull and Mr. Paradise.[1] In the execution of my commissions, I would wish you to attend to the following general rules.

When I name a particular edition of a book, send me that edition and no other.

When I do not name the edition, never send a folio or quarto if there exists an 8vo. or smaller edition. I like books of a handy size.

Where a book costs much higher than the common price of books of that size do not send it, tho I write for it, till you shall have advised me of the price.

I disclaim all pompous editions and all typographical luxury; but I like a fine white paper, neat type, and neat binding, gilt and lettered in the modern stile. But while I remain in Europe it will be better to send my books in boards, as I have found that scarcely any method of packing preserves them from rubbing in a land transportation.

Send my books always by the Diligence which plies 3 or 4 times a week between London and Paris. But, consulting their own convenience only, they are apt to keep packages long by them, if not attended to by the person sending them.

My friend Mr. Trumbull will pay the bill for the parcel of which I now inclose you the catalogue. As some of them will perhaps require time to be found, the rest need not wait for them. Hereafter you will be pleased to send my account once a quarter or once in six months while I remain in Europe. When I return to America, my demands shall be accompanied by the ready money. Be so good as to state the Parliamentary debates, and Hattsel's book in a separate account, as these are not for myself. Let the accounts come by post when you send off the books. I am Sir your very humble servt.,

Th: Jefferson

Adams's essays on the microscope. 4to.
Tyson's Oran-outang, or anatomy of a pigmy.

Raleigh's history of England. 2. vols. 12mo.

Pilpay's fables. 12 mo.

Gregory's comparative view. 12mo.

5th. vol. of Watson's chemical essays. 12mo. Evans. (I have the 4 first)

Whitehurst's attempt toward invariable measures. Bent. 1787.

Pownal's hydraulic & nautical observations. Sayer.

Zimmerman's political survey. 8 vol. Dilly.

Prospects on the Rubicon. Debrett.

Barton's observations on Natural history. Dilly.

Families of plants by the Litchfeild society. 2. vols. 8vo.

Mc.kenzie's strictures on Tarleton's history. Faulder.

Concordance to Shakespeare. Robinsons.

Indian vocabulary. 12mo. Stockdale.

Additions to Robertson's history of Scotland. 8vo. Cadell.

Additions to Robertson's history of America. 8vo. Cadell.

Burns's poems.

Builder's price book. 8vo. Taylor. London. No. 56. opposite great Turn-
stile Holborn. 1781. A later edition if any.

Potter's Aeschylus. 2. vols. 8vo.

Chandler's debates of the Lords and Commons

Hatsell's book on Parliamentary subjects. I do not know the title, but it is
the latest edition, containing a digest of his former publications on
different parts of Parliamentary learning, with some additions.

Spelman's life of Alfred, Saxon, with Wilbur's translation.

Boethius, Anglo-Saxonicé Aelfridi regis. Oxon. 1698.

Thwait's Saxon heptateuch.

Spelman's Saxon psalms.

Mareshall's Saxon gospels.

Saxon homilies (I think some have been published.)

Lye's Junius's etymologicon by Owen. 2. vols. fol. latest edition.

Thompson's translation of Goeffry of Monmouth.

Lye's sacrorum evangeliorum versio Gothica. 4to.

Knitell's fragments of Ulphilas's translation of the epistle to the Romans.
4to.

What is the price of Anderson's history of commerce?

97. TO GEORGE WASHINGTON

Sir   *Paris Nov. 4. 1788.*

Your favor of Aug. 31. came to hand yesterday; and a confidential conveiance offering, by the way of London, I avail myself of it to acknolege the receipt. I have seen, with infinite pleasure, our new constitution accepted by 11. states, not rejected by the 12th. and that the 13th. happens to be a state of the least importance. It is true that the minorities in most of the accepting states have been very respectable, so much so as to render it prudent, were it not otherwise reasonable, to make some sacrifices to them. I am in hopes that the annexation of a bill of rights to the constitution will alone draw over so great a proportion of the minorities, as to leave little danger in the opposition of the residue; and that this annexation may be made by Congress and the assemblies, without calling a convention which might endanger the most valuable parts of the system. Calculation has convinced me that circumstances may arise, and probably will arise, wherein all the resources of taxation will be necessary for the safety of the state. For tho I am decidedly of opinion we should take no part in European quarrels, but cultivate peace and commerce with all, yet who can avoid seeing the source of war in the tyranny of those nations who deprive us of the natural right of trading with our neighbors? The produce of the U.S. will soon exceed the European demand. What is to be done with the surplus, when there shall be one? It will be employed, without question, to open by force a market for itself with those placed on the same continent with us, and who wish nothing better. Other causes too are obvious which may involve us in war; and war requires every resource of taxation and credit. The power of making war often prevents it, and in our case would give efficacy to our desire of peace. If the new government wears the front which I hope it will I see no impossibility in the availing ourselves of the wars of others to open the other parts of America to our commerce, as the price of our neutrality.

The campaign between the Turks and two empires has been clearly in favor of the former. The emperor is secretly trying to bring about a peace. The alliance between England, Prussia and Holland, (and some suspect Sweden also) renders their mediation decisive wherever it is proposed. They seemed to interpose it so magisterially between Denmark and Sweden, that the former submitted to it's dictates, and there was all reason to believe that the war in the North-Western parts of Europe would be quieted. All of a sudden a new flame bursts out in Poland. The king and his party are devoted to Russia. The opposition rely on the protection of Prussia. They have lately become the majority in the confederated diet, and have passed a vote for subjecting their army to a commission independant of the king, and propose a perpetual diet, in which case he will be a perpetual cypher. Russia declares against such a change in their constitution, and Prussia has put an army into readiness for marching at a moment's warning on the frontiers of Poland. These events are too recent to see as yet what turn they will take, or what effect they will have on the peace of Europe. So is that also of the lunacy of the king of England, which is a decided fact, notwithstanding all the stuff the English papers publish about his fevers, his deliriums &c. The truth is that the lunacy declared itself almost at once, and with as few concomitant complaints as usually attend the first developement of that disorder. I suppose a regency will be established, and if it consist of a plurality of members it will probably be peaceable. In this event it will much favor the present wishes of this country, which are so decidedly for peace, that they refused to enter into the mediation between Sweden and Russia, lest it should commit them. As soon as the convocation of the States general was announced, a tranquillity took place thro' the whole kingdom. Happily no open rupture had taken place in any part of it. The parliaments were re-instated in their functions at the same time. This was all they desired, and they had called for the States general only through fear that the crown could not otherwise be forced to re-instate them. Their end obtained, they began to foresee danger to themselves in the States general. They began to lay the foundations for cavilling at the legality of that body, if it's measures should be hostile to them. The court, to clear itself of the dispute, convened the Notables who had acted with general approbation on the former occasion, and referred to them the forms of calling and organizing the States-general. These Notables consist principally of nobility and clergy, the few of the tiers etat among them being either parliament-men, or other privileged persons. The court wished that in the future States general the members of the Tiers-etat should equal those of both the other orders, and that they should form but one house, all together, and vote by persons, not by orders. But the Notables, in the true spirit of priests and nobles, combining together against the people, have voted by 5 bureaux out of 6. that the people or tiers etat shall have no greater number of deputies than each of the other orders separately, and that they shall vote by orders: so that two orders concurring in a vote, the third will be overruled; for it is not here as in England where each of the three branches has a negative on the other two. If this project of theirs succeeds, a combination between the two houses of clergy and nobles, will render the representation of the Tiers etat merely nugatory. The bureaux are to assemble together to consolidate their separate votes; but I see no reasonable hope of their changing this. Perhaps the king, knowing that he may count on the support of the nation and attach it more closely to him, may take on himself to disregard the opinion of the Notables in this instance, and may call an equal representation of the people, in which precedents will support him. In every event, I think the present disquiet will end well. The nation has been awaked by our revolution, they feel their strength, they are enlightened, their lights are spreading, and they will not retrograde. The first states general may establish 3. important points without opposition from the court. 1. their own periodical convocation. 2. their exclusive right of taxation (which has been confessed by the king.) 3. The right of registering laws and of previously proposing amendments to them, as the parliaments have by usurpation been in the habit of doing. The court will consent to this from it's hatred to the parliaments, and from the desire of having to do with one rather than many legislatures. If the states are prudent they will not aim at more than this at first, lest they should shock the dispositions of the court, and even alarm the public mind, which must be left to open itself by degrees to successive improvements. These will follow from the nature of things. How far they can proceed, in the end, towards a thorough reformation of abuse, cannot be foreseen. In my opinion a kind of influence, which none of their plans of reform take into account, will elude them all; I mean the influence of women in the government. The manners of the nation allow them to visit, alone, all persons in office, to sollicit the affairs of the husband, family, or friends, and their sollicitations bid defiance to laws and regulations. This obstacle may seem less to those who, like our countrymen, are in the precious habit of considering Right, as a barrier against all sollicitation. Nor can such an one, without the evidence of his own eyes, believe in the desperate state to which things are reduced in this country from the omnipotence of an influence which, fortunately for the happiness of the sex itself, does not endeavor to extend itself in our country beyond the domestic line.

Your communications to the Count de Moustier, whatever they may have been, cannot have done injury to my endeavors here to open the W. Indies to us. On this head the ministers are invincibly mute, tho' I have often tried to draw them into the subject. I have therefore found it necessary to let it lie till war or other circumstances may force it on. Whenever they are in war with England, they must open the islands to us, and perhaps during that war they may see some price which might make them agree to keep them always open. In the mean time I have laid my shoulder to the opening the markets of this country to our produce, and rendering it's transportation a nursery for our seamen. A maritime force is the only one by which we can act on Europe. Our navigation law (if it be wise to have any) should be the reverse of that of England. Instead of confining *importations* to home-bottoms or those of the *producing* nation, I think we should confine *exportations* to home bottoms or to those of nations *having treaties with us.* Our exportations are heavy, and would nourish a great force of our own, or be a tempting price to the nation to whom we should offer a participation of it in exchange for free access to all their possessions. This is an object to which our government alone is adequate in the gross. But I have ventured to pursue it here, so far as the consumption of our productions by this country extends. Thus in our arrangements relative to tobacco, none can be received here but in French or American bottoms. This is emploiment for near 2000 seamen, and puts nearly that number of British out of employ. By the arret of Dec. 1787. it was provided that our whale oils should not be received here but in French or American bottoms, and by later regulations all oils but those of France and America are excluded. This will put 100 English whale vessels immediately out of employ, and 150. ere long: and call so many of French and American into service. We have had 6000 seamen formerly in this business, the whole of whom we have been likely to lose. The consumption of rice is growing fast in this country, and that of Carolina gaining ground on every other kind. I am of opinion the whole of the Carolina rice can be consumed here. It's transportation employs 2500. sailors, almost all of them English at present, the rice being deposited at Cowes and brought from thence here. It would be dangerous to confine this transportation to French and American bottoms the ensuing year, because they will be much engrossed by the transportation of wheat and flour hither, and the crop of rice might lie on hand for want of vessels: but I see no objections to the extension of our principle to this article also, beginning with the year 1790. However before there is a necessity of deciding on this I hope to be able to consult our new government in person, as I have asked of Congress a leave of Absence for 6. months, that is to say from April to November next. It is necessary for me to pay a short visit to my native country, first to reconduct my family thither, and place them in the hands of their friends, and secondly to place my private affairs under certain arrangements. When I left my own house I expected to be absent but 5. months, and I have been led by events to an absence of 5. years. I shall hope therefore for the pleasure of personal conferences with your Excellency on the subjects of this letter and others interesting to our country, of getting my own ideas set to rights by a communication of yours, and of taking again the tone of sentiment of my own country which we lose in some degree after a certain absence. You know doubtless of the death of the Marquis de Chastellux. The Marquis de la Fayette is out of favor with the court, but high in favor with the nation. I once feared for his personal liberty. But I hope him on safe ground at present.—On the subject of the whale fishery I inclose you some observations[1] I drew up for the ministry here, in order to obtain a correction of their Arret of Sep. last, whereby they had involved our oils with the English in a general exclusion from their ports. They will accordingly correct this, so that our oils will participate with theirs in the monopoly of their markets. There are several things incidentally introduced which do not seem pertinent to the general question. They were rendered necessary by particular circumstances the explanation of which would add to a letter already too long. I will trespass no further then, than to assure you of the sentiments of sincere attachment and respect with which I have the honor to be your Excellency's most obedt. humble servant,

Th: Jefferson

98. TO RICHARD PRICE¹

Dear Sir   *Paris Jan. 8. 1789.*

I was favoured with your letter of Oct. 26. and far from finding any of it's subjects uninteresting as you apprehend, they were to me, as every thing which comes from you, pleasing and instructive. I concur with you strictly in your opinion of the comparative merits of atheism and demonism, and really see nothing but the latter in the being worshipped by many who think themselves Christians. Your opinions and writings will have effect in bringing others to reason on this subject.— Our new constitution, of which you speak also, has succeded beyond what I apprehended it would have done. I did not at first believe that 11. states out of 13. would have consented to a plan consolidating them so much into one. A change in their dispositions, which had taken place since I left them, had rendered this consolidation necessary, that is to say, had called for a federal government which could walk upon it's own legs, without leaning for support on the state legislatures. A sense of this necessity, and a submission to it, is to me a new and consolatory proof that wherever the people are well informed they can be trusted with their own government; that whenever things get so far wrong as to attract their notice, they may be relied on to set them to rights.—You say you are not sufficiently informed about the nature and circumstances of the present struggle here. Having been on the spot from it's first origin and watched it's movements as an uninterested spectator, with no other bias than a love of mankind I will give you my ideas of it. Tho' celebrated writers of this and other countries had already sketched good principles on the subject of government, yet the American war seems first to have awakened the thinking part of this nation in general from the sleep of despotism in which they were sunk. The officers too, who had been to America, were mostly young men, less shackled by habit and prejudice, and more ready to assent to the dictates of common sense and common right. They came back impressed with these. The press, notwithstanding it's shackles, began to disseminate them: conversation too assumed new freedoms; politics became the theme of all societies, male and female, and a very extensive and zealous party was formed, which may be called the Patriotic party, who sensible of the abusive government under which they lived, longed for occasions of reforming it. This party comprehended all the honesty of the kingdom, sufficiently at it's leisure to think: the men of letters, the easy bourgeois, the young nobility, partly from reflection partly from mode; for those sentiments became a matter of mode, and as such united most of the young women to the party. Happily for the nation, it happened that at the same moment, the dissipations of the court had exhausted the money and credit of the state, and M. de Calonnes found himself obliged to appeal to the nation and to develope to it the ruin of their finances. He had no ideas of supplying the deficit by economies; he saw no means but new taxes. To tempt the nation to consent to these some douceurs were necessary. The Notables were called in 1787. The leading vices of the constitution and administration were ably sketched out, good remedies proposed, and under the splendor of these propositions a demand of more money was couched. The Notables concurred with the minister in the necessity of reformation, adroitly avoided the demand of money, got him displaced, and one of their leading men placed in his room. The Archbishop of Thoulouse by the aid of the hopes formed of him, was able to borrow some money, and he reformed considerably the expences of the court. Notwithstanding the prejudices since formed against him, he appeared to me to pursue the reformation of the laws and constitution as steadily as a man could do who had to drag the court after him, and even to conceal from them the consequences of the measures he was leading them into. In his time the Criminal laws were reformed, provincial assemblies and states established in most of the provinces, the States general promised, and a solemn acknolegement made by the king that he could not impose a new tax without the consent of the nation. It is true he was continually goaded forward by the public clamours excited by the writings and workings of the Patriots, who were able to keep up the public fermentation at the exact point which borders on resistance without entering on it. They had taken into their alliance the parliaments also, who were led by very singular circumstances to espouse, for the first time, the rights of the nation. They had from old causes had personal hostility against M. de Calonne. They refused to register his loans or his taxes, and went so far as to acknolege they had no power to do it. They persisted in this with his successor, who therefore exiled them. Seeing that the nation did not interest themselves much for their recall, they began to fear that the new judicatures proposed in their place would be established and that their own suppression would be perpetual. In short they found their own strength insufficient to oppose that of the king. They therefore insisted the states general should be called. Here they became united with and supported by the Patriots, and their joint influence was sufficient to produce the promise of that assembly. I always suspected that the Archbishop had no objections to this force under which they laid him. But the patriots and parliament insist it was their efforts which extorted the promise against his will. The reestablishment of the parliament was the effect of the same coalition between the patriots and parliament: but, once reestablished, the latter began to see danger in that very power, the States general, which they had called for in a moment of despair, but which they now foresaw might very possibly abridge their powers. They began to prepare grounds for questioning their legality, as a rod over the head of the states, and as a refuge if they should really extend their reformations to them. Mr. Neckar came in at this period, and very dexterously disembarrassed the administration of these disputes by calling the Notables to advise the form of calling and constituting the states. The court was well disposed towards the people; not from principles of justice or love to them. But they want money. No more can be had from the people. They are squeezed to the last drop. The clergy and nobles, by their privileges and influence, have kept their property in a great measure untaxed hitherto. They then remain to be squeezed, and no agent is powerful enough for this but the people. The court therefore must ally itself with the people. But the Notables, consisting mostly of privileged characters, had proposed a method of composing the states, which would have rendered the voice of the people, or tiers etat, in the states general, inefficient for the purposes of the court. It concurred then with the patriots in intriguing with the parliament to get them to pass a vote in favor of the rights of the people. This vote balancing that of the Notables has placed the court at liberty to follow it's own views, and they have determined that the tiers etat shall have in the States general as many votes as the clergy and nobles put together. Still a great question remains to be decided: that is, shall the states general vote by orders or by persons? Precedents are both ways. The clergy will move heaven and earth to obtain the suffrage by orders, because that parries the effect of all hitherto done for the people. The people will probably send their deputies expressly instructed to consent to no tax, to no adoption of the public debts, unless the unprivileged part of the nation has a voice equal to that of the privileged; that is to say unless the voice of the tiers etat be equalled to that of the clergy and nobles. They will have the young noblesse in general on their side, and the king and court. Against them will be the antient nobles and the clergy. So that I hope upon the whole, that by the time they meet there will be a majority of the nobles themselves in favor of the tiers etat. So far history. We are now to come to prophecy; for you will ask, to what will all this lead? I answer, if the States general do not stumble at the threshold on the question before stated, and which must be decided before they can proceed to business, then they will in their first session easily obtain 1. the future periodical convocation of the States: 2. their exclusive right to raise and appropriate money, which includes that of establishing a civil list. 3. a participation in legislation; probably, at first, it will only be a transfer to them of the portion of it now exercised by parliament, that is to say a right to propose amendments and a negative: but it must infallibly end in a right of origination. 4. perhaps they may make a declaration of rights. It will be attempted at least. Two other objects will be attempted, viz. a habeas corpus law, and free press. But probably they may not obtain these in the first session, or with modifications only, and the nation must be left to ripen itself more for their unlimited adoption.

Upon the whole it has appeared to me that the basis of the present struggle is an illumination of the public mind as to the rights of the nation, aided by fortunate incidents; that they can never retrograde, but from the natural progress of things must press forward to the establishment of a constitution which shall assure to them a good degree of liberty. They flatter themselves they shall form a better constitution than the English. I think it will be better in some points, worse in others. It will be better in the article of representation which will be more equal. It will be worse, as their situation obliges them to keep up the dangerous machine of a standing army. I doubt too whether they will obtain the trial by jury, because they are not sensible of it's value.

I am sure I have by this time heartily tired you with this long epistle, and that you will be glad to see it brought to an end with assurances of the sentiments of esteem and respect with which I have the honor to be Dear Sir Your most obedient & most humble servt,

Th: Jefferson

99. TO MARIA COSWAY

Paris Jan. 14. 1789.

Fearing, my dear Madam, that I might not be able to write to you by this occasion, I had charged my friend Trumbull to lay my homage at your feet. But this is an office I would always chuse to perform myself. It is very long since I have heard from you: tho I have no right to complain, as it is long since I wrote to you. A great deal of business, and some tribulation must be my excuse. I have for two months past had a very sick family, and have not as yet a tranquil mind on that score. How have you weathered this rigorous season, my dear friend? Surely it was never so cold before. To me who am an animal of a warm climate, a mere Oran-ootan, it has been a severe trial. Yet we have been generally cheered by the presence of the sun, of whose *bright* company at least you have been deprived. The weather has cut off communication between friends and acquaintances here. I have seen the princess Lubomirski but once since her return, and Dancarville not this age. So that I am not able to give you any account of them. But they being more punctual correspondents than myself, have, I expect, given you an account of themselves. It is some time since I heard from Mde. de Brehan, and am sorry to tell you that by what I have heard she is furiously displeased with America. Her love of simplicity, and her wish to find it had made her fancy she was going to Arcadia, in spite of all my warnings to the contrary. My last letter from Mr. Short was dated at Rome. The poetical ground he was treading had almost filled him also with the god. Have you arranged all things for the voiage with Mrs. Church? We are so apt to believe what we wish that I almost believe I shall meet you in America, and that we shall make together the tour of the curiosities of that country. Be this as it may, let us be together in spirit. Preserve for me always a little corner in your affection in exchange for the spacious part you occupy in mine. Adieu ma chere et tres chere amie! Yours respectfully & affectionately,

Th: J.

100. TO EDWARD BANCROFT[1]

Dear Sir   *Paris Jan. 26. 178[9]*
I have deferred answering your letter on the subject of slaves, because you permitted me to do it till a moment of leisure, and that moment rarely comes, and because too, I could not answer you with such a degree of certainty as to merit any notice. I do not recollect the conversation at Vincennes to which you allude, but can repeat still on the same ground, on which I must have done then, that as far as I can judge from the experiments which have been made, to give liberty to, or rather, to abandon persons whose habits have been formed in slavery is like abandoning children. Many quakers in Virginia seated their slaves on their lands as tenants. They were distant from me, and therefore I cannot be particular in the details, because I never had very particular information. I cannot say whether they were to pay a rent in money, or a share of the produce: but I remember that the landlord was obliged to plan their crops for them, to direct all their operations

during every season and according to the weather, but, what is more afflicting, he was obliged to watch them daily and almost constantly to make them work, and even to whip them. A man's moral sense must be unusually strong, if slavery does not make him a thief. He who is permitted by law to have no property of his own, can with difficulty conceive that property is founded in any thing but force. These slaves chose to steal from their neighbors rather than work. They became public nuisances, and in most instances were reduced to slavery again. But I will beg of you to make no use of this imperfect information (unless in common conversation). I shall go to America in the Spring and return in the fall. During my stay in Virginia I shall be in the neighborhood where many of these trials were made. I will inform myself very particularly of them, and communicate the information to you. Besides these, there is an instance since I came away of a young man (Mr. Mayo) who died and gave freedom to all his slaves, about 200. This is about 4. years ago. I shall know how they have turned out. Notwithstanding the discouraging result of these experiments, I am decided on my final return to America to try this one. I shall endeavor to import as many Germans as I have grown slaves. I will settle them and my slaves, on farms of 50. acres each, intermingled, and place all on the footing of the Metayers [Medietarii][2] of Europe. Their children shall be brought up, as others are, in habits of property and foresight, and I have no doubt but that they will be good citizens. Some of their fathers will be so: others I suppose will need government. With these, all that can be done is to oblige them to labour as the labouring poor of Europe do, and to apply to their comfortable subsistence the produce of their labour, retaining such a moderate portion of it as may be a just equivalent for the use of the lands they labour and the stocks and other necessary advances....

101. TO JOHN TRUMBULL

Dear Sir   *Paris Feb. 15. 178[9].*

I have duly received your favor of the 5th. inst. with respect to the busts and pictures. I will put off till my return from America all of them except Bacon, Locke and Newton, whose pictures I will trouble you to have copied for me: and as I consider them as the three greatest men that have ever lived, without any exception, and as having laid the foundation of those superstructures which have been raised in the Physical and Moral sciences, I would wish to form them into a knot on the same canvas, that they may not be confounded at all with the herd of other great men. To do this I suppose we need only desire the copyist to draw the three busts in three ovals all contained in a larger oval in some such forms as this each bust to be the size of the life. The large oval would I suppose be about between four and five feet. Perhaps you

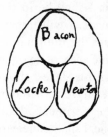 can suggest a better way of accomplishing my idea. In your hands be it, as well as the subaltern expences you mention. I trouble you with a letter to Mrs. Church. We have no important news here but of the revolution of Geneva which is not yet sufficiently explained. But they have certainly reformed their government. I am with great esteem Dr. Sir Your affectionate friend & humble servt.,

Th: Jefferson

102. TO FRANCIS HOPKINSON[1]

Dear Sir   *Paris Mar. 13. 1789.*
Since my last, which was of Dec. 21. yours of Dec. 9. and 21. are received. Accept my thanks for the papers and pamphlets which accompanied them, and mine and my daughter's for the book of songs. I will not tell you how much they have pleased us nor how well the last of them merits praise for it's pathos, but relate a fact only, which is that while my elder daughter was playing it on the harpsichord, I happened to look towards the fire and saw the younger one all in tears. I asked her if she was sick? She said "no; but the tune was so mournful."—The Editor of the Encyclopedie has published something as to an advanced price on his future volumes, which I understand alarms the subscribers. It was in a paper which I do not take and therefore I have not yet seen it, nor can say what it is.—I hope that by this time

you have ceased to make wry faces about your vinegar, and that you have received it safe and good. You say that I have been dished up to you as an antifederalist, and ask me if it be just. My opinion was never worthy enough of notice to merit citing: but since you ask it I will tell it you. I am not a Federalist, because I never submitted the whole system of my opinions to the creed of any party of men whatever in religion, in philosophy, in politics, or in any thing else where I was capable of thinking for myself. Such an addiction is the last degradation of a free and moral agent. If I could not go to heaven but with a party, I would not go there at all. Therefore I protest to you I am not of the party of federalists. But I am much farther from that of the Antifederalists. I approved from the first moment, of the great mass of what is in the new constitution, the consolidation of the government, the organisation into Executive, legislative and judiciary, the subdivision of the legislative, the happy compromise of interests between the great and little states by the different manner of voting in the different houses, the voting by persons instead of states, the qualified negative on laws given to the Executive which however I should have liked better if associated with the judiciary also as in New York, and the power of taxation. I thought at first that the latter might have been limited. A little reflection soon convinced me it ought not to be. What I disapproved from the first moment also was the want of a bill of rights to guard liberty against the legislative as well as executive branches of the government, that is to say to secure freedom in religion, freedom of the press, freedom from monopolies, freedom from unlawful imprisonment, freedom from a permanent military, and a trial by jury in all cases determinable by the laws of the land. I disapproved also the perpetual reeligibility of the President. To these points of disapprobation I adhere. My first wish was that the 9. first conventions might accept the constitution, as the means of securing to us the great mass of good it contained, and that the 4. last might reject it, as the means of obtaining amendments. But I was corrected in this wish the moment I saw the much better plan of Massachusets[2] and which had never occurred to me. With respect to the declaration of rights I suppose the majority of the United states are of my opinion: for I apprehend all the antifederalists, and a very respectable propor-

tion of the federalists think that such a declaration should now be annexed. The enlightened part of Europe have given us the greatest
credit for inventing this instrument of security for the rights of the
people, and have been not a little surprised to see us so soon give it up.
With respect to the re-eligibility of the president, I find myself differ-
ing from the majority of my countrymen, for I think there are but
three states of the 11. which have desired an alteration of this. And indeed, since the thing is established, I would wish it not to be altered
during the life of our great leader, whose executive talents are superior to those I believe of any man in the world, and who alone by the
authority of his name and the confidence reposed in his perfect integrity, is fully qualified to put the new government so under way as to
secure it against the efforts of opposition. But having derived from our
error all the good there was in it I hope we shall correct it the moment
we can no longer have the same person at the helm. These, my dear
friend, are my sentiments, by which you will see I was right in saying
I am neither federalist nor antifederalist; that I am of neither party,
nor yet a trimmer between parties. These my opinions I wrote within
a few hours after I had read the constitution, to one or two friends in
America. I had not then read one single word printed on the subject. I
never had an opinion in politics or religion which I was afraid to own.
A costive reserve on these subjects might have procured me more esteem from some people, but less from myself. My great wish is to go
on in a strict but silent performance of my duty: to avoid attracting
notice and to keep my name out of newspapers, because I find the pain
of a little censure, even when it is unfounded, is more acute than the
pleasure of much praise. The attaching circumstance of my present
office is that I can do it's duties unseen by those for whom they are
done.—You did not think, by so short a phrase in your letter, to have
drawn on yourself such an egoistical dissertation. I beg your pardon
for it, and will endeavor to merit that pardon by the constant sentiments of esteem & attachment with which I am Dear Sir, Your sincere
friend & servant,

Th: Jefferson

103. TO JAMES MADISON

Dear Sir   *Paris Mar. 15. 1789.*
I wrote you last on the 12th. of Jan. since which I have received yours
of Octob. 17. Dec. 8. and 12. That of Oct. 17. came to hand only Feb.
23. How it happened to be four months on the way, I cannot tell, as I
never knew by what hand it came. Looking over my letter of Jan. 12th.
I remark an error of the word 'probable' instead of 'improbable,'
which doubtless however you had been able to correct. Your thoughts
on the subject of the Declaration of rights in the letter of Oct. 17. I
have weighed with great satisfaction. Some of them had not occurred
to me before, but were acknoleged just in the moment they were presented to my mind. In the arguments in favor of a declaration of
rights, you omit one which has great weight with me, the legal check
which it puts into the hands of the judiciary. This is a body, which if
rendered independent, and kept strictly to their own department
merits great confidence for their learning and integrity. In fact what
degree of confidence would be too much for a body composed of such
men as Wythe, Blair, and Pendleton? On characters like these the
'civium ardor prava jubentium'[1] would make no impression. I am
happy to find that on the whole you are a friend to this amendment.
The Declaration of rights is like all other human blessings alloyed
with some inconveniences, and not accomplishing fully it's object. But
the good in this instance vastly overweighs the evil. I cannot refrain
from making short answers to the objections which your letter states
to have been raised. 1. That the rights in question are reserved by the
manner in which the federal powers are granted. Answer. A constitu-
tive act may certainly be so formed as to need no declaration of rights.
The act itself has the force of a declaration as far as it goes: and if it
goes to all material points nothing more is wanting. In the draught of
a constitution which I had once a thought of proposing in Virginia,
and printed afterwards, I endeavored to reach all the great objects of
public liberty, and did not mean to add a declaration of rights. Probably the object was imperfectly executed: but the deficiencies would
have been supplied by others in the course of discussion. But in a con-
stitutive act which leaves some precious articles unnoticed, and raises

implications against others, a declaration of rights becomes necessary by way of supplement. This is the case of our new federal constitution. This instrument forms us into one state as to certain objects, and gives us a legislative and executive body for these objects. It should therefore guard us against their abuses of power within the feild submitted to them. 2. A positive declaration of some essential rights could not be obtained in the requisite latitude. Answer. Half a loaf is better than no bread. If we cannot secure all our rights, let us secure what we can. 3. The limited powers of the federal government and jealousy of the subordinate governments afford a security which exists in no other instance. Answer. The first member of this seems resolvable into the 1st. objection before stated. The jealousy of the subordinate governments is a precious reliance. But observe that those governments are only agents. They must have principles furnished them whereon to found their opposition. The declaration of rights will be the text whereby they will try all the acts of the federal government. In this view it is necessary to the federal government also: as by the same text they may try the opposition of the subordinate governments. 4. Experience proves the inefficacy of a bill of rights. True. But tho it is not absolutely efficacious under all circumstances, it is of great potency always, and rarely inefficacious. A brace the more will often keep up the building which would have fallen with that brace the less. There is a remarkeable difference between the characters of the Inconveniencies which attend a Declaration of rights, and those which attend the want of it. The inconveniences of the Declaration are that it may cramp government in it's useful exertions. But the evil of this is shortlived, moderate, and reparable. The inconveniencies of the want of a Declaration are permanent, afflicting and irreparable: they are in constant progression from bad to worse. The executive in our governments is not the sole, it is scarcely the principal object of my jealousy. The tyranny of the legislatures is the most formidable dread at present, and will be for long years. That of the executive will come in it's turn, but it will be at a remote period. I know there are some among us who would now establish a monarchy. But they are inconsiderable in number and weight of character. The rising race are all republicans. We were educated in royalism: no wonder if some of us retain that idolatry still. Our young people are educated in republicanism. An apostacy from that to royalism is unprecedented and impossible.   I am much pleased with the prospect that a declaration of rights will be added: and hope it will be done in that way which will not endanger the whole frame of the government, or any essential part of it.

I have hitherto avoided public news in my letters to you, because your situation ensured you a communication of my letters to Mr. Jay. This circumstance being changed, I shall in future indulge myself in these details to you. There had been some slight hopes that an accomodation might be effected between the Turks and two empires. But these hopes do not strengthen, and the season is approaching which will put an end to them for another campaign at least. The accident to the king of England has had great influence on the affairs of Europe. His mediation joined with that of Prussia would certainly have kept Denmark quiet, and so have left the two empires in the hands of the Turks and Swedes. But the inactivity to which England is reduced, leaves Denmark more free, and she will probably go on in opposition to Sweden. The K. of Prussia too had advanced so far that he can scarcely retire. This is rendered the more difficult by the troubles he has excited in Poland. He cannot well abandon the party he had brought forward there. So that it is very possible he may be engaged in the ensuing campaign. France will be quiet this year, because this year at least is necessary for settling her future constitution. The States will meet the 27th. of April: and the public mind will I think by that time be ripe for a just decision of the Question whether they shall vote by orders or persons. I think there is a majority of the nobles already for the latter. If so, their affairs cannot but go on well. Besides settling for themselves a tolerably free constitution, perhaps as free a one as the nation is as yet prepared to bear, they will fund their public debts. This will give them such a credit as will enable them to borrow any money they may want, and of course to take the feild again when they think proper. And I believe they mean to take the feild as soon as they can. The pride of every individual in the nation suffers under the ignominies they have lately been exposed to: and I think the states general will give money for a war to wipe off the reproach. There have arisen new bickerings between this court and that of the Hague, and the papers which have passed shew the most bitter acrimony rankling at the heart of this ministry. They have recalled their Ambassador from the Hague without appointing a successor. They have given a note to the Diet of Poland which shews a disapprobation of their measures. The insanity of the King of England has been fortunate for them as it given them time to put their house in order. The English papers tell you the king is well: and even the English ministry say so. They will naturally set the best foot foremost: and they guard his person so well that it is difficult for the public to contradict them. The king is probably better, but not well by a great deal. 1. He has been bled, and judicious physicians say that in his exhausted state nothing could have induced a recurrence to bleeding but symptoms of relapse. 2. The Prince of Wales tells the Irish deputation he will give them a definitive answer in some days: but if the king had been well he could have given it at once. 3. They talk of passing a standing law for providing a regency in similar cases. They apprehend then they are not yet clear of the danger of wanting a regency. 4. They have carried the king to church: but it was his private chapel. If he be well, why do not they shew him publicly to the nation, and raise them from that consternation into which they have been thrown by the prospect of being delivered over to the profligate hands of the prince of Wales. In short, judging from little facts which escape in spite of their teeth, we may say the king is better, but not well. Possibly he is getting well; but still, time will be wanting to satisfy even the ministry that it is not merely a lucid interval. Consequently they cannot interrupt France this year in the settlement of her affairs, and after this year it will be too late.

As you will be in a situation to know when the leave of absence will be granted me which I have asked, will you be so good as to communicate it by a line to Mr. Lewis and Mr. Eppes? I hope to see you in the summer, and that if you are not otherwise engaged, you will encamp with me at Monticello for a while. I am with great and sincere attachment Dear sir Your affectionate friend & servt,

Th: Jefferson

104. TO JOSEPH WILLARD[1]

Sir   *Paris Mar. 24. 1789.*

I have been lately honoured with your letter of Sep. 24. 1788. accompanied by a diploma for a doctorate of laws which the University of Harvard has been pleased to confer on me. Conscious how little I merit it, I am the more sensible of their goodness and indulgence to a stranger who has had no means of serving or making himself known to them. I beg you to return them my grateful thanks, and to assure them that this notice from so eminent a seat of science is very precious to me.

The most remarkable publications we have had in France for a year or two past are the following. Les voiages d'Anacharsis par l'Abbé Barthelemi. 7. vols. 8vo. This is a very elegant digest of whatever is known of the Greeks; unuseful indeed to him who has read the original authors, but very proper for one who reads modern languages only.—The works of the king of Prussia. The Berlin edition is in 16. vols. 8vo. It is said to have been gutted at Berlin; and here it has been still more mangled. There are one or two other editions published abroad, which pretend to have rectified the maltreatment both of Berlin and Paris. Some time will be necessary to settle the public mind as to the best edition.

Montignot has given us the original Greek, and a French translation of the 7th. book of Ptolemy's great work, under the title of 'Etat des etoiles fixes au second siecle,' in 4to. He has given the designation of the same stars by Flamstead and Beyer, and their position in the year 1786. A very remarkeable work is the 'Mechanique Analytique' of La Grange in 4to. He is allowed to be the greatest mathematician now living, and his personal worth is equal to his science. The object of his work is to reduce all the principles of Mechanics to the single one of the Equilibrium, and to give a simple formula applicable to them all. The subject is treated in the Algebraic method, without diagrams to assist the conception. My present occupations not permitting me to read any thing which requires a long and undisturbed attention, I am not able to give you the character of this work from my own examination. It has been received with great approbation in Europe. In Italy, the works of Spallanzani on digestion, and generation, are valuable. Tho perhaps too minute, and therefore tedious, he has developed some useful truths, and his book is well worth attention. It is in 4. vols. 8vo. Clavigero, an Italian also, who has resided thirty six years in Mexico, has given us a history of that country, which certainly merits more respect than any other work on the same subject. He corrects many errors of Dr. Robertson and tho sound philosophy will disapprove many of his ideas, we must still consider it as an useful work, and assuredly the best we possess on the same subject. It is in 4. thin volumes small 4to. De la Land has not yet published a 5th. volume.

The chemical dispute about the conversion and reconversion of air and water, continues still undecided. Arguments and authorities are so balanced that we may still safely believe, as our fathers did before us, that these principles are distinct. A schism of another kind has taken place among the chimists. A particular set of them here have undertaken to remodel all the terms of the science, and to give to every substance a new name the composition, and especially the termination, of which shall define the relation in which it stands to other substances of the same family. But the science seems too much in it's infancy as yet for this reformation: because in fact the reformation of this year must be reformed again the next year, and so on, changing the names of substances as often as new experiments develope properties in them undiscovered before. The new nomenclature has accordingly been already proved to need numerous and important reformations. Probably it will not prevail. It is espoused by the minority only here, and by a very few indeed of the foreign chymists. It is particularly rejected in England.

In the arts, I think two of our countrymen have presentd the most important inventions. Mr. Paine, the author of common sense, has invented an iron bridge which promises to be cheaper by a great deal than stone, and to admit of a much greater arch. He supposes it may be ventured for an arch of 500. feet. He has obtained a patent for it in England, and is now executing the first experiment with an arch of between 90. and 100. feet. Mr. Rumsey has also obtained a patent for his navigation by the force of steam in England and is solliciting a similar one here. His principal merit is in the improvement of the boiler, and, instead of the complicated machinery of oars and paddles proposed by others, the substitution of so simple a thing as the reaction of a stream of water on his vessel. He is building a sea-vessel at this time in England and she will be ready for an experiment in May. He has suggested a great number of mechanical improvements in a variety of branches; and upon the whole is the most original and the greatest mechanical genius I have ever seen.   The return of la Peyrouse (whenever that shall happen) will probably add to our knowlege in Geography, botany and natural history. What a feild have we at our doors to signalize ourselves in! The botany of America is far from being exhausted: it's Mineralogy is untouched, and it's Natural history or Zoology totally mistaken and misrepresented. As far as I have seen there is not one single species of terrestrial birds common to Europe and America, and I question if there be a single species of quadrupeds. (Domestic animals are to be excepted.) It is for such institutions as that over which you preside so worthily, Sir, to do justice to our country, it's productions, and it's genius. It is the work to which the young men, whom you are forming, should lay their hands. We have spent the prime of our lives in procuring them the precious blessing of liberty. Let them spend theirs in shewing that it is the great parent of science and of virtue; and that a nation will be great in both always in proportion as it is free. No body wishes more warmly for the success of your good exhortations on this subject, than him who has the honor to be with sentiments of great esteem & respect Sir your most obedient humble servant,

Th: Jefferson

105. TO MARIA COSWAY

Paris May 21. 1789.

I have not yet, my dear friend, received my leave of absence, but I expect it hourly, and shall depart almost in the hour of receiving it. My absence will be of about six months. I leave here a scene of tumult and contest. All is politics in this capital. Even love has lost it's part in conversation. This is not well, for love is always a consolatory thing. I am going to a country where it is felt in it's sublimest degree. In great cities it is distracted by the variety of objects. Friendship perhaps suffers there also from the same cause but I am determined to except from this your friendship for m[e], and to beleive it distracted by neither time, distance, nor object. When wafting on the bosom of the ocean I shall pray it to be as calm and smooth as yours to me. What shall I say for you to our friend Mrs. Church? I shall see her assuredly, perhaps return with her. We shall talk a great deal of you. In fact you ought to have gone with her. We would have travelled a great deal together, we would have intruded our opinions into the choice of objects for your pencil and returned fraught with treasures of art, science and sentiment. Adieu, my very dear friend. Be our affections unchangeable, and if our little history is to last beyond the grave, be the longest chapter in it that which shall record their purity, warmth and duration.

106. TO RABAUT DE ST. ETIENNE[1]

Sir   *Paris June 3. 1789.*
After you quitted us yesterday evening, we continued our conversation (Monsr. de la Fayette, Mr. Short and myself) on the subject of the difficulties which environ you. The desireable object being to secure the good which the King has offered and to avoid the ill which seems to threaten, an idea was suggested, which appearing to make an impression on Monsr. de la Fayette, I was encouraged to pursue it on my return to Paris, to put it into form, and now to send it to you and him. It is this, that the king, in a *seance royale*, should come forward with a Charter of Rights in his hand, to be signed by himself and by every member of the three orders. This charter to contain the five great points which the Resultat of December offered on the part of the king, the abolition of pecuniary privileges offered by the privileged orders, and the adoption of the National debt and a grant of the sum of money asked from the nation. This last will be a cheap price for the preceding articles, and let the same act declare your immediate separation till the next anniversary meeting. You will carry back to your

constituents more good than ever was effected before without violence, and you will stop exactly at the point where violence would otherwise begin. Time will be gained, the public mind will continue to ripen and to be informed, a basis of support may be prepared with the people themselves, and expedients occur for gaining still something further at your next meeting, and for stopping again at the point of force. I have ventured to send to yourself and Monsieur de la Fayette a sketch of my ideas of what this act might contain without endangering any dispute. But it is offered merely as a canvas for you to work on, if it be fit to work on at all. I know too little of the subject, and you know too much of it to justify me in offering any thing but a hint. I have done it too in a hurry: insomuch that since committing it to writing it occurs to me that the 5th. article may give alarm, that it is in a good degree included in the 4th. and is therefore useless. But after all what excuse can I make, Sir, for this presumption. I have none but an unmeasurable love for your nation and a painful anxiety lest Despotism, after an unaccepted offer to bind it's own hands, should seize you again with tenfold fury. Permit me to add to these very sincere assurances of the sentiments of esteem & respect with which I have the honor to be Sir Your most obedt. & most humble servt.,

Th: Jefferson

DRAFT OF A CHARTER OF RIGHTS

A Charter of Rights solemnly established by the King and Nation.

1. The States general shall assemble, uncalled, on the 1st. day of November annually, and shall remain together so long as they shall see cause. They shall regulate their own elections and proceedings, and until they shall ordain otherwise, their elections shall be in the forms observed in the present year, and shall be triennial.

2. The States-general alone shall levy money on the nation, and shall appropriate it.

3. Laws shall be made by the States-general only, with the consent of the king.

4. No person shall be restrained of his liberty but by regular process from a court of justice, authorized by a general law: (except

that a Noble may be imprisoned by order of a court of justice on the prayer of 12. of his nearest relations.) On complaint of an unlawful imprisonment, to any judge whatever, he shall have the prisoner immediately brought before him, and shall discharge him if his imprisonment be unlawful. The officer in whose custody the prisoner is shall obey the orders of the judge, and both judge and officer shall be responsible civilly and criminally for a failure of duty herein.

5. The Military shall be subordinate to the Civil authority.

6. Printers shall be liable to legal prosecution for printing and publishing false facts injurious to the party prosecuting: but they shall be under no other restraint.

7. All pecuniary privileges and exemptions enjoyed by any description of persons are abolished.

8. All debts already contracted by the king are hereby made the debts of the nation: and the faith thereof is pledged for their paiment in due time.

9. 80. millions of livres are now granted to the king, to be raised by loan and reimbursed by the nation: and the taxes heretofore paid shall continue to be paid to the end of the present year, and no longer.

10. The States general shall now separate and meet again on the 1st. day of November next.

Done, on behalf of the whole nation, by the King and their representatives in the States general, at Versailles, this ———— day of June 1789.

> *Signed by the king, and by every member individually, and in his presence.*

107. TO MARIA COSWAY

Paris July 25. 1789.

My letter of May 21. my dear Madam, was the last I expected to have written you on this side the Atlantic for the present year. Reasons, which I cannot devine, have prevented my yet receiving my Congé. In the mean time we have been here in the midst of tumult and violence.

The cutting off heads is become so much á la mode, that one is apt to feel of a morning whether their own is on their shoulders. Whether this work is yet over, depends on their catching more of the fugitives. If no new capture re-excites the spirit of vengeance, we may hope it will soon be at rest, and that order and safety will be reestablished except for a few of the most obnoxious characters. My fortune has been singular, to see in the course of fourteen years two such revolutions as were never before seen. But why should I talk of wars and revolutions to you who are all peace and goodness. Receive then into your peace and grace the bearer hereof Mr. Morris,[1] a countryman and friend of mine of great consideration in his own country, and who deserves to be so every where. Peculiarly gifted with fancy and judgment, he will be qualified to taste the beauties of your canvas. The Marquis de la Luzerne, an old and intimate acquaintance of his, will bear witness to you of his merit. But do not let him nestle me out of my place; for I still pretend to have one in your affection, tho' it is a long time since you told me so. I must soon begin to scold, if I do not hear from you. In order to be quiet, I persuade myself that you have thought me in, on, or over the Deep. But wherever I am, I feed on your friendship. I therefore need assurances of it in all times and places. Accept in return those which flow cordially from the heart of Your

Th: Jefferson

108. TO DIODATI[1]

à Paris ce 3me. Aout, 1789

Je viens de recevoir, mon chere Monsieur, l'honneur de votre lettre du 24. Juillet. La peine avec laquelle je m'exprime en Francois feroit que ma reponse seroit bien courte s'il ne m'etoit pas permis de repondre que dans cette langue. Mais je sçais qu'avec quelque connoissance de la langue Angloise vous meme, vous aurez une aide tres suffisante dans Madame la comtesse que j'ose prier d'ajouter a ses amitiés multipliées devers moi celle de devenir l'interprete de ce que vais ecrire en ma propre langue, et qu'elle embellira en la rendant en François.[2]

I presume that your correspondents here have given you a history of all the events which have happened. The Leyden gazette, tho' it contains several inconsiderable errors gives on the whole a just enough idea. It is impossible to conceive a greater fermentation than has worked in Paris, nor do I believe that so great a fermentation ever produced so little injury in any other place. I have been thro' it daily, have observed the mobs with my own eyes in order to be satisfied of their objects, and declare to you that I saw so plainly the legitimacy of them, that I have slept in my house as quietly thro' the whole as I ever did in the most peaceable moments. So strongly fortified was the despotism of this government by long posession, by the respect and the fears of the people, by possessing the public force, by the imposing authority of forms and of faste,³ that had it held itself on the defensive only, the national assembly with all their good sense, could probably have only obtained a considerable improvement of the government, not a total revision of it. But, ill informed of the spirit of their nation, the despots around the throne had recourse to violent measures, the forerunners of force. In this they have been completely overthrown, and the nation has made a total resumption of rights, which they had certainly never before ventured even to think of. The National assembly have now as clean a canvas to work on here as we had in America. Such has been the firmness and wisdom of their proceedings in moments of adversity as well as prosperity, that I have the highest confidence that they will use their power justly. As far as I can collect from conversation with their members, the constitution they will propose will resemble that of England in it's outlines, but not in it's defects. They will certainly leave the king possessed completely of the Executive powers, and particularly of the public force. Their legislature will consist of one order only, and not of two as in England: the representation will be equal and not abominably partial as that of England: it will be guarded against corruption, instead of having a majority sold to the king, and rendering his will absolute: whether it will be in one chamber, or broke into two cannot be foreseen. They will meet at certain epochs and sit as long as they please, instead of meeting only when, and sitting only as long as, the king pleases as in England. There is a difference of opinion whether the king shall have an absolute, or only a qualified Negative on their acts. The parliaments will probably be suppressed; and juries provided in criminal cases perhaps even in civil ones. This is what appears probable at present. The Assembly is this day discussing the question whether they will have a declaration of rights. Paris has been led by events to assume the government of itself. It has hitherto worn too much the appearance of conformity to continue thus independently of the will of the nation. Reflection will probably make them sensible that the security of all depends on the dependance of all on the national legislature. I have so much confidence in the good sense of man, and his qualifications for self-government, that I am never afraid of the issue where reason is left free to exert her force; and I will agree to be stoned as a false prophet if all does not end well in this country. Nor will it end with this country. Here is but the first chapter of the history of European liberty.

The capture of the Baron Besenval is very embarrassing for the States general. They are principled against retrospective laws, and will make it one of the corner stones of their new building. But it is very doubtful whether the antient laws will condemn him, and whether the people will permit him to be acquitted. The Duke de la Vauguyon also and his son are taken at Havre.—In drawing the parallel between what England is, and what France is to be I forgot to observe that the latter will have a real constitution, which cannot be changed by the ordinary legislature; whereas England has no constitution at all; that is to say there is not one principle of their government which the parliament does not alter at pleasure. The omnipotence of parliament is an established principle with them.—Postponing my departure to America till the end of September I shall hope to have the pleasure of seeing you at Paris before I go, and of renewing in person to yourself and Madame la Comtesse assurances of those sentiments of respect and attachment with which I have the honor to be Dear Sir Your most obedient humble servt.,

Th: Jefferson

109. TO JAMES MADISON

Dear Sir   *Paris September 6. 1789.*
I sit down to write to you without knowing by what occasion I shall
send my letter. I do it because a subject comes into my head which I
would wish to develope a little more than is practicable in the hurry
of the moment of making up general dispatches.

The question Whether one generation of men has a right to bind another, seems never to have been started either on this or our side of the
water. Yet it is a question of such consequences as not only to merit decision, but place also, among the fundamental principles of every government. The course of reflection in which we are immersed here on
the elementary principles of society has presented this question to my
mind; and that no such obligation can be so transmitted I think very capable of proof.—I set out on this ground, which I suppose to be self evident, *'that the earth belongs in usufruct to the living'*: that the dead have
neither powers nor rights over it. The portion occupied by any individual ceases to be his when himself ceases to be, and reverts to the society. If the society has formed no rules for the appropriation of it's lands
in severality, it will be taken by the first occupants. These will generally
be the wife and children of the decedent. If they have formed rules of
appropriation, those rules may give it to the wife and children, or to
some one of them, or to the legatee of the deceased. So they may give
it to his creditor. But the child, the legatee, or creditor takes it, not by
any natural right, but by a law of the society of which they are members, and to which they are subject. Then no man can, by *natural right,*
oblige the lands he occupied, or the persons who succeed him in that
occupation, to the paiment of debts contracted by him. For if he could,
he might, during his own life, eat up the usufruct of the lands for several generations to come, and then the lands would belong to the dead,
and not to the living, which would be the reverse of our principle.

What is true of every member of the society individually, is true of
them all collectively, since the rights of the whole can be no more than
the sum of the rights of the individuals.—To keep our ideas clear
when applying them to a multitude, let us suppose a whole generation
of men to be born on the same day, to attain mature age on the same

day, and to die on the same day, leaving a succeeding generation in the moment of attaining their mature age all together. Let the ripe age be supposed of 21. years, and their period of life 34. years more, that being the average term given by the bills of mortality to persons who have already attained 21. years of age. Each successive generation would, in this way, come on, and go off the stage at a fixed moment, as individuals do now. Then I say the earth belongs to each of these generations, during it's course, fully, and in their own right. The 2d. generation receives it clear of the debts and incumberances of the 1st. the 3d of the 2d. and so on. For if the 1st. could charge it with a debt, then the earth would belong to the dead and not the living generation. Then no generation can contract debts greater than may be paid during the course of it's own existence. At 21. years of age they may bind themselves and their lands for 34. years to come: at 22. for 33: at 23. for 32. and at 54. for one year only; because these are the terms of life which remain to them at those respective epochs.—But a material difference must be noted between the succession of an individual, and that of a whole generation. Individuals are parts only of a society, subject to the laws of the whole. These laws may appropriate the portion of land occupied by a decedent to his creditor rather than to any other, or to his child on condition he satisfies the creditor. But when a whole generation, that is, the whole society dies, as in the case we have supposed, and another generation or society succeeds, this forms a whole, and there is no superior who can give their territory to a third society, who may have lent money to their predecessors beyond their faculties of paying.

What is true of a generation all arriving to self-government on the same day, and dying all on the same day, is true of those in a constant course of decay and renewal, with this only difference. A generation coming in and going out entire, as in the first case, would have a right in the 1st. year of their self-dominion to contract a debt for 33. years, in the 10th. for 24. in the 20th. for 14. in the 30th. for 4. whereas generations, changing daily by daily deaths and births, have one constant term, beginning at the date of their contract, and ending when a majority of those of full age at that date shall be dead. The length of that term may be estimated from the tables of mortality, corrected by the circumstances of climate, occupation &c. peculiar to the country of the contractors. Take, for instance, the table of M. de Buffon wherein he states 23,994 deaths, and the ages at which they happened. Suppose a society in which 23,994 persons are born every year, and live to the ages stated in this table. The conditions of that society will be as follows. 1st. It will consist constantly of 617,703. persons of all ages. 2ly. Of those living at any one instant of time, one half will be dead in 24. years 8. months. 3dly. 10,675 will arrive every year at the age of 21. years complete. 4ly. It will constantly have 348,417 persons of all ages above 21. years. 5ly. And the half of those of 21. years and upwards living at any one instant of time will be dead in 18. years 8. months, or say 19. years as the nearest integral number. Then 19. years is the term beyond which neither the representatives of a nation, nor even the whole nation itself assembled, can validly extend a debt.

To render this conclusion palpable by example, suppose that Louis XIV. and XV. had contracted debts in the name of the French nation to the amount of 10,000 milliards of livres, and that the whole had been contracted in Genoa. The interest of this sum would be 500. milliards, which is said to be the whole rent roll or nett proceeds of the territory of France. Must the present generation of men have retired from the territory in which nature produced them, and ceded it to the Genoese creditors? No. They have the same rights over the soil on which they were produced, as the preceding generations had. They derive these rights not from their predecessors, but from nature. They then and their soil are by nature clear of the debts of their predecessors.

Again suppose Louis XV. and his cotemporary generation had said to the money-lenders of Genoa, give us money that we may eat, drink, and be merry in our day; and on condition you will demand no interest till the end of 19. years you shall then for ever after receive an annual interest of * 12⅚ per cent. The money is lent on these conditions, is divided among the living, eaten, drank, and squandered. Would the present generation be obliged to apply the produce of the earth and of their labour to replace their dissipations? Not at all.

---

* 100£, at a compound interest of 5. per cent, makes, at the end of 19. years, an aggregate of principal and interest of £252-14, the interest of which is 12£-12s-7d which is nearly 12⅚ per cent on the first capital of 100.£.

I suppose that the recieved opinion, that the public debts of one generation devolve on the next, has been suggested by our seeing habitually in private life that he who succeeds to lands is required to pay the debts of his ancestor or testator: without considering that this requisition is municipal only, not moral; flowing from the will of the society, which has found it convenient to appropriate lands, become vacant by the death of their occupant, on the condition of a paiment of his debts: but that between society and society, or generation and generation, there is no municipal obligation, no umpire but the law of nature. We seem not to have percieved that, by the law of nature, one generation is to another as one independant nation to another.

The interest of the national debt of France being in fact but a two thousandth part of it's rent roll, the paiment of it is practicable enough: and so becomes a question merely of honor, or of expediency. But with respect to future debts, would it not be wise and just for that nation to declare, in the constitution they are forming, that neither the legislature, nor the nation itself, can validly contract more debt than they may pay within their own age, or within the term of 19. years? And that all future contracts will be deemed void as to what shall remain unpaid at the end of 19. years from their date? This would put the lenders, and the borrowers also, on their guard. By reducing too the faculty of borrowing within it's natural limits, it would bridle the spirit of war, to which too free a course has been procured by the inattention of money-lenders to this law of nature, that succeeding generations are not responsible for the preceding.

On similar ground it may be proved that no society can make a perpetual constitution, or even a perpetual law. The earth belongs always to the living generation. They may manage it then, and what proceeds from it, as they please, during their usufruct. They are masters too of their own persons, and consequently may govern them as they please. But persons and property make the sum of the objects of government. The constitution and the laws of their predecessors extinguished then in their natural course with those who gave them being. This could preserve that being till it ceased to be itself, and no longer. Every constitution then, and every law, naturally expires at the end of 19 years. If it be enforced longer, it is an act of force, and not of right.—It may be said that the succeeding generation exercising in fact the power of repeal, this leaves them as free as if the constitution or law had been expressly limited to 19 years only. In the first place, this objection admits the right, in proposing an equivalent. But the power of repeal is not an equivalent. It might be indeed if every form of government were so perfectly contrived that the will of the majority could always be obtained fairly and without impediment. But this is true of no form. The people cannot assemble themselves. Their representation is unequal and vicious. Various checks are opposed to every legislative proposition. Factions get possession of the public councils. Bribery corrupts them. Personal interests lead them astray from the general interests of their constituents: and other impediments arise so as to prove to every practical man that a law of limited duration is much more manageable than one which needs a repeal.

This principle that the earth belongs to the living, and not to the dead, is of very extensive application and consequences, in every country, and most especially in France. It enters into the resolution of the questions Whether the nation may change the descent of lands holden in tail? Whether they may change the appropriation of lands given antiently to the church, to hospitals, colleges, orders of chivalry, and otherwise in perpetuity? Whether they may abolish the charges and privileges attached on lands, including the whole catalogue ecclesiastical and feudal? It goes to hereditary offices, authorities and jurisdictions; to hereditary orders, distinctions and appellations; to perpetual monopolies in commerce, the arts and sciences; with a long train of et ceteras: and it renders the question of reimbursement a question of generosity and not of right. In all these cases, the legislature of the day could authorize such appropriations and establishments for their own time, but no longer; and the present holders, even where they, or their ancestors, have purchased, are in the case of bonâ fide purchasers of what the seller had no right to convey.

Turn this subject in your mind, my dear Sir, and particularly as to the power of contracting debts; and develope it with that perspicuity and cogent logic so peculiarly yours. Your station in the councils of our country gives you an opportunity of producing it to public consideration, of forcing it into discussion. At first blush it may be rallied, as a theoretical speculation: but examination will prove it to be solid and salutary. It would furnish matter for a fine preamble to our first law for appropriating the public revenue; and it will exclude at the threshold of our new government the contagious and ruinous errors of this quarter of the globe, which have armed despots with means, not sanctioned by nature, for binding in chains their fellow men. We have already given in example one effectual check to the Dog of war by transferring the power of letting him loose from the Executive to the Legislative body, from those who are to spend to those who are to pay. I should be pleased to see this second obstacle held out by us also in the first instance. No nation can make a declaration against the validity of long-contracted debts so disinterestedly as we, since we do not owe a shilling which may not be paid with ease, principal and interest, within the time of our own lives.—Establish the principle also in the new law to be passed for protecting copyrights and new inventions, by securing the exclusive right for 19. instead of 14. years. Besides familiarising us to this term, it will be an instance the more of our taking reason for our guide, instead of English precedent, the habit of which fetters us with all the political heresies of a nation equally remarkable for it's early excitement from some errors, and long slumbering under others.

I write you no news, because, when an occasion occurs, I shall write a separate letter for that. I am always with great & sincere esteem, dear Sir Your affectionate friend & servt,

Th: Jefferson

110. TO MARIA COSWAY

Cowes Octob. 14. 1789.

I am here, my dear friend, waiting the arrival of a ship to take my flight from this side of the Atlantic and as we think last of those we love most, I profit of the latest moment to bid you a short but affectionate Adieu. Before this, Trumbull will have left you: but we are more than exchanged by Mrs. Church who will probably be with you in the course of the present month. My daughters are with me and in good health. We have left a turbulent scene, and I wish it may be tranquilized on my return, which I count will be in the month of April.[1] Under present circumstances, aggravated as you will read them in the English papers, we cannot hope to see you in France. But a return of quiet and order may remove that bugbear, and the ensuing spring might give us a meeting at Paris with the first swallow. So be it, my dear friend, and Adieu under the hope which springs naturally out of what we wish. Once and again then farewell, remember me and love me.

111. "ON SENDING AMERICAN YOUTH TO EUROPE"[1]

[1785?]

Government. Pure Despotism
   Powers of king. Legislative—registg. of parl.
                Executive.   Military
                           Lettres de cachet
                           Printing.
              Aristocracy. Oppressions
                           Pensions, &c.
              Finances.   Abuses in
                           Unproductive of revenue
              Judiciary. Venality
                         Protections
                                 Effects of these on commerce
                                 Grand seigneurs never pay
                                 Poor man not venture to force
                                     them
                               Others therefore pay higher price.
              Commerce affected by preceding circumstances
                          by internal duties
                          by difficulties at bureaux
                          by unwritten agreement
                          by taste for pleasure
              Manufactures. Silks, cloths, linen, household
                             furniture, bijouterie & [montres?]
                             looking glass, books

Productions.	Wine, oil, fruits, brandy, marble plaister
Fine arts.	Painting, statuary, architecture.
	Music, poetry, gardening.
Science	
Society	Love
	Friendship
	Charity
	Religion
	Children
	Dogs
	Theatres
	Concerts
	Balls
	Meals
	Talkativeness
	Sexes have changed business
	Convents
Paris.	Streets. No trottoirs. Lighted. Sewers.
	Buildings. Portes cocheres. Courts. Little houses. Gardens.
	(Littlehouses)
	(Sewers)
	Police
	Filles de joie
	Fiacres
	(Lamps)
	Public gardens
The country.	Soil
	Climate. Compare with America
	Agriculture
	Inclosures

	Animals.	Horses
		Cattle
		Mules
		Asses.

NOTES

PREFACE

1. TJ to Charles Bellini, Sept. 30, 1785, *The Papers of Thomas Jefferson,* ed. Julian P. Boyd et al. (Princeton, 1950–), 8:568; hereafter *Papers.*
2. TJ to James Monroe, March 18, 1785, *Papers,* 8:43.
3. TJ to Bellini, *Papers,* 8:569.
4. TJ to Samuel H. Smith, Sept. 21, 1814, *The Works of Thomas Jefferson,* ed. Paul Leicester Ford, Federal Edition, 12 vols. (New York: G. P. Putnam's Sons, 1905), 11:430.
5. Gouverneur Morris, *A Diary of the French Revolution,* ed. Beatrix Cary Davenport, 2 vols. (Boston: Houghton Mifflin Company, 1939), I:83.
6. John Adams to Henry Knox, Dec. 15, 1785, in *Papers,* 7:383*n.*
7. Abraham Lincoln to Mrs. M. J. Green, Sept. 22, 1860, *The Collected Works of Abraham Lincoln,* ed. Roy P. Basler et al. (New Brunswick: Rutgers University Press, 1953), IV:118.
8. Merrill D. Peterson, *The Jefferson Image in the American Mind* (New York: Oxford University Press, 1960), 64.

1. REASONS IN SUPPORT OF THE NEW PROPOSED ARTICLES IN THE TREATIES OF COMMERCE . . .

1. Enclosure to letter of the three American Commissioners for Negotiating

Treaties of Amity and Commerce (Jefferson, John Adams, and Benjamin Franklin) to the Minister of Prussia. It exemplifies Jefferson's attempt to apply Enlightenment ideas to diplomacy.

2. TO JAMES MADISON

1. The *Encyclopédie méthodique*, Charles Joseph Panckoucke's expansion and rearrangement by subject of the great encyclopedia of Diderot and d'Alembert.
2. Jefferson had witnessed the hydrogen balloon ascension of the Robert brothers from the Tuileries gardens on September 19. The first successful manned flight had taken place in Paris in November 1783.
3. Aimé Argand's patented lamp, with cylindrical wick and glass chimney.
4. Coast carrying trade.

3. TO JAMES CURRIE

1. Jefferson's lifelong friend Dr. Currie (1745–1807) was a prominent physician in Richmond, Virginia.
2. The Palais Royal, recently enlarged by the Duc de Chartres (later Duc d'Orléans), housed restaurants and cafés, clubs and luxury shops.

4. TO JAMES MONROE

1. Until Monroe (1758–1831) left the Confederation Congress in 1786, Jefferson relied on him for information about the Virginia delegation.

5. TO ABIGAIL ADAMS

1. Summary: The ambassador proceeds on his embassy to the princess, who has two swollen cheeks to his one. He makes known to her the king's ardor with an offer of half his kingdom for that of her bed. He carries back the princess's reply, happy to add to the honor of seeing her the pleasure of leaving her.
2. J. F. Pilâtre de Rozier had been killed June 15 attempting to cross the English Channel in a balloon.
3. The salon of Élisabeth Sophie de Lalive de Bellegarde, Comtesse d'Houdetot (1730–1813), the inspiration for Rousseau's *La Nouvelle Héloïse*.

6. TO ELIZABETH HOUSE TRIST

1. Mrs. Trist had learned of the death of her husband on her arrival in New Orleans.

8. TO JOHN JAY

1. Jay (1745–1829), later the first chief justice of the United States, was at this time secretary for foreign affairs.

9. TO FRANCIS EPPES

1. Jefferson's in-laws, Henry and Anne Wayles Skipwith.
2. James Hemings (1762–1801), a slave brought by Jefferson from Monticello to France for training in French cookery.

10. TO JAMES MADISON WITH A LIST OF BOOKS

1. Jefferson had privately printed two hundred copies of his *Notes on the State of Virginia* in May.
2. The Maison Carrée at Nîmes.
3. A letter-copying machine, patented by James Watt in 1780; Jefferson had received his in May.
4. Jefferson's symbol for the *livre tournois,* then the equivalent of one-sixth of an American dollar.

11. TO CHASTELLUX, WITH ENCLOSURE

1. Chastellux's *Travels in North America,* published in 1786.
2. Jefferson means his fellow Virginians.

12. TO ABIGAIL ADAMS

1. The Abbés Arnoud and Chalut, friends of both Jefferson and the Adamses.
2. The Hôtel de Langeac, on the corner of the Champs-Elysées and the Rue de Berri, where Jefferson lived for the remainder of his residence in France.

13. TO JAMES MADISON

1. Charles Louis Clérisseau (1721–1820).
2. Edmund Randolph (1753–1813).

14. TO ABIGAIL ADAMS

1. In 1792 Jefferson was finally paid the equivalent of a year's salary for his "outfit," that is, the costs of clothing, carriage and horses, and household furniture.

15. TO RALPH IZARD

1. Izard (1741/2–1804), former congressman and future senator, was actively pursuing agricultural improvements on his plantation near Charleston, South Carolina.

17. TO CHARLES BELLINI

1. A native of Florence, Italy, Bellini (1735–1804) was professor of modern languages at the College of William and Mary in Williamsburg, Virginia.

18. TO REV. JAMES MADISON

1. Uranus, discovered by William Herschel in 1782.

19. TO G. K. VAN HOGENDORP

1. Count van Hogendorp (1762–1834) was a Dutch nobleman whom Jefferson had met in Annapolis early in 1784.
2. The great French naturalist Georges Louis Leclerc, Comte de Buffon (1707–1788), was at this time director of the Jardin du Roi (now Jardin des Plantes).

20. TO JOHN BANISTER, JR.

1. Banister (d. 1788), the son of Jefferson's friend John Banister of Battersea, near Petersburg, Virginia, was making the Grand Tour. He later fell vic-

tim to "the allurements of Paris" and Jefferson had to lend him over five hundred dollars.

22. TO ARCHIBALD CARY

1. Jefferson's old family friend Archibald Cary (1721–1787) of Chesterfield County was speaker of the Virginia Senate.
2. Tuckahoe, once Jefferson's childhood home, was the residence of Thomas Mann Randolph (1741–1793).

23. TO ARCHIBALD STUART

1. Stuart (1757–1832), later a jurist and legislator, had read law with Jefferson. He lived in Staunton, Virginia.

24. TO JAMES BUCHANAN AND WILLIAM HAY

1. Buchanan and Hay were directors for Virginia public buildings.

25. TO JAMES MADISON

1. Diderot and d'Alembert's *Encyclopédie, ou Dictionnaire raisonné des sciences, des arts et des métiers,* first published beginning in 1751; the new one was Panckoucke's *Encyclopédie méthodique.*
2. Jefferson had commissioned French sculptor Jean Antoine Houdon to make a statue of George Washington for the state of Virginia; it now stands in the Capitol in Richmond.
3. F. I. J. Hoffman, whose Imprimerie Polytype also produced a journal using a process similar to stereotype.

26. NOTES OF TOUR OF ENGLISH GARDENS

1. Thomas Whately, *Observations on Modern Gardening* (London, 1770).
2. Jefferson and William Stephens Smith made a tour of Surrey and Middlesex landscape gardens, several the work of William Kent, on April 2 and 3. Chiswick, Claremont, Hampton Court, and Painshill have been maintained or restored and are open to the public. Esher Place, Alexander Pope's Twickenham garden, and Woburn Farm, the foremost example of

the ornamented farm, or *ferme ornée*, retain little of their eighteenth-century appearance.

3. "Ah! Edith, best of mothers, most beloved of women, Farewell."

4. From April 4 to 9, Jefferson and John Adams toured landscape gardens and battlefields between London and Birmingham. Stowe, Hagley Hall, and Blenheim are still open to the public. Caversham Park, near Reading, and Wotton House, near Thame, are not. The poet William Shenstone's The Leasowes had influenced Jefferson long before he saw it.

5. Chaste.

6. Henry II, who according to legend, kept his "Fair Rosamond," Rosamond Clifford, in a mazelike house nearby.

7. Jefferson made day trips from central London to view William Pitt's Enfield Chase, "Capability" Brown's landscape at Moor Park, and the gardens at Kew.

27. TO JOHN PAGE

1. Jefferson and his close friend Page (1743–1808), later a U.S. congressman and governor of Virginia, had been students together at the College of William and Mary.

28. FROM JEFFERSON'S OBSERVATIONS ON DÉMEUNIER'S MANUSCRIPT ON THE UNITED STATES

1. Jean Nicolas Démeunier (1751–1814) was the author of the section on the United States in the *Encyclopédie méthodique*. This extract, part of over thirty pages of corrections, was used by Démeunier almost in its entirety.

29. TO WILLIAM STEPHENS SMITH

1. Dutch and French bankers.

2. While in London Jefferson had designed a portable version of the Watt copying press, in the form of a small writing desk.

30. TO GEORGE WYTHE

1. Wythe (1726–1806), Jefferson's "second father" and law teacher, was at this time professor of law at the College of William and Mary and one of the three judges of the Virginia high court of chancery.

2. The Greek word for "best." The motto has been translated: "Not to seem but to be."

33. TO EZRA STILES

1. Jefferson had visited Stiles (1727–1795), president of Yale College, in New Haven in June 1784.
2. F. I. J. Hoffman

34. TO MARIA COSWAY

1. Jefferson had fallen and dislocated his wrist two weeks earlier.

35. TO MARIA COSWAY

1. The new grain market, with a dome designed by J. G. Legrand and Jacques Molinos; the Bourse du Commerce occupies its site today.
2. The Désert de Retz, west of Paris, was an Anglo-Chinese garden with a dwelling house in the form of a ruined column; the structures are now being restored.
3. Haman is hanged from his own gallows in the biblical book of Esther.
4. J. P. Claris de Florian's short comedy, which Jefferson had seen, probably with Maria Cosway, at the Opéra-Comique.
5. Approximately: "Without wit, without feelings, without either beauty or youth (or virginity), in France one can have the first lover (the King): Of this Pompadour is proof."

36. TO MARIA COSWAY

1. "Happy Day," a song from Sacchini's *Dardanus,* included the line "In these [isolated] places to which she delays coming."

37. TO WILLIAM STEPHENS SMITH

1. Jefferson had drawn a new map of Virginia, based on his father's 1751 map, to accompany his *Notes on the State of Virginia.*

43. TO MARIA COSWAY

1. One of Maria Cosway's *Songs and Duets,* "Ogni Dolce," included the phrase "Here I await her/him and she/he never comes."

44. TO ST. JOHN DE CRÈVECOEUR

1. Crèvecoeur (1735–1813), author of *Letters from an American Farmer* (1782), was on leave in Europe from his post as French consul in New York.
2. John Viny, wheel manufacturer at Blackfriar's Bridge, London.

46. TO EDWARD CARRINGTON

1. With the departure of James Monroe from Philadelphia, Carrington (1748–1810) became Jefferson's principal contact with the Virginia delegation to Congress.
2. The "tumults" in western Massachusetts, known as Shays' Rebellion.

47. TO JAMES MADISON

1. "I prefer dangerous freedom to servitude."
2. Jefferson's views on public characters were written partly in code. Words set in italic type here indicate text originally written in code.
3. William Carmichael (d. 1795), American chargé d'affaires at the court of Spain.
4. David Salisbury Franks (c. 1740–1793) held several minor public appointments in Europe from 1784 to 1787.
5. William Bingham of Philadelphia.
6. French foreign minister.

48. TO ANNE WILLING BINGHAM

1. The theaters.
2. The fashion periodical *Magasin des modes nouvelles, françaises et anglaises.*

49. TO ABIGAIL ADAMS

1. Adrien Petit, Jefferson's—and formerly the Adamses'—*maître d'hôtel.*

50. TO MADAME DE TOTT

1. *Marius at Minternes,* by Jean Germain Drouais, depicted the Roman general after his defeat by Sulla in 86 B.C. See also letter 57, page 140.

51. TO WILLIAM SHORT

1. Jefferson's Goochland County plantation.
2. Small horse.

52. TO MADAME DE TESSÉ

1. The text given here is taken from Jefferson's retained copy and, where this is illegible, from a transcription he made during his retirement, many years later. While his purpose in transcribing this remarkable letter is unknown, certain changes he made in the text suggest a wish not only to improve its style but to make its author appear a better prophet. For Jefferson's changes, see *Papers*, 11:228.

55. TO WILLIAM SHORT

1. The *Diana and Endymion* by Slodtz. See also mention in letter 52, page 131.

56. TO CHASTELLUX

1. See item 62, under Tours, page 169.

57. TO MADAME DE TOTT

1. Possibly at the same time and for the same unknown reasons he made a transcription of letter 52 in his retirement, Jefferson copied this letter as well, making minor but interesting alterations. For these, see *Papers*, 11:273.
2. Letter 50, page 129.

60. TO MARTHA JEFFERSON

1. Petrarch's Laura.

62. EXTRACTS FROM NOTES OF A TOUR . . .

1. Here Jefferson uses "corn" in the British sense, to mean wheat, or whatever cereal grain is the local staple.

2. Unpublished.
3. Holm oak.
4. At this point in a 1799 transcript of this entry, Jefferson added: "I attended in a dairy from sunrise to sunset, and wrote down the preceding process as it was executed under my view."
5. Vine-shoots.

63. TO MADAME DE CORNY

1. Marguerite Victoire de Corny was one of the "little coterie" of friends that included Jefferson and Maria Cosway.

64. TO JOHN ADAMS

1. That is, the Farmers General, merchants granted a monopoly by the government to purchase American tobacco.

65. TO MARIA COSWAY

1. See letter 35, note 2.

67. TO NICHOLAS LEWIS

1. Anna Scott Jefferson Marks (1755–1828).
2. Tithables were all free males and slaves of either sex of working age, that is, over twelve years old.

68. TO PETER CARR, WITH ENCLOSURE

1. "the noble"
2. "on a forked frame"

69. TO GEORGE GILMER

1. Dr. Gilmer (d. 1796), who lived at Pen Park several miles north of Charlottesville, was Jefferson's friend and family physician.

70. TO DAVID HUMPHREYS

1. Jefferson's meaning is that ceremonial attire, complete with sword and dress-coat, has given way to the less formal frock-coat.

71. TO EDITOR OF THE *JOURNAL DE PARIS*

1. Jefferson wrote, but never sent, this response to a Paris newspaper's misrepresentation of the events of July 1 and 2, 1776.
2. In brief, the offending paragraph, citing Mayer, erroneously stated that John Dickinson's tie-breaking change of vote led to Congress's resolution for independence. In Mayer's words, "America owes Dickinson eternal gratitude; it is he who freed her."

72. TO JOHN ADAMS

1. Louis XVI's brother, the Comte de Provence, later Louis XVIII.

74. TO CHARLES THOMSON

1. Thomson (1729–1824) was secretary of the Continental Congress and fellow member of the American Philosophical Society.
2. Prehistoric mounds on the Ohio River.

76. TO JAMES MADISON

1. Accompanied by his sister-in-law and (unknown to Jefferson) lover, Madame de Bréhan, the Comte de Moustier was leaving to take up his post as minister to the United States. His embassy was short-lived. Moustier was disenchanted with the new republic, while Americans found his conduct "politically and morally offensive."

77. TO JOHN ADAMS

1. Chief minister Étienne Charles Loménie de Brienne, Archbishop of Toulouse.
2. "Cried like a child."
3. A wax disk, for sealing papers.

79. TO JAMES MADISON

1. The coded portion of Madison's Oct. 24 letter notified Jefferson that his reappointment for three years had passed without a dissenting vote.
2. Safeguard.

80. TO MARIA COSWAY

1. Actually, *en petit comité,* "among close friends."

81. TO ALEXANDER DONALD

1. Jefferson's friend since the 1760s, the merchant Alexander Donald formed the prominent London and Richmond, Virginia, commission house Donald & Burton.

83. NOTES OF A TOUR THROUGH HOLLAND AND THE RHINE VALLEY

1. Windlass or capstan.
2. A Dutch work on mills by Johannes van Zyl.
3. The "vibrating," or "pendulum," boats operated on a system somewhat analogous to the principle of the pendulum, in which the ferry is the bob and the rope corresponds to the rod.
4. Wild boar.
5. Deer.
6. Jefferson's "moldboard of least resistance" was one of few inventions.

84. TO WILLIAM SHORT

1. Graveled road.

85. TO MARIA COSWAY

1. The tale of Diego's arrival in Strasbourg from the Promontory of Noses appears in Laurence Sterne's *Tristram Shandy.*

88. HINTS TO AMERICANS TRAVELING IN EUROPE

1. A contemporary travelers' guide to France, *Itinéraire des routes les plus fréquentées,* by M. L. Dutens.

90. TO WILLIAM GORDON

1. William Gordon (1728–1807), Massachusetts clergyman, drew much of his *History of the Rise, Progress, and Establishment, of the Independence of the United States of America* (London, 1788) from the London *Annual Register.*

2. A Latin proverb: "[You can recognize] Hercules from his foot."

92. TO MARIA COSWAY

1. A reference to Cosway's painting depicting the dancing "Hours," available as a print in the Paris shops.

94. TO ANGELICA SCHUYLER CHURCH

1. A character in Laurence Sterne's *A Sentimental Journey.*

96. TO THOMAS PAYNE

1. Payne's name had been provided in response to Jefferson's request for the "best classical bookseller" in London.

97. TO GEORGE WASHINGTON

1. *Observations on the Whale-Fishery,* prepared by Jefferson in early November.

98. TO RICHARD PRICE

1. Jefferson had first met author and nonconformist minister Dr. Price (1723–1791) in London in 1786.

100. TO EDWARD BANCROFT

1. Massachusetts-born Dr. Edward Bancroft (1744–1821) was a respected figure in American and British political and scientific circles. His role as a double agent during the American Revolution was not revealed until a century later.
2. Tenants who make in-kind payments, similar to sharecroppers.

102. TO FRANCIS HOPKINSON

1. Hopkinson (1737–1791), jurist, political satirist, and musician, was part of Jefferson's Philadelphia circle of friends.
2. Massachusetts ratified the proposed Constitution and amendments to it at the same time.

103. TO JAMES MADISON

1. The "base passion of the mob." Horace, *Odes* 3.3.

104. TO JOSEPH WILLARD

1. Willard (1738–1804), founder of the American Academy of Arts and Sciences, was president of Harvard College.

106. TO RABAUT DE ST. ETIENNE

1. Jean Paul Rabaut de Saint Etienne (1743–1793), a champion of religious freedom, was a deputy of the Third Estate in the Estates-General.

107. TO MARIA COSWAY

1. Gouverneur Morris (1752–1816), who would succeed Jefferson as minister to France.

108. TO DIODATI

1. Count Diodati, minister plenipotentiary of the Duke of Mecklenburg-Schwerin to the Court of Louis XVI, was at this time in Switzerland.
2. "I have just received, dear Sir, the honor of your letter of 24 July. The difficulty with which I express myself in French would mean that my response would be very short if I was permitted to reply only in this language. But I know that, with some knowledge of the English language yourself, you will have a sufficient assistant in the Comtesse [Diodati's wife], and I dare to ask to add to her many kindnesses to me that of becoming the interpreter of what I am going to write in my own language, and what she will embellish in turning it into French."
3. Pomp, ostentation.

110. TO MARIA COSWAY

1. Jefferson fully intended to return to France the following spring, but once back in America, he was prevailed upon by President George Washington to join his cabinet as secretary of state.

111. "ON SENDING AMERICAN YOUTH TO EUROPE"

1. This undated document in Jefferson's hand appears to be the outline of something he intended to write on France. Evidently part of his efforts to focus the attentions of American visitors, particularly younger ones, it suggests the range and character of his own views of French society.

INDEX

A NOTE ON THE TYPE

The principal text of this Modern Library edition
was set in a digitized version of Janson,
a typeface that dates from about 1690 and was cut by Nicholas Kis,
a Hungarian working in Amsterdam. The original matrices have
survived and are held by the Stempel foundry in Germany.
Hermann Zapf redesigned some of the weights and sizes for Stempel,
basing his revisions on the original design.